Commentary on the Sermon on the Mount

Commentary on the Sermon on the Mount

Martin Luther

Translated by Charles A. Hay, D. D.

LEXHAM PRESS

Commentary on the Sermon on the Mount

Copyright 2017 Lexham Press

Lexham Press, 1313 Commercial St., Bellingham, WA 98225
LexhamPress.com

Originally published by the Lutheran Publication Society, Philadelphia, 1892.

ISBN 9781577997955

Cover Art: Jan Brueghel the Elder, *The Sermon on the Mount*, 1598. Public domain.
Typesetting: boundlesspen.com

Contents

Translator's Preface

The forty-third volume of the Erlangen edition of Luther's works contains his exposition of the *"Sermon on the Mount."* Dr. Irmischer, the editor of this edition, prefaces the volume with these remarks:

"During Bugenhagen's absence Luther preached a long while for him, regularly, on the fifth, sixth and seventh chapters of Matthew, beginning Nov. 9, 1530. These sermons were then published, first in 1532, at Wittenberg, under Joseph Klug, in quarto; in 1533 at Marburg, in octavo; and in 1539, again in Wittenberg, in quarto, under Johann Weiss. In 1533 they were also translated into Latin by Vincent Obsopoeus."

In this Irmischer edition these sermons are thrown into the form of a running commentary, and as such they are now presented to the English reading public by the Lutheran Publication Society.

When requested by a committee of this Board to translate this work, I called attention to the peculiar roughness and even fierceness of Luther's way of expressing himself and of denouncing the minions of the papacy. But the committee judged it best that Luther should be allowed to speak for himself, presuming that intelligent English readers will make due allowance for the style of speech common in that day, and for the peculiarly aggravating circumstances under which that noble man of God was called to labor. An admirable vindication of these "Asperities" appeared in the ninth volume of our excellent Quarterly Review, in 1881; it is from the pen of Rev. Dr. Morris, one of Luther's most enthusiastic admirers.

Charles A. Hay.

Gettysburg, Feb. 11, 1892.

Luther's Preface

I am truly glad that my exposition of the three chapters of St. Matthew, which St. Augustine calls the Lord's Sermon on the Mount, are about to be published, hoping that by the grace of God it may help to preserve and maintain the true, sure and Christian understanding of this teaching of Christ, because these sayings and texts are so very common and so often used throughout all Christendom. For I do not doubt that I have herein presented to my friends, and all others who care for these things, the true, pure Christian meaning of the same.

And it is hard to understand how the very devil himself has by his apostles so cunningly twisted and perverted especially the fifth chapter, as to make it teach the very opposite of what it means. And though Christ purposely intended thereby to antagonize all false teaching, and to exhibit the true meaning of God's commands, as he expressly says: "I am not come to destroy the law;" and takes it up piece by piece to make it perfectly clear; yet the infernal Satan has not found a single text in the Scriptures which he has more shamefully perverted, and made more error and false doctrine out of, than just this one which was by Christ himself ordered and appointed to neutralize false doctrine. This we may call a masterpiece of the devil.

First of all there have fallen upon this chapter the vulgar hogs and asses, jurists and sophists, the right hand of the pope and his Mamelukes. They have sucked this poison out of this beautiful rose, and scattered it everywhere; they have covered up Christ with it and have exalted and maintained the antichrist, namely, that Christ here does not wish everything which he teaches in the fifth chapter to be regarded by his Christians as commanded and to be observed by them; but that much of it was given merely as advice to such as wish to become perfect, and any who wish may observe these parts; despite the fact that Christ there threatens wrathfully:—no one shall enter heaven who sets aside one of the least of these commands,—and he calls them in plain words *commands*.

Thus they have invented twelve gospel counsels [consilia evangelii], twelve items of good counsel in the gospel, which one may heed if he wants to be something over and above other Christians (higher and more perfect); they have thus made not only Christian salvation, yes even perfection also, dependent aside from faith upon works, but they have made these same works voluntary. That is, as I understand it, to forbid really and truly good works, which is just what these nasty revilers accuse us of doing. For they cannot deny this, and no covering and smoothing over will help them as long as this fifth chapter of Matthew abides. For their books and glosses are at hand, along with their former and present daily impenitent life that they lead in accordance with this their teaching. And the teaching of those twelve "evangelical counsels" is very common among them, viz., not to require wrong doing, not to take vengeance, to offer the other cheek, not to resist evil, to give the cloak along with the coat, to go two miles for one, to give to every one that asks, to lend to him who borrows, to pray for persecutors, to love enemies, to do good to them that hate, etc., as Christ here teaches. All this (they disgustingly say) is not commanded, and the monks at Paris honestly assign their reasons, saying, this Christian teaching would be much too hard if it were loaded with such commands as these, etc.

This is the way the jurists and sophists have hitherto ruled and taught the church, so that Christ with his teaching and interpretation, has had to be their fool and juggler; and they still show no signs of repentance for this, but are eager to defend it, and to put forward again their cursed shabby canons, and to crown again their cunning pope. God grant, however, that I may live and may have to give clasps and jewels for this crown; then he, God willing, shall be called rightly crowned.

Therefore, dear brother, if you please, and have nothing better, let this my preaching serve you, in the first place, against our squires, the jurists and sophists, I mean especially the canonists, whom they themselves indeed call asses, and such they really are, so that you may keep the teaching of Christ for yourself pure in this place of Matthew, instead of their ass's cunning and devil's dung.

In the second place also against the new jurists and sophists, namely, the factious spirits and Anabaptists, who in their crazy fashion are making new trouble out of this fifth chapter. And just as the others go too much to the left in holding nothing at all of this teaching of Christ, but have condemned and obliterated it, so do these lean too much to the right, and teach that one should have nothing of his own, should not swear, should not act as ruler or judge, should not protect or defend, should forsake wife and child, and much of such miserable stuff.

So completely does the devil mix things up on both sides, that they know no difference between an earthly and a heavenly kingdom, much less what is to be taught and to be done differently in each kingdom; but we, God be thanked, can boast that we in these sermons have clearly and diligently shown and exhibited it, so that whoever hereafter errs, or will err, we are freed from all responsibility on his account, having faithfully presented our opinion for the benefit of all. Let their blood be upon their own head; our reward for this we await, namely, ingratitude, hatred, and all sorts of hostility, and we say *deo gratias*.

Since we then learn and know by such abominable examples, of both papistic and factious jurists, what the devil is aiming at, and especially how he seeks to pervert this fifth chapter of St. Matthew and thereby to exterminate the pure Christian doctrine, every preacher or rector is entreated and exhorted to watch faithfully and diligently against it in the little charge committed to him, and help to preserve the true interpretation of this text. For, as long as the devil lives and the world abides, he will not cease to attack this chapter. For his object is thereby to entirely suppress good works, as has been done in the papacy; or to instigate false good works and a feigned holiness, as he has now begun to do through the new monks and the factious spirits.

And even if both the popish and the mobocratic jurists and the monks were to perish, he would still find or raise up others. For he must have such followers, and his kingdom has been governed by monks ever since the world began. Although they have not been called monks, yet their doctrine and life have been monkish, that is, they have been other than and peculiar or better than what God has commanded; as among the people of Israel were the Baalites, the idolatrous priests (camarim) and such like, and among the heathen the castrated priests (Galli) and the vestal virgins.

Therefore we can never be safe against him. For from this fifth chapter have come the pope's monks, who claim to be a perfect class, in advance of other Christians, basing their claim upon this chapter; and yet we have shown that they are full of avarice, of arrogance, and of late full of all sorts of devils. Christ, our dear Lord and Master, who has opened up to us the true meaning, desires to give it additional force for us, and besides to help us live and act accordingly. To whom be grateful praise, together with the Father and the Holy Spirit forever, Amen.

Part I: The Fifth Chapter of St. Matthew

1

Verses 1 and 2

AND SEEING THE MULTITUDES, HE WENT UP
INTO A MOUNTAIN: AND WHEN HE WAS SET, HIS
DISCIPLES CAME UNTO HIM: AND HE OPENED
HIS MOUTH, AND TAUGHT THEM, SAYING:

Here the evangelist with a formal stately preface declares how Christ disposed himself for the sermon he was about to deliver; that he went upon a mountain, and sat down, and opened his mouth; so that we see he was in earnest. These are the three things, it is commonly said, that mark a good preacher; first, that he take his place; secondly, that he open his mouth and say something; thirdly, that he know when to stop.

To take his place, that means that he assume a position as a master or preacher, who can and ought to do it, as one called for this purpose and not coming of his own accord, but to whom it is a matter of duty and obedience; so that he may say: "I come, not hurried hither by my own purpose and preference, but I must do it, by virtue of my office.

This is said as against those who have heretofore been causing us so much vexation and tribulation, and indeed are still doing it, namely the factious spirits and fanatics, that are running up and down through the country, poisoning the people, before the pastors or those in office and authority find it out, and thus befoul one family after another until they have poisoned a whole city, and from the city a whole country. To guard against such sneaking renegades one ought not to allow any one to preach who has not been duly and officially appointed; also no one should venture, though he should be a preacher, if he hears a lying preacher in a popish or other church, who is misleading the people, to preach against him; nor should any one go about into the houses and get up private preachings, but he should remain at home and mind his own official business, or keep silent, if he neither will or can publicly take his place in the pulpit.

For God does not want us to go wandering about with his word, as though we were impelled by the Holy Spirit and had to preach, and thus were seeking preaching places and corners, houses or pulpits, where we are not officially called. For even St. Paul himself, though called as an apostle by God, did not want to preach in those places where the other apostles had preached before. Therefore we are here told that Christ boldly and publicly goes up upon the mountain, when he begins his official ministry, and soon afterwards says to his disciples: "Ye are the light of the world;" and: "Neither do men light a candle and put it under a bushel, but on a candlestick; and it giveth light to all that are in the house." For the office of the ministry and the word of God are hence to shine as the sun, and not go sneaking and plotting in the dark, as in the play of blind-man's buff; but all must be done in broad daylight, that it may be clearly seen that both preacher and hearer are sure of this, that the teaching is rightly done, and that the office has been rightly conferred, so that there is no need for concealment. Do thou likewise. If you are in office, and are commissioned to preach, take your place openly and fear nobody, that you may glory with Christ: "I spake openly to the world, * * in secret have I said nothing." John 18:20.

But you say, "How? Is no one then to teach anything except in public? Or is the head of a family not to teach his servants in his house, or to have a scholar or some one about him who recites to him?" Answer: Certainly, that is all right, and all just in place. For every head of a family is in duty bound to teach his children and servants, or to have them taught. For he is in his house as a pastor or bishop over his household, and he is commanded to take heed what they learn, and he is responsible for them. But it is all wrong for you to do this away from your own house, and to force yourself into other houses or to neighbors, and you should not allow any such sneak to come to you and to carry on special preaching in your house for which he has no authorization. But if any one comes into a house or city let him be asked for the evidence that he is known, or let him show by letter and seal that he has been duly authorized. For one must not trust all the stragglers that boast of having the Holy Spirit, and insinuate themselves thereby here and there into the homes. In short, it means that the gospel, or the preaching of it, should not be heard in a corner, but up upon a mountain, and openly in the free daylight. That is one thing that Matthew wants to show here.

The next thing is that he opens his mouth. That belongs (as above said) also to a preacher, that he do not keep his mouth shut, and not only publicly perform his official duty so that every one must keep silence and let him take his proper place as one who is divinely authorized and commanded, but also that he briskly and confidently open his mouth, that is, to preach the truth and what has been committed to him; that he be not silent or merely mumble, but bear witness, fearless and unterrified, and speak the truth out frankly, without regarding or sparing any one, no matter who or what is struck by it.

For that hinders a preacher very much if he looks about him and concerns himself as to what the people do or do not like to hear, or what might occasion for him disfavor, harm or danger; but as he stands high up, upon a mountain, in a public place, and looks freely all around him, so he is also to speak freely and fear nobody, although he sees many sorts of people, and to hold no leaf before his mouth, nor to regard either gracious or wrathful lords and squires, either money, riches, honor, power, or disgrace, poverty or injury, and not to think of anything further than that he may speak what his office requires, even that for which he stands where he does.

For Christ did not institute and appoint the office of the ministry that it might serve to gain money, possession, favor, honor, friendship, or that one may seek his own advantage through it, but that one should openly, freely proclaim the truth, rebuke evil, and publish what belongs to the advantage, safety and salvation of souls. For the word of God is not here for the purpose of teaching how a maid or man servant is to work in the house and earn his or her bread, or how a burgomaster is to rule, a farmer to plough or make hay. In short, it neither gives nor shows temporal good things by which one maintains *this* life, for reason has already taught all this to every one; but its purpose is to teach how we are to attain to *that* life, and it teaches thee to use the present life, and to nourish the belly here as long as it lasts; yet, so that thou mayest know where thou art to abide and live when this must come to an end.

If now the time comes for preaching of another life that we are to be concerned about, and for the sake of which we are not to regard this one as if we wanted to remain here forever, then contention and strife begin, so that the world will not endure it. If then a preacher cares more for his belly and worldly living, he does not do his duty; he stands up indeed and babbles in the pulpit, but he does not preach the truth, does not really open his mouth; if there seems to be trouble ahead he keeps quiet and avoids hitting anybody. Observe, this is why Matthew prefaces his account with the statement that Christ, as a true preacher, ascends the mountain and cheerfully opens his mouth, teaches the truth, and rebukes both false teaching and living, as we shall hear in what follows.

2

Verse 3

BLESSED ARE THE POOR IN SPIRIT, FOR
THEIRS IS THE KINGDOM OF HEAVEN.

This is a delightful, sweet and genial beginning of his sermon. For he does not come, like Moses or a teacher of law, with alarming and threatening demands; but in the most friendly manner, with enticements and allurements and pleasant promises. And indeed, if it had not been thus recorded, and if the first uttered precious words of the Lord Christ had not been given to us all, an over-curious spirit would tempt and impel everybody to run after them even to Jerusalem, yes, to the end of the world, if one might hear but a word of it all. Then there would be plenty of money forthcoming to build a good road, and every one would boastingly glory how he had heard or read the very words that the Lord Christ had spoken. O what a wonderfully happy man would he be held to be who should succeed in this! That is just the way it surely would be if we had none of our Saviour's words written, although much might have been written by others; and every one would say: Yes, I hear indeed what St. Paul and his other apostles have taught, but I would much rather hear what he himself said and preached. But now that it is so common, that every one has it written in a book, and can read it daily, nobody regards it as something special and precious. Yes, we grow tired of them and neglect them, just as if not the high Majesty of heaven, but some cobbler, had uttered them. Therefore we are duly punished for our ingratitude and contemptuous treatment of these words by getting little enough from them, and never feeling or tasting what a treasure, force and power there is in the words of Christ. But he who has grace only to recognize them as the words of God and not of man, will surely regard them as higher and more precious, and never grow tired or weary of them.

Kindly and sweet as this sermon is for Christians, who are our Lord's disciples, just so vexatious and intolerable is it for the Jews and their great saints. For he hits them a hard blow in the very beginning with these words, rejects and condemns their doctrine and preaches the direct contrary; yes, he denounces woe against their way of living and teaching, as is shown in the sixth chapter of Luke. For the substance of their teaching was this: If it goes well with a man here upon earth, he is happy and well off; that was all they aimed at, that God should give them enough upon earth, if they were pious and served him; as David says of them in Psalm 144: "Our garners are full, affording all manner of store; our sheep bring forth thousands and ten thousands in our streets; our oxen are strong to labor; there is no breaking in or going out; there is no complaining in our streets." These they call happy people, etc.

Against all this Christ opens his mouth and says there is something else needed than having enough here upon earth; as if to say: You dear disciples, if you come to preach among the people, you will find that they all teach and believe thus: He who is rich, powerful, etc., is altogether happy; and again, he who is poor and miserable is rejected and condemned before God. For the Jews were firmly fixed in this belief: if it went well with a man, that was a proof that God was gracious to him; and the reverse. This is explained by the fact that they had many and great promises from God of temporal and bodily good things that he would bestow upon the pious. They relied upon these, and supposed that if they had this they were well off. This is the theory that underlies the book of Job. For in regard to this his friends dispute with and contend against him, and insist strongly upon it that he must have knowingly committed some great crime against God, that he was so severely punished. Therefore he ought to confess it, be converted and become pious, then God would take away the punishment again from him, etc.

Therefore it was needful that his sermon should begin with overturning this false notion and tearing it out of their hearts, as one of the greatest hindrances to faith, that strengthens the real idol mammon in the heart. For nothing else could follow this teaching than that the people would become avaricious, and every one would care only for having plenty and a good time, without want and discomfort; and every one would have to infer: If he is happy who succeeds and has plenty, I must see to it that I am not left in the lurch.

This is still to-day the common belief of the world, especially of the Turks, who completely and thoroughly rely upon it, and thence conclude that it would not be possible that they should have so much success and victory if they were not the people of God and he were not gracious towards them above all others. Among ourselves also the whole papacy believes the same thing, and their teaching and life are based upon the fact that they only have enough and besides have secured for themselves all manner of worldly property; as everybody can see. In short, this is the greatest and most widely diffused belief or religion upon earth, whereupon all men of mere flesh and blood rely, and they cannot count anything else as happiness.

Therefore he here preaches an altogether different new sermon for Christians, viz. that if it does not go well with them, if they suffer poverty and have to do without riches, power, honor and a good time, they are still to be happy and not to have a temporal, but a different, an eternal reward; that they have enough in the kingdom of heaven.

Do you now say: How, must Christians then all be poor, and dare no one have money, property, honor, power, etc.? Or, what are the rich, as princes, lords, kings, to do? Must they give up all their property, honor, etc., or buy the kingdom of heaven from the poor, as some have taught? No; it is not said that we are to buy from the poor, but we are to be ourselves poor and be found among those poor, if we are to have the kingdom of heaven. For it is said plainly and bluntly: Blessed are the poor; and yet there is another little word along with that, viz. spiritually poor, so that nothing is accomplished by any one's being bodily poor, and having no money and property. For, outwardly to have money, property and people, is not of itself wrong, but it is God's gift and arrangement. No one is blessed, therefore, because he is a beggar and has nowhere anything of his own; but the expression is, spiritually poor. For I said already in the beginning that Christ is here not at all treating of secular government and order, but is speaking only of what is spiritual—how one aside from and over and above that which is outward is to live before God.

It belongs to secular government that one should have money, property, honor, power, land and people, and without these it could not exist. Therefore a lord or prince must and cannot be poor; for he must have all sorts of possessions suited to his office and rank. Therefore it is not meant that one must be poor and have nothing at all of his own. For the world could not exist in such a way that we should all be beggars and have nothing. For no head of a family could maintain his family and servants, if he himself had nothing at all. In short, to be bodily poor decides nothing. For we find many a beggar who gets bread at our door more proud and evil-disposed than any rich man, and many a miserly farmer with whom it is harder to get along than with any lord or prince.

Therefore be bodily and outwardly poor or rich, as may be your lot, God does not ask about that; and he knows that every one must be before God, that is spiritually and in his heart, poor; that is, not to place his confidence, comfort and assurance in temporal possessions, nor fix his heart upon them and make mammon his idol. David was an excellent king and had indeed his purse and his chest full of money, his barns full of grain, the country full of all sorts of goods and stores; yet along with this he had to be spiritually a poor beggar, as he sings about himself: "I am poor, and a stranger in the land, as all my fathers were." Notice, the king who sits in the midst of such possessions, a lord over land and people, dare not call himself anything else than a stranger or a pilgrim who goes upon the highway and has no place where he can abide. That means a heart that does not cling to property and riches; but, although it has, yet it is as though it had not, as St. Paul boasts of the Corinthians, 2 Cor. 6:10: "As poor, yet making many rich; as having nothing, and yet possessing all things."

The meaning of all that has been said is that one is to use all temporal good and bodily necessities, whilst he lives here, not otherwise than as a stranger in a strange place, where he spends the night and leaves in the morning. He needs no more than food and lodging, and dare not say: "This is mine, here will I stay nor dare he take possession of the property as tho' of right it belonged to him; else he would soon hear the host say to him: "Friend, do you not know that you are a stranger guest here? Go your way, where you belong." Just so here; that you have worldly goods, that is the gift of God to you for this life, and he allows you indeed to make use of it and to fill with it the worm-bag (Madensack) that you wear about your neck; but not that you fix and hang your heart upon it as though you were to live forever; but you are to be always going farther and thinking about another higher and better treasure that is your own and is to endure forever.

This is roughly said for the common man, that one may learn to understand (speaking according to the Scriptures) what it means to be spiritually poor or poor before God, not to reckon outwardly as to money and property, or as to want or superfluity, since we see (as above said) that the poorest and most miserable beggars are the worst and most desperate scoundrels, and dare to commit all sorts of knavery and evil tricks, which decent, honest people, rich citizens or lords and princes, are not guilty of; on the other hand also, many saintly people that have had plenty of money, honor, land and people, and yet with so much property have been poor; but we must reckon according to the heart, that it must not be much concerned whether it has anything or nothing, much or little, and always to treat what it has as though one did not have it, and had to be ready at any time to lose it, keeping the heart always fixed upon the kingdom of heaven.

Again, he is called rich according to the Scriptures who, although not having any worldly possessions, still scrambles and scratches after them, so that he never can get enough. These are the very ones whom the gospel calls rich bellies, who amid great possessions have the very least, and are never satisfied with that which God gives them. For it looks into the heart which is sticking full of money and worldly goods, and judges accordingly, although there is nothing in the purse or money box. Again it judges him poor in heart, though he has chest, house and hearth full. Thus Christian faith moves straight forward; it regards neither poverty nor riches; it asks only how the heart stands. If there be an avaricious belly there, the man is said to be spiritually rich; and again, he is spiritually poor who does not cling to such things and can empty his heart of them, as Christ elsewhere says: "He who forsakes houses, lands, children, wife, etc., he shall have a hundred fold again, and besides eternal life," that he may bear away their hearts from earthly good, so that they do not regard it as their treasure, and that he may comfort his own, who have to forsake it, that they shall receive much more and better, even in this life, than what they relinquish.

Not that we are to run away from property, home, wife and child, and wander about the country burdening other people, as the Anabaptist crowd does, that accuse us of not preaching the gospel aright because we keep our home and stay by wife and child. No, such crazy saints he does not want; but the true meaning is: Let a man be able in heart to leave his earthly home, his wife and child, though staying in the midst of them, nourishing himself along with them and serving them through love, as God has commanded, and yet able, if need be, to give them up at any time for God's sake. If thou art thus disposed, thou hast forsaken all things in such a way that thy heart is not taken captive, but remains pure from avarice and from clinging to other things for comfort and confidence. A rich man may properly be called spiritually poor, and need not therefore throw away his earthly possessions, except when he must needs forsake them; then let him do it in God's name, not for the reason that he would rather be away from wife, child and home, but would rather keep them as long as God grants it and is served by his so doing, and yet willing if he wishes to take them from him again. So you see what it means to be spiritually and before God poor, or spiritually to have nothing and forsake all.

Now look also at the promise that Christ adds, and says: "For of such is the kingdom of heaven." This is indeed a great, excellent, glorious promise, that we are to have a beautiful, glorious, great, eternal possession in heaven, since we are here gladly poor and regardless of earthly good. And as thou here givest up a very small matter that thou wouldst still gladly use as long and as much as thou canst have it, thou shalt instead thereof attain a crown, that thou mayest be a citizen and a lord in heaven. This ought to influence us, if we wanted to be Christians, and if we held his words to be true. But no one cares who it is that says this, and still less what he says; they let it pass through their ears in such a way that no one concerns himself about it any more nor lays it to heart.

But he shows with these words that no one understands this unless he is already a true Christian. For this trait and all the rest that follow are simply fruits of faith which the Holy Spirit himself must work in the heart. Where now faith is not, there the kingdom of heaven also will be wanting, nor will spiritual poverty, meekness, etc., follow, but only sordid raking and scraping, quarreling and noisily contending for worldly goods. Therefore all pains are lost upon such worldly hearts, so that they never learn or know what spiritual poverty is, nor do they believe or care for what he says and promises about the kingdom of heaven; although for their sake he so orders and ordains it that he who will not be spiritually poor in God's name, and for the sake of the kingdom of heaven, must still be poor in the devil's name and get no thanks for it. For God has so hung the greedy to their belly that they are never satiated with their greedily gained good, nor can they ever be happy. For squire greediness is such a merry guest, who never lets any one rest; he seeks, pushes and hunts without ceasing, so that he dare not enjoy his dear treasure for an hour; as Solomon the preacher too wonders and says: "A man to whom God hath given riches, wealth and honor, so that he wanteth nothing for his soul of all that he desireth, yet God giveth him not power to eat thereof, but a stranger eateth it. This is vanity, and it is an evil disease." He must always be afraid and anxiously concerned how he may keep what he has, and add to it, that it perish not, or be diminished, and is so completely tied up that he dare not cheerfully spend a penny. But if there were a heart that could be content and satisfied, it would have rest and the kingdom of heaven besides; otherwise along with great possessions, or indeed with its greediness, it must have purgatory here and there hellish fire besides, and as they say: Travel here with a barrow and there with a wheel; that is, have here trouble and anxiety and there bitter grief.

Notice, God always overrules it so that his word must remain true, and no one be saved or satisfied except Christians; and the rest, although they have everything, yet they are none the better off—indeed are not as well off, and must still be poor beggars, as far as the heart is concerned; only that the former are willingly poor and are looking forward to an imperishable eternal possession, that is to the kingdom of heaven, and are blessed children of God; but the latter are greedy for worldly good and still do not get what they want, and must besides be all the time martyrs of the devil. And there is, in short, no difference between a beggar before the door, and such a wretched greedy-gut, except that the one has nothing and can be put off with a crust of bread, whilst the other, the more he has the harder he is to fill, even though he should get all the world's money and goods in a heap.

Therefore this sermon, as I said, is of no account for the world, and answers for it no good purpose; for it insists upon being sure of its case, and will not take anything upon faith, but must see it and handle it, and says, it is better to have a sparrow in your hand than to be gaping at a crane in the air. Therefore Christ lets them go, does not want to force anybody or drag him to him by the hair; but he gives his kind counsel to all who are willing to be advised, and holds out before us the most precious promise. If thou wilt, thou hast here peace and rest in heart, and there forever what thy heart shall desire. If thou wilt not, then go along and have rather here and there all manner of misery and misfortune. For we see and know that all depends upon being satisfied and not clinging to worldly good; as many a one is whose heart God can fill, though he has only a bit of bread, so that he is cheerful and better contented than any prince or king. In short, he is a rich lord and emperor; need have no care, trouble or sorrow.

That is the first part of this sermon: He who wants to have enough here and there, let him take heed that he be not greedy and avaricious, but accept and use what God gives, and earn his daily bread in faith, then he will have here his paradise and even the kingdom of heaven, as Paul says, 1 Tim. 4:8, "Godliness is profitable unto all things, having promise of the life that now is and of that which is to come."

3

Verse 4

BLESSED ARE THEY THAT MOURN, FOR THEY SHALL BE COMFORTED.

As he began this sermon against the teaching and faith of the Jews (and indeed not of them alone, but of the whole world, even where it is at its best, which clings to the notion that it is well off if it only has possessions, honor, and its mammon, and it serves God only for this end), he now continues and shows the folly of what they regarded as the best, most blessed life upon earth, viz., having good, quiet days and suffering no discomfort, as some are described in the seventy-third Psalm: "They are not in trouble as other men, neither are they plagued like other men." For that is the chief thing that men desire, that they may have joy and pleasure and have no trouble. Now Christ turns the leaf over, states the exact opposite, and calls those blessed that have sadness and suffering, and so throughout, all these statements are made in direct opposition to the world's way of thinking, as it would like to have it. For it does not want to suffer hunger, trouble, disgrace, contempt, injustice and violence, and those who can be free from all this it counts blessed.

So that he means here to say that there must be another life than the one they seek and care for, and that a Christian must see to it that he is a sufferer and sorrow-bearer in this life. He who will not do this may indeed have a good time here, and live according to all his heart's desire, but he will have to suffer forever hereafter, as Luke says, 6:25, "Woe unto you that laugh now! For ye shall mourn and weep." So it went with the rich man, Lk. 16, who lived sumptuously and joyfully every day, clothed in purple and fine linen, and thought he was a great saint and well off before God because he had given him so much that was good, though he at the same time let poor Lazarus lie daily before his door full of sores, in hunger and distress and great misery. But what kind of a judgment did he hear at last when he was lying in hell? "Remember thou in thy lifetime didst receive thy good things and Lazarus his evil things, therefore thou art now tormented and he is comforted," etc. See, that is exactly our text: "Blessed are they that mourn, for they shall be comforted;" and again, as much as to say: Those who here seek and have nothing but joy and pleasure shall weep and howl forever.

Do you ask again: What then are we to do? Are those all to be damned that laugh, sing, dance, dress well, eat and drink? We surely read about kings and holy people that were cheerful and lived well. And especially Paul is a wonderful saint, who insists upon it that we be always cheerful, Phil. 4:4, and says, Rom. 12:15, "Rejoice with them that do rejoice," and again: "Weep with those that weep." Observe, that seems inconsistent, to rejoice evermore and yet weep and mourn with others. Answer: Just as I said before, that to have riches is no sin, nor is it forbidden; just so to be cheerful, to eat and drink well, is no sin, nor is it condemnatory; in like manner it is not wrong to have honor and a good name; and yet I am to be blessed if I do not have this, or can do without it, and instead of this suffer poverty, wretchedness, disgrace and persecution. So both of these things are here, and must be, to mourn and be cheerful, to eat and suffer hunger, as Paul boasts concerning himself, Phil. 4:11 seq.: "I have learned, in whatsoever state I am, therewith to be content. I know both how to be abased and how to abound: everywhere and in all things I am instructed both to be full and to be hungry, both to abound and to suffer need." Also, 2 Cor. 6:8 seq.: "By honor and dishonor, by evil report and good report: as dying, and behold we live; as sorrowful, yet always rejoicing," etc.

Therefore, the meaning is: Just as not he is called spiritually poor who has no money or anything of his own, but he who does not hanker after it or put his confidence in it as if it were his kingdom of heaven: so also not he is said to mourn who is always outwardly of downcast countenance, looking gloomy and never laughing; but he who does not comfort himself with having a good time and living sumptuously, as the world does—that cares for nothing but having constant joy and pleasure, and revels in it, and does not think or care how it goes with God or the people.

Thus many excellent, great people, kings and others, that were Christians, have had to mourn and bear trouble, although they lived splendidly before the world; as David everywhere in the Psalms complains about his weeping and sorrowing. And also now I could easily give examples of great people, lords and princes, who have had the same bitter experience with reference to the precious gospel; as, now at the late diet at Augsburg and on other occasions, although they got along very well outwardly, and were clothed in princely style in silk and gold, and to all appearance were like those who walk upon roses, yet they had to be daily right among poisonous serpents, and they had to experience at heart such unheard-of arrogance, insolence and shame, so many evil tricks and words from the shameful papists, who took pleasure in embittering their hearts and as far as they could in preventing them from having a single cheerful hour, so that they had to chew the cud of inward misery and do nothing but lament before God with sighs and tears. Such people know something of what it means to mourn and be sorrowful, although they do not at once show it, but eat and drink with others, and sometimes with laughing and jesting, to conceal their sorrow. For you must not think that mourning means only weeping and lamenting, or wailing, like children and women; this is not yet the real deep grief, if it has found its way to the heart and pours itself out through the eyes; but that is it, when the real hard blows come that strike and crush the heart, so that one cannot weep or dare complain to any one.

Therefore mourning is not a rare plant among Christians, although it makes no outward show, even if they would gladly be cheerful in Christ, and also outwardly as much as they can. For when they look at the world they must daily see and be painfully conscious of so much malice, arrogance, contempt for and blasphemy of God and his word, and besides so much misery and misfortune that the devil occasions, both in church and state, that they cannot have many cheerful thoughts, and their spiritual joy is very weak. And if they were to look at such things all the while, and did not sometimes turn their eyes away, they could never be cheerful at all; it is enough that this really happens oftener than they would wish, so that they need not go far to find it.

Therefore only begin and be a Christian, and you will soon learn what mourning means. If you cannot do better take a wife, and settle yourself, and make a living in faith, so that you love the word of God and do what belongs to your calling; then you will soon learn, both from neighbors and in your own house, that things will not go as you would like, and you will be everywhere hindered and hedged so that you will get enough to suffer and must see what will make you sad at heart. Especially however the dear preachers must learn this thoroughly, and be daily exercised with it, so that they must take to heart all manner of envy, hatred, scorn and ridicule, ingratitude, contempt besides, and revilement, so that they are inwardly pierced and uninterruptedly tormented.

But the world will have none of this mourning, therefore it seeks those callings and modes of living in which it can have a good time and need not suffer anything from anybody, as the monks' and priests' calling used to be. For it cannot endure that it should in a divinely given calling serve other people with constant care, trouble and labor, and get nothing for this but ingratitude and contempt and other malicious treatment as a reward. Therefore when things do not go with it as it wishes, and one is scowled at by another, they can do nothing but pound away with cursing and swearing, yes, and with their fists besides, and are ready to sacrifice property and reputation, land and people. But God orders it so, that they still must not get off so easily, that they need not see or suffer any misery, and he awards to them as a recompense, because they try to avoid it, that they still must suffer, and even make this twofold greater and heavier by their wrath and impatience, and cannot have any comfort and good conscience. But Christians have this advantage, that although they mourn they shall be comforted and be blessed both here and there.

Therefore, whoever does not want to be out and out a worldling, but to have part with Christians, let him be counted in as one who helps to sigh and mourn, so that he may be comforted, as this promise tells. We read of a case of this kind in the prophecy of Ezekiel, chapter nine, how God sent six men with deadly weapons to the city of Jerusalem. But he commissioned one among them to go through the midst of the city with "a writer's inkhorn by his side," to "set a mark upon the foreheads of the men that sigh and that cry for all the abominations that be done in the midst thereof." Those thus marked were to remain alive, but the rest were all to be slain. See, this is the advantage of Christians, that although they must see only sorrow and misery in the world, yet at last it comes to pass, when the world is most secure and is moving along in full enjoyment, that the little wheel turns, and suddenly a misfortune overtakes them in which these must remain and perish, whilst the others are snatched out of it and delivered, as in the case of dear Lot at Sodom, when they had long vexed his heart (as St. Peter says) "with their filthy conversation." Therefore let the world now laugh and live in revelry, according to its lust and wantonness. And though you have to mourn and weep, and daily see what grieves your heart, submit and hold fast to the saying [of our text], that you may be satisfied and comfort yourself with it, and also outwardly refresh yourself and be as cheerful as you can.

For those who thus mourn may properly have and take joy when they can, so that they do not utterly sink through sadness. For Christ also added these very words and promised this consolation, that they should not despond in their sorrow, or let the joy of their heart be entirely taken away and extinguished, but should mingle this mourning with consolation and refreshment, otherwise, if they never had any comfort or joy, they would have to pine and shrivel away. For no man can endure nothing but mourning; for it sucks out the very juices of the body, as the wise man says: "Grief has killed many people." Also: "A gloomy spirit dries up the marrow in the bones." Therefore we should not only avoid this, but we should commend and urge such people to be cheerful sometimes, if possible; or at least to moderate their grief and partly forget it.

Therefore Christ does not wish that there should be nothing but mourning and sadness here, but warns against those who will not mourn at all, who want to have only a good time and all their comfort here; and he wants to teach his Christians, if it goes badly with them and they have to mourn, that they may know that this is God's good pleasure, and it should also be theirs, and that they should not swear, or rage, or despair, as though their God had no mercy. When this is the case, the little bitter draught is to be mixed with honey and sugar, and so made less repulsive; that is the purpose of this promise, that this is well pleasing to him, and that he calls them blessed, besides that he comforts them here, and there they shall be entirely relieved of sorrow.

Therefore bid good-bye to the world and all that harm us, in the name of their lord, the devil, and let us sing this song and be cheerful, in the name of God and Christ. For it will surely not end with them as they wish; but, although they now rejoice at our misfortune, and do much to injure us, we will still keep up good courage, and shall live to see that they will have to weep and lament when we are comforted and happy.

4

Verse 5

BLESSED ARE THE MEEK, FOR THEY SHALL INHERIT THE EARTH.

This beatitude follows admirably upon the first when he said: Blessed are the poor in spirit, etc. For as he there promised the kingdom of heaven and an eternal inheritance, so he here adds a promise of this present life and possessions here upon earth.

But how does this agree together? to be poor and to possess the land? It seems to me that the preacher has forgotten how he began. For, if one is to possess the land and worldly goods, he cannot be poor. But he does not mean to say here that to own the land and have all kinds of possessions here upon earth, means, that every one is to possess a whole country; else God would have to create more worlds; but he refers to the blessings that God bestows upon each one, that he gives to one wife, children, cattle, house and home, and what is implied in this, that he may abide in the land (where he lives) and have control of his worldly goods, as the scriptures usually speak, and it is repeatedly said in Psalm thirty-seven: "those that wait upon the Lord shall inherit the earth;" also, "such as be blessed of him shall inherit the earth," etc. Therefore, he himself adds here the gloss, that to be spiritually poor, of which he spoke before, does not mean to be a beggar, or to throw away money and goods. For he teaches here that they are to remain and dwell in the land and have to do with earthly possessions; as we shall hear bye and bye.

Now, what does it mean to be meek? Here you must, in the first place, be again reminded, that Christ is not speaking at all about the government and its official authority; for it does not belong to this to be meek (sanft-müthig, as we use the word Sanftmuth in German); for it holds the sword, that it may punish the wicked, and it has a wrath and vengeance that are called the wrath and vengeance of God; but he is speaking only of individual persons, how each one is to conduct himself towards others, aside from official position and control; as father and mother, if they do not live as father and mother towards their children, nor perform their official duty as father and mother, that is, towards those who are not called father or mother, as neighbors and others. For I have elsewhere often said that we must make a wide difference between these two, office and person. He who is known as Jack or Martin is a very different man from him who is called Elector, or Doctor, or Preacher.

For here we have two different persons in one man. One, in which we are created and born, according to which we are all alike, man, woman, child, young, old, etc. But when we have now been born, God makes of you another person, makes you a child, me a father; one a master, another a servant; this one a prince, that one a citizen, etc. That means then a divine person, holding a divine office, and moves clothed with its own dignity, and is not called simply Jack or Nicholas, but a prince of Saxony, or father and master. Here he says nothing about these, but lets them move on in their office and rank, as he has ordered it; but he is speaking of the mere, single, natural person, what each is to do for himself, as a man, towards others.

Therefore, if we hold official and authoritative position, we must be strict and rigid, be wrathful and punish, etc. For here we must do what God places within our reach and of his own accord commands us to do. Beyond this, in what is unofficial, let every one learn for himself that he be mild towards everybody, that is, not to deal with and treat his neighbor unreasonably, with a hateful or revengeful spirit, like those who rush through headlong, never willing to bear anything or yield an inch, but turning the world upside down, never listening to anybody or excusing him for anything, but pile on the bundles at once and never stop to think, only how they may take vengeance and strike back again. Rulers are not hereby forbidden to punish and enforce retribution by divine authority; but also no license is here granted for a judge, burgomaster, lord or prince, who is a villain, and confounds the two persons and goes beyond his official authority through personal malice, or from envy, hatred and hostility (as often happens) under the mantle of office and legal right: as if our neighbors, under the name of the authorities, wanted to carry out something against us which they could not otherwise accomplish.

And especially he is here talking again with his Jews, as he had begun, who always insisted upon it that they were not to suffer anything from a heathen and a stranger, and that they were always right if they unhesitatingly avenged themselves, and quoted for this purpose the sayings of Moses, as Deut. 28:13: "The Lord shall make thee the head and not the tail; and thou shalt be above only and not beneath," etc., which would be all right enough. But the meaning is, if God himself does this, then it is well done. For it is altogether another matter if he orders it and says: I will do it, and if we do it ourselves, without authority. What he says, that shall and must be done. What we say, that happens if it can, or perhaps it does not happen at all. Therefore you have no right to apply to yourself this promise, and take confidence from it when you want to do something which he ought to do, and you will not wait till he tells you to do it.

Observe, Christ is here rebuking those wild saints who think every one is master in the whole world and has a perfect right to bear no suffering, but only to make a racket and bluster, and with violence to defend his own; and he teaches us that he who wishes to rule and possess his own, his property, home, etc., in peace, must be meek, so that he may overlook things and act reasonably, and suffer just as much as he can. For it cannot be otherwise but that your neighbor will sometimes take advantage of or injure you, either accidentally or through malice. If it was done accidentally, you make it no better on your part if you neither can nor will endure anything. If it was done maliciously, you only aggravate him by scratching and pounding, whilst he is laughing at you and making merry that he is worrying and vexing you, so that you still can have no peace or quietly enjoy your own.

Therefore choose one of the two, whichever you please: either to live with meekness and patience among the people and keep what you have with peace and a good conscience, or with racket and rumpus to lose your own, and besides have no peace. For this is settled, the meek shall inherit the earth. And look only yourself at those queer characters that are always quarreling and disputing about property and other matters, and yielding to nobody, but are determined to rush everything through, whether they do not squander more by quarreling and contending than they could ever gain, and at last lose land and people, house and home, with unrest and a bad conscience besides; and God adds his sanction to it, which says: "Be then not meek, so that you do not keep the land, nor enjoy your mite with peace." But if you want to live rightly and have rest, then let your neighbor's malice and hostility smother and extinguish itself; otherwise you cannot better please the devil, or more greatly harm yourself, than by getting up an angry racket. Have you a government over you? report the case and let them attend to it. For it is the business of the government not to permit the innocent to be much oppressed; and God will also overrule in such a way that his word and ordinance abides, and you according to this promise come to possess the land. Thus you will have peace and blessing from God, but your neighbor will have unrest, together with God's displeasure and curse.

But this sermon is intended only for those who are Christians, and believe, and know that they have their treasure in heaven, that is secure for them, and cannot be taken from them; therefore they must have enough also here, although they do not have chests and pockets full of red ducats. Since you know this, why will you let your joy be disturbed and taken from you—yes, why even make disquiet for yourself and rob yourself of this excellent promise?

Observe, you have now three points with three rich promises, so that he who is a Christian must have enough, both temporal and eternal, though he must here suffer much, both inwardly, in heart, and outwardly. Again, the worldlings, because they will not endure poverty, nor trouble, nor violence, neither have nor enjoy either the kingdom of heaven or worldly good with peace and quiet. You can read more about this in Psalm thirty-seven, which is the real commentary upon this passage, and richly describes how the meek inherit the earth and the ungodly are to be cut off.

5

Verse 6

BLESSED ARE THEY WHICH DO HUNGER AND THIRST AFTER RIGHTEOUSNESS, FOR THEY SHALL BE FILLED.

Righteousness must here not be understood as being the Christian righteousness in general, whereby the person becomes pious and acceptable before God. For I have before said that these eight beatitudes are nothing else than a teaching about the fruits and good works of a Christian, which must be preceded by faith, as the tree and main body or sum of his righteousness and blessedness, without any work or merit, out of which these beatitudes must all grow and follow. Therefore understand here the outward righteousness before the world, which we observe among ourselves towards others, that this is the meaning, short and simple, of these words: he is a really blessed man who perseveringly and assiduously strives to promote the general welfare and the right conduct of every one, and who helps to maintain and carry this out with word and deed, with counsel and act.

This is now also an excellent beatitude, which comprehends very many good works, but which is by no means common. For instance, that we may illustrate, if a preacher wishes to be counted as hungering and thirsting for righteousness, he must be ready to instruct and help every one in his calling, that he may conduct it properly and do what belongs to it, and when he sees that there is something wanting, and things do not go right, that he be on hand, warn, rebuke, and correct as well and by such means as he can: thus that I, as a preacher, be faithful to my office, and others to theirs, that they follow my teaching and preaching, and thus on both sides the right thing is done. Where now there are such people as take a special and earnest interest in gladly doing what is right, or in being found rightly at work, these may be said to be hungering and thirsting after righteousness. If this were the case there would be no knavery or injustice, but complete righteousness and blessedness on earth. For what is the righteousness of the world else than that every one do in his calling what is due? That means that every one's rights should be duly regarded, those of the man, the woman, the child, the man servant and maid servant in the family, the citizen or the city in the land; and it all amounts to this, that those who are to oversee and rule other people execute this office with diligence, careful-ness and fidelity, and that the others also faithfully and willingly render to these due service and obedience.

Nor does he without cause use the phrase: "Hunger and thirst after righteousness;" he means thereby to indicate that in order to attain it one must have great earnestness, a yearning eagerness and incessant diligence: that where there is a lack of this hunger and thirst, all will amount to noth-ing. The reason is this; for there are too many and great hindrances, both on the part of the devil, who is everywhere blocking the way, and on the part of the world, (namely his children,) which is so wicked that it cannot endure a pious man, who wants to do right or help others to do it; but it so annoys and worries him that in the end he loses patience and is out of humor about it. For it is painful to see how shamefully people act, and reward whole-hearted kindness with ingratitude, contempt, hatred and persecution. Hence also many persons who could not bear to witness this base conduct, at last grew desperate about it and took refuge in the wilder-ness, fleeing from human society and becoming monks, so that the saying has often been verified: "Despair makes a monk;" either, that one does not trust to make his own living and runs into a monastery for his stomach's sake, as the great crowd has done; or, that one despairs of the world and does not trust to remain pious in it or to help other people.

But this is not hungering and thirsting after righteousness. For he who wants to preach or rule in such a way, that he allows himself to be made weary and impatient, and to scamper off into a corner, he will be slow to help other people. It is not your duty to creep into a corner or into the wilderness, but to come out briskly, if you were therein, and offer both your hands and feet and your whole body for use, and hazard everything that you have and can do; and you are to be such a man as can be hard against hard, so as not to allow himself to be frightened off or dumfounded, or be overcome by the ingratitude or malice of the world: but you should always push along and persevere as much as possible. In short, you should have such a hunger and thirst after righteousness that will never diminish or cease and cannot be satiated, so that you care for nothing else, only so that you may accomplish and maintain what is right, despising on the other hand everything that would hinder you. If one cannot make the world altogether pious, let him do what he can. It is enough, that he has done his own duty, and has helped some, if only one or two. If the others will not follow, then let them go, in God's name. One must not run off because of the wicked, but conclude: it was not undertaken for their sake, nor for their sake was it dropped; perhaps bye and bye some of them may come to their senses, or there may be fewer of them, and they may somewhat improve.

For here you have a consolatory, certain promise, with which Christ allures and attracts his Christians, that those who hunger and thirst after righteousness shall be filled; that is, that they shall be delightfully rewarded for their hunger and thirst by seeing that they have not labored in vain, and that at last some have been reached who have been benefited; and it will be manifest not only here upon earth, but still more hereafter, when every one will see what such people have accomplished by their diligence and perseverance, although things do not now go as they would like, and they have nearly lost heart; as when a pious preacher has snatched so many souls out of the jaws of the devil and brought them to heaven; or a pious faithful ruler has helped many lands and people, who bear this testimony of him and praise him before the whole world.

Just the opposite, are the sham saints who out of great sanctity forsake the world and run into the wilderness, or hide themselves in corners, so that they may escape the trouble and worry that they must otherwise endure, and pay no regard to what is going on in the world; never once thinking upon it that they ought to help or advise other people with doctrine, instruction, exhortation, reproof and correction, or at least with praying and supplication to God. Yes, they are disgusted with it, and grieve over it, that other people become pious, for they want to be considered the only holy ones, so that whoever wants to get to heaven must buy from them their good works and merit. In short, they are so full of righteousness that they look contemptuously upon other poor sinners, just as the great saint Pharisee, Lk. 18, intoxicated with self-sufficiency, blurts out his contempt for the poor publican, is profuse in his self-congratulations, so that he pays his respects to God, and is thankful that he alone is pious and other people bad.

Observe, these are the people against whom Christ here speaks—the proud, self-sufficient spirits that tickle themselves with and find joy and pleasure in the fact that other people are not pious, whereas they ought to pity, compassionate and help them; they cannot do anything else but despise, backbite, judge and condemn everybody; and everything must be stench and filth except what they themselves do. But, that they should go and instruct and benefit a poor faulty sinner, that they shun as they would shun the devil. Therefore they will have to hear again, how Christ exclaims about them, Lk. 6:25: "Woe unto you that are full, for ye shall hunger." For as those shall be filled, who now hunger and thirst; so must those forever hunger, who now are so full and satiated, and yet no one can get any good from them, or boast that they have ever helped any one or led him in the right way. Now you have in a word the meaning of this beatitude, which (as above said) comprehends many good works, yes all good works, wherewith every one may live aright by himself among the people and help to give success to all sorts of offices and callings; as I have often shown elsewhere.

6

Verse 7

BLESSED ARE THE MERCIFUL, FOR THEY SHALL OBTAIN MERCY.

This is also an excellent fruit of faith, and follows well upon the preceding: he who is to help others and contribute to the common well-being and success, should also be kind and merciful—that is, that he should not be ready to raise a racket and make a disturbance if something be wanting, and things do not go as they should, whilst there is still hope of improvement. For that is one of the virtues of sham sanctity that it can have no compassion for or mercy upon the fallible and weak, but insists upon the extremest strictness and most careful selection, and as soon as there is the slightest failure, all mercy is gone and they do nothing but fume and fret; as also St. Gregory shows how to recognize this, and say: Vera justitia compassionem habet, falsa indignationem—true holiness is merciful and compassionate, but false holiness can do nothing but be angry and rage; and yet they say: Pro zelo justitiae, (as they boast), that is, we do it through love and zeal for righteousness.

For all the world is coming to see that they have been carrying on their mischievous and outrageous tricks under the beautiful, excellent semblance and cover that they were doing it for the sake of righteousness. Just as they have heretofore exhibited and are still exhibiting their hostility to and treachery against the gospel under the name of protecting the truth and exterminating heresy; they claim thereby to merit that God is to crown them for this and raise them to heaven, as those who out of great thirst and hunger for righteousness persecute, strangle and burn his saints. For they claim, forsooth, to have the name, even more than the true saints, of hungering and thirsting after righteousness, and put on such a sanctimonious appearance and use such admirable words, that they think even God himself will not know any better.

But the noble tree is known by its fruits. For, when they should insist upon righteousness, that both spiritual and temporal affairs be rightly conducted, they do not do it, do not think of instructing and improving any one, live themselves in constant vice, and if any one rebukes their conduct, or does not praise it and do as they wish, he must be a heretic and let himself be damned to hell. See, just so is surely every sham saint. For his self-righteousness makes him so proud that he despises everybody else, and can have no kind, merciful heart. Therefore is this a necessary warning against these abominable saints, so that every one may take care, if he has to do with his neighbor, whom he should help and rectify in his way of living, that he still may be able to be merciful, and forgive, that it may be seen that you are honestly aiming at righteousness, and not wishing to gratify your own malice and anger, and that you are so righteous that you deal amicably and gently with him who is willing to desist from unrighteousness and become better, that you bear with and endure his fault or weakness until he comes to terms. If, however, you try all this, and still find no hope of improvement, then you may give him up and turn him over to those whose place it is to punish him.

This is now one side of mercifulness, that one takes pleasure in forgiving sinners and those at fault. The other is to be beneficent also towards those who are externally in need or require help, which we call works of mercy, from Matt. 25:35. This feature too the ostentatious Jewish saints knew nothing about. For with them there was nothing but ice and frost, yes a heart hard as a block or a stone, and not an affectionate drop of blood that found pleasure in doing good to a neighbor, and no mercifulness to forgive sin; they cared and planned alone for their own belly, although another might die of hunger; so that there is much more mercifulness among open sinners than in such a saint; as it cannot be otherwise, since they praise only themselves and count themselves holy, despising every one else as of no account, and suppose that all the world must serve them and give them plenty; but they are not under obligation to give anything to or to serve anybody.

Therefore this sermon and exhortation is despised by and of no account among such saints, and finds no scholars except those who are already cleaving to and believing on Christ, who know of no holiness of their own, but who, as already described, are poor, wretched, meek, really hungering and thirsting, and so disposed that they despise nobody, but compassionately sympathize with the need of everybody else. To these applies now the comforting promise: It is well for you that are merciful, for you will find again abundant mercy, both here and hereafter, and such mercy as inexpressibly far exceeds all human benefactions and mercifulness. For there is no comparison between our mercifulness and that of God, nor between our possessions and the eternal treasures in the kingdom of heaven; and he is so pleased with our benefactions to our neighbor that he promises us for a penny a hundred thousand ducats, if it were necessary for us, and for a drink of water the kingdom of heaven.

Now, if any one will not suffer himself to be moved by this excellent, comforting promise, let him turn the other side of the page and hear another sentence: "Woe to the unmerciful, and let them be cursed, for no mercy shall be shown to them; as now the world is full of such people, among the nobility and citizens and farmers, who so wondrously sin against the dear gospel that they not only give nothing to poor pastors and preachers, but besides take and torment, where they can, and act just as if they meant to starve it out and drive it out of the world, and notwithstanding go along quite securely, thinking that God must keep quiet about it and let them do just as they please." But they will be struck some day, and, I fear, somebody will come who will make of me (who have given warning enough) a prophet, and he will treat them with perfect heartlessness, and besides take from them reputation and property, body and life, that God's word may remain true, and he experience unmitigated wrath and eternal displeasure who will not show or have mercy, as St. James says: "He shall have judgment without mercy that hath showed no mercy."

Therefore also Christ at the last day will adduce this unmercifulness as the worst injury done against himself, even all that we have done out of uncharitableness, and will himself utter the curse: "I was hungry and thirsty and ye gave me no meat, ye gave me no drink, etc. Depart ye, therefore, ye cursed, into everlasting, hellish fire," etc. He warns and exhorts us faithfully from pure grace and mercy. Whoever will not accept this, let him choose the worse and eternal damnation. Consider the rich man, Lk. 16:19 seq., who, although he saw poor Lazarus daily lying at his gate full of sores, had not charity enough to give him a bundle of straw or allow him the crumbs from under his table. But see how fearfully he was requited, that in hell he would gladly have given a hundred thousand ducats if he could only boast of having given him a thread.

7

Verse 8

BLESSED ARE THE PURE IN HEART,
FOR THEY SHALL SEE GOD.

This beatitude is somewhat obscure, and not so easily understood by us who have such gross carnal hearts and minds, and it is hidden, too, from all the sophists, who should really be the most learned, so that none of them can say what it means to have a pure heart, and still less, what it means to see God; they busy themselves with mere dreams and evil thoughts, about matters of which they know nothing themselves by experience.

Therefore we must look at these words according to the Scriptures, and learn to understand them correctly. A pure heart, they fancy, means that a man runs off from the community into a corner, a monastery, or the wilderness, and does not think upon the world, nor concern himself about worldly affairs and business, but amuses himself with nothing but heavenly thoughts; they have by this fanciful teaching not only befooled and dangerously misled themselves and other people, but have committed the murderous fault of holding as unclean the doing of things and holding of positions in society that are unavoidable in the world and indeed are by God himself appointed.

But the Scripture speaks of this pure heart and mind, that it is quite consistent with it that one be a husband, love his wife and children, think about them and care for them, and busy himself about other matters that belong to such a relation. For all this God has ordained. But what God has ordained, that cannot be impure—yes, it is the very purity with which we see God. Thus, when a judge acts in his official capacity and condemns a criminal to death, that is not his office and work, but God's. Therefore it is a good, pure and holy work (if he be indeed a Christian) which he could not do if he had not already a pure heart. Also, that must be called a pure work and heart, although a man or maid-servant in the house performs a dirty, filthy task, as hauling manure, or washing and cleaning children. Therefore it is a shameful perversion when one pays so little attention to the relations that are embraced in the ten commandments, and gapes after other, special, showy works; just as if God had not as pure a mouth or eyes as we, or as pure a heart and hand when he makes both man and woman: how should then such works or thoughts make an impure heart? But thus they shall become blind and fools who despise the word of God and measure purity only by the outward mask and display of works, and meanwhile have to make mischief with their own wandering thoughts, and stand gaping to climb up to heaven and feel after God, until in the effort they break their own necks.

Therefore, let us understand rightly what Christ means by a pure heart; and notice again, that this sermon was principally aimed at and sharply directed against the Jews. For, as they wanted to have no suffering, but coveted a life of ease, pleasure and joy, and would not hunger, nor be merciful, but to be self-satisfied and the only pious ones, besides judging and despising others; so their holiness, too, was this, that they must be outwardly clean, in body, skin, hair, clothes and food, so that not even a little spot dare be upon their clothing. And if any one touched a dead body, or had a scab or the itch upon his person, he dared not approach other people; that they regarded as purity. But that is not what constitutes being pure, said he; but those I praise who take pains to be of a pure heart, as he says, Matt. 23:25: "Ye make clean the outside of the cup and of the platter, but within are full of extortion and excess." Also: "Ye are like unto whited sepulchres, which indeed appear beautiful outwardly, but are within full of dead men's bones and of all uncleanness;" just as is the case with our clergy at present, altho' they lead outwardly a decent life, and conduct the public worship with such formality and display that it is something beautiful to see. But he does not ask for such purity, but wants to have the heart pure, though it be one who is outwardly a scullion in the kitchen, black, sooty and begrimed, and doing all sorts of dirty work.

What then is a pure heart? or in what does it consist? Answer: It is easily told, and you need not climb to heaven nor run into a monastery after it and make it out with your own thoughts; but be guarded against all such thoughts as you call your own, as against so much mud and filth, and know, that a monk in the monastery, when he is sitting in his deepest contemplativeness, and thinking of his Lord God, as he paints and imagines him to himself, is sitting (if you will pardon me) in the dirt, not up to his knees, but over head and ears. For he is following his own notions, without any word of God, which is simply lying and delusion; as the Scriptures everywhere testify. But that is a pure heart, that is ever on the lookout for God's word, and takes this in place of its own thoughts. For only that is pure before God, yes purity itself, through which everything that comes in contact with it and belongs to it is and is called pure. So with a common rough mechanic, a cobbler or a smith, who sits at home, though he be personally unclean and sooty, or smells badly on account of being blackened and soiled, and thinks: My God has made me a man and given me a house, wife and child, and ordered me to love them, and with my labor to nourish them, etc. Now observe, he is making a heart matter of it with God, and, although outwardly he stinks, inwardly he is perfectly fragrant before God. But if he gets to be highly pure, so that he also embraces the gospel and believes on Christ (without which indeed that purity cannot be), then he is pure through and through, inwardly at heart towards God, and outwardly towards everything that is under him upon earth, so that everything that he is and does, whether he goes, stands, eats and drinks, etc., is pure to him, and nothing can make him impure; so when he looks at his own wife or sports with her, as the patriarch Isaac, Gen. 26:8, which to a monk is disgusting and makes him impure. For there he has the word of God, and knows that God has given her to him. But if he forsook his wife and took up another, or neglected his trade or office and injured or worried other people, he would be no longer pure; for that would be against the command of God.

As long, however, as he is faithful in these two particulars, namely, in the word of faith towards God, by which the heart becomes pure, and in the word of the knowledge of what he is to do towards his neighbor in his calling, everything is pure to him, even if with his fists and his whole body he is busy with dirt. A poor servant girl, if she does what she ought to, and along with it is a Christian, she is before God in heaven a beautiful, pure maid, so that all the angels applaud her and love to look at her. On the other hand, the very strictest Carthusian, though he fasts and castigates himself to death, does nothing but weep for pure devotion, and never thinks about the world, and yet is without faith in Christ and love towards his neighbor, is a mere stench and pollution, both inside and outside, so that both God and the angels abominate and are disgusted with him.

So you see how all depends upon the word of God, so that what is comprehended in and moves with that, must all be called clean, pure and snow-white as to God and man. Therefore St. Paul says, Titus 1:15: "To the pure all things are pure," and again: "Unto them that are defiled and unbelieving is nothing pure." Why so? Because both their mind and conscience are impure. How can that be? For they say they know God, but with works they deny it; for it is these that are abominable in the sight of God, etc. Observe how the apostle paints them in horrible colors, and how he denounces the great Jewish saints. For, take as an example a Carthusian monk, who thinks, if he lives after his strict rule, in obedience, in poverty, unmarried, cut off from the world, he is in every respect pure. What else is that than their own way of thinking, aside from the word of God and faith, originating in their own heart? In this way they consider themselves alone pure, and other people impure. That St. Paul calls an impure mind, that is, everything that they think and imagine.

Since now this notion and thinking is impure, everything that they do accordingly must also be impure for them, and as their mind is so is also their conscience, so that, though they should and could be useful to other people, they have a conscience that takes its hue from their way of thinking and is tied up with their hoods, cloisters and rules: they think if for a minute they should neglect this routine to serve their neighbor and have anything to do with others, they would have committed the most heinous sin and have quite polluted themselves. That all comes of not recognizing the word of God and his creatures, although as St. Paul says, "with their mouths they profess that they do." For if they knew how and for what purpose they had been created by God, they would not despise these callings in society, nor set up so highly their own standard, but they would acknowledge these as the works and creatures of God to be pure, and would honor them, and themselves gladly abide in them and be helpful to their neighbor. That would then be to recognize God aright, both in his word and in his creatures, and to keep pure both heart and conscience, which thus believes and reasons: What God does and orders, that must be pure and good, for he makes nothing impure, and sanctifies everything through the word that he has affixed to all callings and creatures.

Therefore guard yourself against all your own thoughts, if you wish to be pure before God, and see to it that your heart is established and fixed upon the word of God, then you are pure over and above all Carthusians and saints in the world. When I was young, they gloried in this proverb: Love to be alone and your heart will stay pure; and they quoted in proof a saying of St. Bernard, who said whenever he was among the people he befouled himself—as we read in the lives of the fathers of a hermit, who would not have any one come near him or talk with anybody, and said: "The angels cannot come to him who moves among men." We read also of two others who would not let their mother see them; and as she often watched her opportunity and once took them by surprise, they presently closed the door and left her standing without a long while weeping, until they finally persuaded her to go away and wait until they would see each other in a future life.

Behold, that was called a noble deed, and the height of sanctity and most perfect purity. But what was it? There is the word of God: "Thou shalt honor thy father and thy mother." Had they regarded that as holy and pure, they would have shown their mother and their neighbor all honor, love and friendship: on the contrary, following their own notions and self-chosen holiness, they cut themselves off from them, and by their very attempt to be the purest they most shamefully defiled themselves before God; just as though the most desperate scoundrels could not have such thoughts and put on such an appearance that one would have to say: "These are living saints, they can despise the world and hold intercourse only with spirits;"—yes, with spirits from the bottom of hell. The angels like nothing better, than when we familiarly handle the word of God; with such they love to dwell. Therefore let the angels be undisturbed up there in heaven, and look for them here below, upon earth, in your neighbor, father and mother, child and others, that you may do to them what God has commanded, and the angels will not be far away from you.

I speak thus, that one may learn in this matter of purity to order himself aright, and not go so far to hunt for it as the monks do, who have thrown it quite out of the world and stuck it in a corner or into a hood; all of which is stench and filth, and the true harboring place of the devil; but let it be where God has placed it, namely in the heart that clings to God's word, and uses its calling and all creatures in accordance therewith, in such a way that both the entire purity of faith toward God is embraced therein, also outwardly shown in this life, and everything is done in obedience to the word and command of God, whether it be bodily clean or unclean. So I have said above, concerning a judge who has to condemn a man to death, and thus shed blood and pollute himself with it, which a monk holds to be an abominably unclean deed; but the Scripture calls this serving God; as St. Paul, Rom. 13:1-4, calls "the higher powers" that "bear the sword," "the minister of God;" and it is not their work and command but his, that he lays upon them and demands from them. Now you have the meaning of a pure heart that acts in accordance with the clean and pure word of God.

What is however their reward, or what does he promise them? It is this, that they shall see God. A glorious title and a splendid treasure! But what does it mean to see God? The monks have here again their dreams, that it means to sit in the cells and meditate heavenward, and lead a contemplative life—so they call it, and have written many books about it. But it will never do to call that seeing God, when you come harping on your own notions and scrambling heavenward; as the sophists and our factious spirits and crazy saints insist upon measuring and mastering God and his word and works by their own brains: but it is this, if thou hast a true faith that Christ is thy Saviour, etc., then thou seest at once that thou hast a gracious God. For faith leads thee up, and opens for thee the heart and will of God, where thou beholdest nothing but superabundant grace and love. That is exactly what it means, to see God, not with bodily eyes, (for with these no one can see him in this life,) but with faith, that beholds his paternal, friendly heart, in which there is no wrath or disfavor. For he who regards him as wrathful, does not see him aright, but has drawn a veil and cover, yes, a dark cloud, over his face. But to behold his face, as the Scripture expresses it, means to recognize him aright as a gracious, benevolent father, upon whom one can rely for everything good; and this comes only through faith in Christ.

Accordingly also, if thou livest in thy calling after the word and command of God, with thy husband, wife, child, neighbor and friend, thou canst see what is the mind of God in regard to these relations, and canst conclude that he is pleased, as that is not thine own dream, but his word and command, that never belies or deceives us. Now it is a most excellent thing, and a treasure above all that one can think or wish, to know that one is standing and living aright towards God: in such a way, that not only the heart can comfort itself with the assurance of his grace and glory in it, but that one can know that his external walk and conversation is pleasing in his sight; whence it follows that he can cheerfully and heartily do and suffer everything and let nothing alarm or dishearten him. None of these things can they do who do not have this faith and a pure heart that is guided only by God's word; as all the monks have openly taught that no man can know whether he is in a gracious state or not; and it serves them just right, that, because they despise faith and real godly works, and seek a purity of their own devising, they must never see God, nor know how they stand with him.

For if you ask some one, who has most diligently observed his hours for prayer, held his masses daily, and fasted, whether he is sure too that God is pleased with this, he must say he does not know that, and is doing it all at a venture; if it succeeds, let it succeed. It is not possible for any one to say anything else. For no one can boastingly say: God gave me this hood, or ordered me to wear it; he commanded me to hold this mass, etc. We have all been groping in this blindness hitherto, when we were doing so many so-called good works, making contributions, fasting, praying rosaries, and yet we never dared to say: This work is well pleasing to God; I am sure of this, and will die upon it. Therefore no one can say that in all his doing and living he has ever seen God. Or if any one should presumptuously glorify such works, and think that God must regard them favorably and reward them, that would mean seeing not God, but the devil in place of God. For there is no word of God for that, but it is all devised by men, grown out of their own hearts. Therefore it can nevermore make any heart sure or satisfied, but it remains hidden under presumption until the last hour comes, when it all vanishes and drives into despair, and so it never comes to pass that one sees the face of God.

But he who lays hold upon the word of God and abides in the faith, can maintain his stand before God and look upon him as his gracious Father, and need not fear that God is standing behind him with a club; is sure that God is looking graciously and smilingly upon him, together with all the angels and saints in heaven. See, that is what Christ means by this word, that only those behold God who have this pure heart; whereby he cuts off and sets aside all other sorts of purity, so that, where this kind is not, although otherwise everything be pure in a man, it avails nothing before God, and he can never see God. On the other hand, if the heart is pure, everything is pure, and it matters not if outwardly everything be impure, yes, even if the body is full of sores, scabs and leprosy all over.

8

Verse 9

BLESSED ARE THE PEACEMAKERS; FOR THEY
SHALL BE CALLED THE CHILDREN OF GOD.

Here the Lord honors with a high title and excellent praise those who find
pleasure in diligently trying to make peace, not only so far as they are
themselves concerned, but also among other people, that they may help
to settle ugly and tangled disputes, endure contention, guard against and
prevent war and bloodshed; which is indeed a great virtue, but very rare
in the world and among the sham saints. For those who are not Christians
are both liars and murderers, like their father, the devil. Therefore they
serve no other purpose than to create strife, contention, war, etc.; as we
now find among the priests, bishops and princes hardly anything but bloodhounds, who by many tokens have abundantly shown, that there is nothing they would rather see than that we should all swim in blood. Thus, if
a prince becomes angry, he thinks at once that he must begin a war; then
he inflames and incites everybody, until there has been so much warring
and shedding of blood that he begins to be sorry for it, and gives a thousand ducats for the souls of those that were slain. These are nothing but
bloodhounds; they cannot rest until they have taken vengeance and sated
their rage, until they have dragged their land and people into wretchedness and misery; and yet they want to be called Christian princes and have
a good cause.

There is more needed to begin a war than that you have a good cause. For although we are not forbidden here to carry on a war, as above said, that Christ here does not mean to detract anything from the powers that be and their official authority, but is teaching only individual people who wish to lead for themselves a Christian life; yet it is not right that a prince determines to have a war with his neighbor, even though (I say) he has a good cause and his neighbor is in the wrong; but the meaning is: Blessed are the peacemakers; so that he who wants to be a Christian and a child of God, not only does not begin war and strife, but helps and advises for peace, wherever he can, although there was reason and cause enough for going to war. It is enough, if one has tried his best for peace and all avails nothing, that one acts on the defensive, to protect land and people. Therefore not Christians, but the children of the devil are those to be called, the quarrelsome fellows, who rush to their rapiers and jerk their sword from its sheath for a word; still more, however, those who now persecute the gospel, and cause its preachers to be innocently burned or murdered, who have done them no harm, but only good, and have served them with body and soul. But of these we say nothing now, but of those only who maintain that they are right and have a good cause, and think that they, as high and princely persons, ought not to suffer, although other people would suffer.

It is also meant here, if injustice and violence are done to you, that it is not right for you to consult your own foolish head, and begin right away to take vengeance and strike back; but you are to think over it and try to bear it and have peace. If that will not answer, and you cannot endure it, you have law and governmental authority in the land, where you can seek relief in a regular way. For the powers that be are ordained to guard against this injustice and punish it. Therefore he who injures you, sins not only against you, but rather against the authority itself, for the order and command to keep the peace was given to it and not to you. Therefore let your judge, whose business it is, avenge and punish this, for against him your opponent has done the wrong. If you, however, take vengeance into your own hands, you do still greater wrong, for you make yourself guilty of the same sin as he who sins against the powers that be, and interferes with their office; and by so doing you put your own good cause in the wrong.

For the common saying is: "He who strikes back is in the wrong, and striking back makes a quarrel."

Notice now this is one thing that Christ here demands against the revengeful and uproarious; and he calls those peacemakers, in the first place, who help to make peace among the people, as pious princes, counselors or jurists, and persons in authority, who hold their governmental position for the sake of peace. In the second place, pious citizens and neighbors, who by their salutary good counsel adjust, harmonize and settle contention and strife (that has been occasioned by bad, poisonous tongues) between husband and wife, or among neighbors; as St. Augustine boasted of his mother, Monica, that when she saw two at outs she always spoke the best on both sides, and whatever of good she heard about the one party that she brought to the other, but whatever of evil she heard that she kept quiet, or mildened it as much as she could, and thus she often effected a reconciliation. For it is among the women particularly that the shameful vice of slander is prevalent, often so that great trouble is occasioned through an evil tongue. To this those bitter and poisonous brides of the devil largely contribute, who if they hear a word about anybody give it a point and edge, and intense bitterness against others, so that sometimes wretchedness and murder are the result.

This all comes from the fact that there is naturally sticking to us the shameful, devilish filth, that every one likes to hear and tell the worst about his neighbor, and is tickled if he sees a fault in some one else. If a woman were as beautiful as the sun, and had any mark or little spot upon her body, one should forget everything else and look only for the spot, and talk about that. So, if some one were the most renowned for honor and virtue, yet a poisonous tongue shall come along and say she had been seen once laughing with somebody, and so defame her as to eclipse all her praise and honor. Such are real poisonous spiders that can suck nothing but poison out of a beautiful, lovely rose, and ruin both the flower and the sap, whilst a little bee sucks nothing but honey out of it and leaves the roses uninjured.

That is the way those act, who discern nothing in other people, unless there is something faulty or impure in them, which they can blame; on the other hand, what there is good in them, they do not see; for men have many virtues which the devil cannot destroy, and yet he hides or defaces them that they shall not be seen. So, in the case of a woman, though she be very full of faults and have no other virtue, yet she is a creature of God, and can at least carry water and wash clouts; and there is no person upon earth so bad that there is not something in him that one must praise. How is it, then, that we leave out of view the good and feast our eyes upon what is impure, as if we took delight (by your leave) in looking only at a man's behind, when God himself has covered the uncomely parts of the body, and (as Paul says, 1 Cor. 12:24) "has given more abundant honor to that part which lacked?" And we are such a filthy set, that we seek only after that which is dirty and stinks, and wallow in it like hogs.

See, those too are real children of the devil, who himself gets his name from doing that, so that he is called *diabolus*, that is, a disgracer and reviler, who finds his pleasure in this, that he puts us most completely to shame, and embitters us among ourselves, so that he may occasion only murder and misery, and allow no peace or concord between brethren and neighbors, husband and wife.

I once heard of a case of this kind, of two married persons who lived together in such love and harmony that they were the town's talk, and when the devil could not hinder this in any way, he sent an old hag to the woman, who told her that her husband was going with another woman and meant to kill her; she thus embittered her heart against her husband, and advised her to conceal a knife about her person, that she might get ahead of him. When she had accomplished this, she went to the husband and told him the same about her, that she meant to murder him, and in proof of it (said she) he would find at night a knife beside her in bed. That he then found, and cut off her head with it. Whether this be true or not, it shows at all events what wicked, poisonous tongues can do, even between those who heartily love each other, so that they may properly be called devil's-mouths or female devils, as he, the devil, diabolus, signifies nothing else than a bitter, poisonous, evil mouth.

Therefore be on your guard against such as these, that you pay no attention to them, and learn to put the best construction upon, or even to conceal, what you hear about your neighbor, so that you may make and keep peace and harmony; then you can be called with all honor a child of God before all the world and the angels in heaven. You should let yourself be drawn and attracted by this honor—yes, you should run after it, if that were possible for you, even to the end of the world, and gladly give for it all that you have. Now you have it here offered to you and spread before you for nothing, do not need to do or give anything for it, except that if you want to be a child of God, that you also show yourself to be that, and do the works of your Father towards your neighbor. For thus has our Lord Christ done for us when he reconciled us to the Father and secured his favor, and still daily intercedes for us and pleads our cause. Do thou likewise, that thou mayest be a pacificator and mediator between thy neighbors, and carry the best to both sides, but withhold the bad, that the devil has inspired, or explain it as well as you can. If you come to Margaret, do as was said of Monica, the mother of Augustine, and say: O, dear M., why are you so bitter? She surely don't mean it ill; I see nothing else about her but that she would like to be your dear sister, etc. In like manner, if you meet with Catharine, do the same with her. Then as a true child of God you would have effected on both sides a peace, as far as you could.

But if you will or must speak of the evil, then do as Christ has taught you. Do not carry it to others, but go to him who has done the wrong and exhort him to do better; not in such a way that you make a display of it when you come, and expose the person concerned; that you speak when you should be silent, and be silent when you should speak. This is one and the first way that you should deal alone between yourself and your neighbor. If, however, you must tell it to others, if the other course does not answer, then tell it to those whose duty it is to punish, father and mother, master or mistress, burgomaster and judge, etc. That is the right and regular course to pursue, that what is wrong may be done away or punished. Otherwise, if you spread it among other people, the person remains unbenefited, and the evil unrebuked, and will besides be reported abroad by yourself and others, so that it will be on everybody's tongue. Notice how a pious physician does with a sick child; he does not run about among the people and herald it abroad, but he goes to the child and examines his pulse, or whatever is necessary, not that he may gratify his pleasure at the child's expense, or make fun of him, but with the good and kind intention of helping him. So we read of the holy patriarch Joseph, Gen. 37:2, 10, who was with his brothers, by the cattle, and when they were badly reported of, he went and told it to their father, as their master, in whose place it was to look into the matter and punish them, for they would not hear him.

But you may say: Why then do you yourself publicly attack the pope and others, and do not keep the peace? Answer: One must advise and help all he can for peace, and keep silence as well as he can. But, when the sin is public, and becomes too widely spread, or does public injury (as the pope's teaching), then it is no longer right to be silent, but to protest and rebuke, especially for me and others, who are in public office, whose duty it is to teach and warn everybody. For the command and duty has been laid upon me, as a preacher and doctor, who am to watch that no one is misled, so that I may give account of this at the last judgment. So St. Paul, Acts 20:28, commands the preachers, that they are to watch and guard the whole flock against the wolves that would appear among them, etc. So it becomes me to rebuke those who sin publicly, that they may do better, just as a judge must publicly convict and punish the evil-doers by virtue of his office. For we have said it often enough that Christ is not speaking here of a public office, but of all Christians in general, according as we are all alike before God.

9

Verse 10

BLESSED ARE THEY WHICH ARE PERSECUTED
FOR RIGHTEOUSNESS' SAKE, FOR THEIRS
IS THE KINGDOM OF HEAVEN.

I have said above that these statements and promises must all be understood as matters of faith, and as said concerning things that are not seen nor heard, and they have no reference to outward appearances. For how can those be said to be prosperous and blessed outwardly who are poor and mouru, and besides must suffer all sorts of persecution, which things the whole world and reason call adversity and which they teach to avoid? Therefore whoever wants to have the blessedness and the good things that Christ here speaks of, he must lift up his heart above all senses and reason, and not judge himself by his feelings, but must argue thus: Am I poor, then am I not poor. Poor I am outwardly, according to the flesh, but before God in faith I am rich. So, when he feels sad, dejected and worried, he must not judge accordingly and say he is an unhappy man, but he must turn about and say: I feel sadness, indeed, misery and inward sorrow, but nevertheless I am blessed, cheerful and comfortably fixed upon the word of God. Just the opposite of this is the case, too, in the world, so that those who are called rich and happy are not so. For Christ utters his woe against them, and calls them unhappy, although it appears as if they were well off and succeeding admirably. Therefore they should raise their thoughts above riches and a good time which they are enjoying, and should say: I am indeed rich and live in the midst of enjoyment, but alas for me if I have nothing else than this! For amid all this there must assuredly be abundant misery, wretchedness and sorrow, that will overtake me before I am aware of it. The same is true of all these sayings, that every one of them has a different aspect before the world from that it wears according to these words.

Now we have hitherto treated nearly all the parts of a Christian mode of living and the spiritual fruits of faith in these two aspects: First, as to his person, that he is poor, sad, miserable, suffers want and hunger, and along with this, towards others is a useful, beneficent, merciful, peaceable man, and does nothing but good works. Here he now adds the last, how he is treated for all this—that although he is full of good works, even towards enemies and evil men, he must get this reward from the world, that he is persecuted, and lose body, life and everything for it.

Therefore, if you wish to be a Christian, consider this well, that you may be unterrified, and not on that account become out of heart and impatient, but be cheerful and content with it all, and know that you are not badly off when this happens to you. For the same thing happened to himself and all the saints, (as is soon hereafter stated,) and to those who wish to be Christians it is for this reason thus foretold, that they shall and must suffer persecution. Therefore you must make your choice. You have two ways open before you, either towards heaven and eternal life, or towards hell; either with Christ or with the world. But you must know this: If you live so that you will have a good time here, and no persecution, then you will not get to heaven with Christ, and the converse; and you must, in short, either let Christ and heaven go, or choose this, that you will suffer all manner of persecution and evil treatment in the world. In a word, he who will have Christ, must forfeit personal ease, life, goods, honor, the favor of the world, and not be frightened at contemptuous treatment, ingratitude or persecution. The reason is this: The devil is a wicked, wrathful spirit, and neither can nor will endure it that a man enters the kindom of God. If any one undertakes to do this, he throws himself in his way, and stirs up and tries all the opposition against him that he can.

Therefore, if you wish to be a child of God, get ready for persecution, as the wise man says, and Paul in 2 Tim. 3:12: "All that will live godly in Christ Jesus shall suffer persecution." Also Christ himself: "The disciple is not above his Master. Have they persecuted me? they will also persecute you." It cannot be otherwise, therefore it is said: "Blessed are those that are persecuted for righteousness' sake;" so that one may know with what to console himself. For otherwise it is a trying, unhappy condition, outwardly viewed, and has a bad influence, to be sitting constantly in bodily and pecuniary danger. But when faith takes hold, he can lift himself above it all and think: Now Christ has nevertheless said that I am blessed and well off. Because he has said it, I let this be my comfort and it gives me great delight. The word shall enlarge my heart—yea, make it greater than heaven and earth. For what are all that persecute me contrasted with this man or his word? Is it one or two that are persecuting us? Those who are on our side, who encourage, console and congratulate us, are many more, yes ten thousand angels to one of them, together with all the saints, who side with Christ and God himself. Therefore we must not let this word lie so cold and simple, but inflate it well and magnify it, and set it in opposition to all persecution; thus we will see and learn that all our suffering is to be despised as nothing at all, in contrast with this great consolation and eternal blessing.

But he adds significantly this expression: "for righteousness' sake;" to show that it is not enough to be persecuted if this be wanting. For the devil and bad people must also endure persecution, and one scoundrel often quarrels with another, and they are not mutually friendly; as one murderer persecutes another, a Turk makes war upon a Tartar, but these are not for that reason happy; but it is true only of those who are persecuted for righteousness' sake; as also Peter, 1 Pet. 4:15, says: "Let no one among you suffer as a murderer, or thief, or evil-doer," etc. Therefore it all amounts to nothing for any one without this [i. e., righteousness] to boast and make an ado about great suffering; as the graceless monks have misled the poor people whom they have led out to punishment for their evil-doing, and have told them for their comfort that they were paying for their sin by their death. But do you beware of the death that is to atone for your sin. For this belongs to the bottom of hell. There must first be righteousness and the death of Christ the Lord.

Therefore see to it, that you have in the first place a real divine cause for the sake of which you must suffer persecution, and are really sure of it, so that your conscience can safely rest upon it, even if the whole world were opposed to you. Therefore, first of all, the word of God must be confidently and firmly grasped, so that no doubt or hesitation can arise from that source. As, if now the emperor, bishops or princes wanted to forbid married life, liberty to eat, using both forms in the sacrament, etc., and would persecute you on that account: then you must see to it, that your heart is sure of the matter and firmly convinced that the word of God has made these things free and unforbidden, yes, commands us to make a serious matter of them and stake even life upon them. Thus you can confidently say: this cause is not mine, but it is that of my Lord Christ. For I have not concocted it out of my own head, nor have I undertaken or begun it of my own accord, or at the advice or suggestion of any one else; but I have received it from the mouth of Christ, brought down and announced from heaven, who never belies or deceives me, but is himself pure truth and righteousness. Upon the word of this man I will venture to suffer, to do and leave undone whatever is befitting, and his word, by itself, shall avail more to comfort and strengthen my heart, than the raging and threatening of all devils and of the world can avail to terrify me.

For what does it amount to, if a prince or emperor is foolishly furious in his rage, and threatens with sword, fire or the gallows, if my Saviour on the contrary, friendly communes with my heart and comforts me with these assurances that I am blessed, and in hearty sympathy with my God in heaven, and all the heavenly host and holy beings call me blessed? If my heart and mind are in such a state that I can suffer for the sake of his word and work, why should I allow myself to be frightened by these wretched people, who indeed rage and foam in hostility against God, but who suddenly vanish like smoke or like poor soap-bubbles? As the prophet Isaiah says, 51:12 sq.: "I, even I, am he that comforteth you: who art thou, that thou shouldest be afraid of a man that shall die, and of the son of man which shall be made as grass; and forgettest the Lord thy Maker, that hath stretched forth the heavens and laid the foundations of the earth," etc., that is, he is everlasting and almighty who comforts thee and has pleasure in thee: when they all shall have vanished he will still be sitting above there, and thou too. Why will you then care more for the threatening and fuming of a miserable, stinking maggot-bag, than for this divine consolation and approbation? You should rather thank God, and be heartily glad of it, that you are worthy to suffer thus, as the apostles went forth (Acts 5:41) "rejoicing that they were counted worthy to suffer shame for his name."

See, are we not now highly blessed with these words, if we only accept it with loving gratitude? for there is no lack of persecution. And we have along with it the great advantage, that our enemies themselves cannot condemn our cause, and must confess (no thanks to them for it) that it is right and the truth; but there is this wanting in the matter, that we should teach it, for they will not learn or accept from us, what has never happened or been heard of before. Therefore, what we suffer on this account is a holy, blessed suffering, as they must themselves bear witness, and it is now no longer a human, but a real devilish persecution, so that they say we must and shall not call it the word of God, but must hold our tongue and not preach, unless we first go and fall at the feet of the Pope, and submit to be judged as it may please him and his minions.

Therefore let us suffer, so much the more willingly and joyfully, everything that they can do against us, because we have the strong, sure consolation, and great, glorious satisfaction, that our teaching and cause are confirmed by their own mouth; besides that, we hear in this place the excellent charming promise that we shall be well rewarded in heaven, and are to rejoice and exult in this, as those who do not need to look forward to heaven, but have it already; and they with their persecuting only the more help us thitherward, yes, actually drive us toward heaven. Now see, whether these simple, short words cannot give as much courage as the whole world can do, and inspire more comfort and joy than all the suffering and torment that our enemies can inflict upon us; if we do not hastily skim over them, but heartily appropriate them and duly consider them.

This we have to say as to the persecution that is carried on by actual violence and affects person or property, when Christians are seized and tortured, burned, hanged and massacred; as happens now, and has happened heretofore. Beyond this there is another kind of persecution which is called defamation, disgracing, putting to shame, which concerns our honor and good name, in which way Christians above all others have to suffer. Of this Christ now further treats.

10

Verse 11

BLESSED ARE YE, WHEN MEN SHALL REVILE YOU,
AND PERSECUTE YOU, AND SHALL SAY ALL MANNER
OF EVIL AGAINST YOU FALSELY, FOR MY SAKE.

This is also a great, severe persecution, and (as above said) the real suffering of Christians, that they are most bitterly and poisonously slandered and defamed. For, although other people too must suffer persecution, so that they are violently and unjustly treated; yet men are satisfied with allowing them to retain their honor and good name. This is therefore still no real Christian suffering. For to this it is not enough that all manner of tortures and torments are imposed upon them; but along with this their name must be most shamefully spit upon and slandered, so that the world loudly boasts, when it murders the Christians, that it has executed the worst scoundrels, whom the earth could no longer carry, and that it has done God the greatest and most acceptable service, as Christ says, John 16:2; so that there is no name upon earth so slandered and disgraced as that of a Christian, and no people so bitterly opposed and attacked by such malicious, poisonous tongues as the Christians.

They are showing this now thoroughly in their treatment of the dear gospel and its preachers, by such slanderous abuse, lying, deception, evil artifices, and malicious misrepresentations, that one would rather die ever so often than endure these poisonous, malicious darts. Here comes the Pope hurling his thunderbolts and damning us under nine hells, as children of the very worst devil. In like manner his hangers-on, bishops and princes, are raging and roaring with such an abominable vilifying and reviling as to strike one through and through, so that one would at last have to become weary, and be no longer able to endure it, if we had not a stronger and mightier consolation than all their malice and rage amounts to. Therefore we let them rage and defame, that they may plague themselves and have the scorching misery with their poisonous insatiable hatred and envy. But we are well satisfied and in good spirits. If they are determined to be very angry and rage, we can, on the other hand, laugh and be cheerful.

Therefore I say again: Let him who wants to be a Christian know that he must expect to suffer such persecution from poisonous, wicked, slanderous tongues, especially where they can do nothing with their fists, that he may let all the world sharpen their tongues upon him, and aim at him, sting and strike him, and he on the other hand only defiantly despise all this, and besides laugh in God's name, and let them rage in the name of their god, the devil, in the comfortable assurance (as above said) that our cause is right, and is God's own, which they must themselves confirm, although they indeed condemn us, and yet say it is the truth; besides, our heart and conscience before God are assured that we are teaching aright. For we are not teaching out of our own head and reason or wisdom, nor are we seeking our own advantage, property or honor thereby before the world; but we preach and praise only God's word and his doings.

On the other hand they, our enemies, glory in nothing but their own works, merits and holiness, and us, who do not practice these things with them, they persecute on that account. For they do not persecute us as if we were adulterers, robbers or thieves, etc.; they can indeed tolerate amongst them the most desperate scoundrels and villains; but they raise a terrible hue and cry, because we will not approve their doctrine and life, and praise only the gospel, Christ, faith and really good works, and thus suffer not for ourselves, but everything for the sake of Christ the Lord. Therefore we will sing the whole tune with them, and we will show them that our head is harder than theirs. For, in a word, they must let the man alone, whether they like it or not.

11

Verse 12

REJOICE AND BE EXCEEDING GLAD, FOR
GREAT IS YOUR REWARD IN HEAVEN.

These are surely sweet, comforting words, that ought to make our heart cheerful and courageous against all sorts of persecution. Ought one not to regard as dearer and of more account the word and consolation of the dear Lord, than that of an impotent maggot-bag, or the raging, threatening, excommunicating, cursing and thundering of the abominable Pope, even if he were to pour out upon us the very dregs and whole hell of his wrath and cursing, like a cloudburst; because I hear that Christ my Lord is so heartily pleased, and orders me to be myself happy along with it, besides he promises me such an excellent reward, that the kingdom of heaven shall be mine and everything that Christ has, along with all saints and all Christendom; in short, such a treasure and consolation that I ought not to exchange it for all the world's possessions, joy and music, although every leaf and blade of grass were a tongue that sang my praises. For here it is not a Christian that calls one blessed, yes, not an angel, but the Lord of all the angels, at whose feet both they and all creatures must fall and offer supplication. Therefore they, along with all other creatures, even the very leaves and grass, must cheerfully join in singing about me and dancing in my praise.

And what on the other hand are they who slander and curse me but mere nits and lousy fellows (pardon the expression), yes, much more infamous than can be told. Even if all creatures, the leaves and blades of grass in the forest, and the grains of sand along the sea-shore, were so many tongues to rebuke and annihilate them, what would all that be in contrast with the single word of this man? For his voice sounds so clearly that heaven and earth must be filled and resound with it, whilst on the other hand the slobbery, hoarse scratching and coughing of his enemies are no longer heard.

See, thus we ought to learn a little how to use and take advantage of these words, that do not stand here in vain, but were spoken and written to strengthen and comfort us, with which he as our dear Master and faithful Shepherd or Bishop, equips us to be unterrified and well prepared to suffer, if they impose upon us all manner of torment and misfortune for his sake, both by words and deeds, and that we may despise all that is offensive to us, and condemn it despite our reason and heart.

For, if we are led by our own thoughts and feelings, we have a hard time of it, and it hurts that one should serve, help, advise and benefit the world and everybody, and get no thanks for it but the very worst, most bitter hatred, and cursed, poisonous tongues, so that, if flesh and blood were to rule here, it would soon say: If I am to get nothing else for this, then let who will cling to the gospel and be a Christian, and let the devil henceforth help the world, if it will have it so. Hence too everybody is now complaining and crying—the gospel is making much discord, strife and disturbance in the world, and everything is worse since it has been published than it was before, when everything moved along quietly, and there was no persecution, and the people lived together as good friends and neighbors.

But this is what it means: If you will not have the gospel or be a Christian, then go and be a worldling, and nobody will persecute you, and you will be a friend of the world. But if you will have the gospel and Christ, then you must expect to have trouble, contention and persecution wherever you go. Reason: because the devil won't allow it to be otherwise, or cease to egg the people on against the gospel, so that all the world is incensed against it;

just as now farmers, citizens, noblemen, princes and lords, who are hostile to the gospel from sheer wantonness, and do not themselves know why.

Therefore I make this reply to these idle talkers and grumblers: There neither can nor ought to be a peaceful, quiet state of things. For how could it be so where the devil is ruling, and is a deadly enemy to the gospel? And this, indeed, not without reason, for it hurts him in his kingdom, so that he feels it; and if he would let it move on unhindered, his kingdom would soon be totally destroyed. But if he is to resist and hinder it, then he must rally all his art and power, and stir up against it whatever he can. Therefore do not hope for any peace and quietness as long as Christ and his gospel are in the midst of the devil's kingdom. And woe upon the pleasant and comfortable time that used to be, and upon those who now wish to have it back again! For this is a sure sign that the devil is ruling with great power, and no Christ is here; as I, alas! am concerned, lest it be so again, and the gospel be taken away from us Germans all too soon, which is what these noisy fellows are struggling for.

But we have this assurance, that it is not our fault that things are not going right. For we would be heartily glad if everything went right, and have done our part by teaching, exhorting, beseeching, entreating and yielding, even towards our enemies, offering them peace, and everything that we ought to do; yet we accomplish nothing, except that they persecute, slander and abuse us most shamefully, and cannot cease until they may cool their rage in our blood. As it will not therefore be otherwise, we let them go on at last with their threatening, raging and defaming, and take to ourselves the comfort of which we have heard, assured, that they cannot accomplish what they desire unless they first have hurled Christ from heaven, and made him, with all that he has said, a liar.

"For thus persecuted they the prophets that were before you."

You are not alone (he means to say) in suffering thus. Look about you and count backward to all the holy fathers that ever lived before you, and you will find that they were served the same way. What special treatment do you expect? Is he to change his plan on your account? He had to suffer it in the case of his dear patriarchs and prophets, that they were persecuted and slain, besides being persecuted and traduced by everybody, and made the mock of the world, as we see in the Scriptures, that it was a common proverb, if one wishes to name a prophet, one names for them a fool; as in the history of Jehu, 2 K. 9:11, they said of a prophet: "Wherefore came this mad fellow to thee?" And Isaiah shows, 57:4, how they "made a wide mouth and drew out the tongue" against him. But what did they gain thereby? For now the dear prophets and saints have honor and praise in all the world, and besides are ruling forever with Christ the Lord; but they are an abominable stench and are accursed. This you are to expect for yourselves (says Christ) assuredly, that you shall be rewarded as they are, only more abundantly and gloriously than you can believe, or even dare to desire. For you belong to the same company.

See, this is surely an excellent, precious Preacher and faithful Master, who omits nothing that serves to strengthen and console, both by word and promise, besides by the example and testimony of all the saints and of himself; and with this agree all the angels in heaven and all creatures. What more, then, should we have and desire? Should we not in consideration of such consolation, for his sake patiently endure the wrath and insolence of the world and the devil? What would we do, if we had not a righteous divine cause, and such excellent assurances, and still had to suffer like other people who have no consolation? For it cannot be in the world that one need not suffer anything, and there must be (as above said) some suffering on account of the gospel, that the pious may thereby be tested and helped to their promised consolation, joy and blessedness; but the wicked and despisers or enemies of the gospel be punished and damned.

Thus now, has Christ hitherto prepared and instructed his Christians, how they are to live and suffer in the world, and especially those who are to hold public office in the Church; although even aside from this, every Christian ought to be always ready to stand by himself, where it is necessary, to confess his Lord, and to represent his faith, and be always ready-armed against the world, the devil, the mob, and whatever may be arrayed against him. Now he goes further, and means to commit to them the office, and teach them how to administer it; afterward also to lay upon their lips what and how they are to preach. For with these characteristics a Christian is entirely perfect if he personally lives right and suffers variously because of this, if he afterwards also properly administers his office, in which he is to serve and help others. Thus he now adds:

12

Verse 13a

YE ARE THE SALT OF THE EARTH; BUT IF THE SALT HAVE
LOST HIS SAVOR, WHEREWITH SHALL IT BE SALTED?
IT IS THENCEFORTH GOOD FOR NOTHING, BUT TO BE
CAST OUT, AND TO BE TRODDEN UNDER FOOT OF MEN.

With the word salt he indicates (as above said) what their office is to be.
For salt is not salt for itself; it cannot salt itself; but this is the use of it, that
one salts meat with it, and other things needed in the kitchen, so that they
retain their taste, remain fresh, and do not decay. So, says he, Ye are also
salt; not that which belongs to the kitchen, but that with which this flesh,
which is the whole world, may be salted. This is indeed a glorious office, and
a great, excellent honor, that God should call them his salt, and adds, that
they are to salt everything that is upon earth. But to be this a man is needed,
who is ready, as Christ has hitherto taught, to be poor, wretched, thirsty,
meek, etc., and to suffer all kinds of persecution, reviling and defamation.
If this be wanting, the man will never be a preacher who will do the right
kind of salting, but he will be a savorless salt, that is of no manner of use.

For it is asking a great deal, and heaping it on too heavily, that the poor
fishermen or any poor despised man should be called before God a salt of the
earth, and undertake to lay hold and salt everything that is of human kind
upon earth. Reason and nature cannot do it; for it grows weary of it, and
cannot bear that it must get from it only disgrace, shame and misfortune,

and would soon say: Let the devil salt the world for me. Therefore our holy fathers, bishops, monks and hermits have acted shrewdly in neglecting preaching and attending to other matters, or have withdrawn from intercourse with the people; for they saw that it costs too much to sit in constant danger of losing honor, property and life, and they thought, we will hand it over to others, and meanwhile creep into corners and serve God, having a good time. Hence it is a difficult matter to be an apostle or preacher, and fill such an office; yes, impossible, judging according to flesh and blood. But there must be such people as do it willingly for the sake of God and Christ the Lord, who does not wish to force any one to it or drive him with commands. For to be a Christian demands a willing heart; he who does not heartily desire it had better let it alone.

But our joyful and defiant confidence is this, when we are in trouble, the world and the devil looking askance at us, and doing us all the harm they can, that he says to us: Ye are the salt of the earth. When this word shines into the heart, so that a man can rely upon it, and be absolutely sure that he is God's salt, then let him be wrathful and malicious who will not laugh. I can be more confident and boast more upon his single word than they upon all their power, swords and guns. For because he recognizes me as being that, and gives the evidence of it through his word, all the angels in heaven, yes, sun and moon, together with all creatures, must confirm it and stand by us against the world and the devil. And even if that were not so, we would still have enough in his single word, that he thus names and baptizes us. That they must let stand; and we will surely be before them in honor as long as Christ and his word endures.

Now it is easy to understand how it is with this salting, namely, that one must stand up and say: everything that is born and lives upon earth, is of no account, it is rotten and corrupt before God. For, because he says bluntly and plainly, they shall be a salt of the earth, that is, as to everything that the world is; then it must follow, that everything that is in the world, and is called flesh, or mankind, must be rebuked and thoroughly salted, so that we condemn the sanctity, the wisdom and the divine worship of all the world, self-devised, aside from the word of God, as coming from the devil and belonging to the pit of hell, if it do not hold to Christ alone.

This is then a harsh style of preaching; it makes us disagreeable to the world, and deserves that men get angry at us and strike us in the mouth. For the world could easily endure that we preach aright about Christ and all the articles of the faith; but if we want to lay hold of them and salt them by showing that their wisdom and sanctity are of no account, yes, are blind and damned, this it cannot and will not endure, and it charges the preachers with not being able to do anything but scolding and biting; it blames us with having disturbed society and created discord, with having maligned the clergy and good works.

But what can we do about it? If we are to salt, it must bite. And although they denounce us as biters, we know that it has to be so, and Christ has ordered this, and he means that the salt shall be sharp and bite away, as we shall hear. So St. Paul also does constantly; he rebukes the whole world and denounces all its living and acting, if there be no faith in Christ; and Christ says, John 16:8, "when the Holy Ghost comes, he shall reprove the world of sin," etc., that is, he shall attack everything that he finds in the world, shall make no exception or difference, shall not rebuke some and praise others, or punish only thieves and scoundrels: but he will seize all, all in a mass, one with another, whether one be great, small, pious, wise, holy, or whatever he may be; in short, everything that is not Christ. For the Holy Ghost does not need to come into the world or send preachers into the world that he may exhibit and punish outwardly gross sins, adultery, murder, etc., which the world itself can very well know and punish; but that which it regards as the most precious, and in which it is at its best, claiming to be pious and holy, and meaning thereby to serve God.

Therefore it is all wrong, that some now sophistically assert that it is enough that a preacher tell every one what is right, and simply preach the gospel, but that one dare not touch the Pope, the bishops, princes and other ranks or persons, whereby much discord and contention are occasioned; but the real meaning is: If you will preach the gospel and be of use to the people, you must be sharp and rub the salt into the wounds, that is, must show the opposite and rebuke what is not right, as now the mass, monkery, indulgences, etc., and everything that is connected with them, so that these scandals are removed and no one is thereby deceived. Therefore we must keep on here with our salting, that we may protest and leave no room for its coming back again or being sneakingly introduced; for this will happen, if the salting is not diligently kept up, as used to be the case in Christendom, so that miserable rotten human teaching ruled and ruined everything; which would not have been the case, if the salt had remained. For there would have been no lack of sound doctrine, because by the grace of God still the Scriptures, the gospel, the sacraments, the pulpits remained in the Church, if only the bishops and preachers had attended to this, and had employed these means for salting with them whatever is of the old Adam.

Therefore Christ here exhorts and warns the disciples so diligently that they see to it that this salting is always attended to, and says: If the salt have lost his savor, wherewith shall it then be salted? Salt that has lost its savor means that which has lost its strength and sharpness, and no longer seasons or bites; that is, when the office in Christendom deteriorates so that one ceases to reprove the people, and does not show them their misery and their inability, nor insist upon repentance and self-knowledge, lets them live along as if they were pious and all right, and thus allows their wrong notions of self-righteousness and self-chosen worship to prevail so long, until the true doctrine concerning faith is entirely wrecked, and Christ is lost, and things come to such a pass that there is no help for it.

This he foresaw as here intimated, and he predicted the future danger, even the injury and corruption of Christendom, that this salting or official rebuking would be neglected, and instead of it there would arise a swarm of parties and sects, when every one would herald his own hobby as a true doctrine and worship, when all this is nothing else than worldy, carnal notions, originating in our own head and reason, wherewith we tickle ourselves and thus actually rot in them, as in a mass of natural, stinking, rotten flesh, upon which salting and rebuking are thrown away.

From this you see how much importance is attached to this matter, so that Christ with good reason treats of it here, before all the rest, and commends it so earnestly. For without this Christendom cannot exist, and Christ cannot endure, nor can there be proper thinking or living: so that there is indeed no great injury or corruption of Christendom, except where the salt, wherewith everything else should be seasoned and salted, has lost its savor. And this happens so easily. For it is a poison of such a kind that it is pleasant to take, and exactly suits the old Adam. For he does not like to stand in such danger, risk life and limb or suffer persecution, disgrace and defamation.

Hence our bishops and clergy are the shrewdest people upon earth, in this matter, (though they are not good enough to be called salt that has lost its savor, but are the very devil himself, for they do not at all attend to their bishop's office, but are themselves the greatest persecutors); for they preach in such a way, as to keep out of danger, and have money and property, besides honor and power; for whoever has to rebuke the world at large, emperors, kings, princes, wise men, learned men, and say that their way of living is damned before God, he must have his head taken off. But if I act the hypocrite before them, and say they are all right, then I go scot free, keep my favor and honor, etc., and meantime flatter myself that I mean nevertheless along with this to preach the gospel. But despite all that, I have become salt that has lost its savor. For in that way I let the people stick in their own old crazy notion and carnality, so that they go to the devil, and I at the head of them.

This office thus encounters many temptations and hindrances, both on the right and left, so that many keep silence either through fear of the danger of harm and persecution, or for the sake of honor, property or enjoyment. Besides, we are weak, lazy and averse to this duty, so that we are easily led to neglect it, and grow weary, when we see that things do not go as we like, and it looks as though it were of no use, and the people act contemptuously, yes, even become worse the more we rebuke them.

Therefore we must be firmly set against all this, and have respect only to the command of Christ, who imposes this office upon us, and means that we are to open our mouths promptly, and rebuke what is to be rebuked; paying no attention to our own danger, inconvenience or advantage and enjoyment, neither to the malice and contempt of other people, and take comfort from the fact that he makes us his salt, and will support us in doing our duty. And he commands us confidently to salt, without giving heed to it or allowing ourselves to be alarmed about it, whether the world will not endure it, and consequently persecute us; nor are we to despair although, as we think, we are accomplishing nothing. For what he commands us to do, we should be pleased and satisfied with, and let him decide what and how much he may accomplish through us. If the people will not hear or accept it, we are nevertheless salt and have done our official duty. Then we can with all honor and cheerfulness stand before the bar of God and testify that we have faithfully told every man his duty, and have stuck nothing under the bench, so that they have no excuse, as if they did not understand, and it had not been told them.

But those who allow themselves to be scared, and are silent for the sake of favor, honor or worldly good, they will have at the last day to hear it said of them: This was our preacher, and he did not tell us of it; and he will not excuse them, although they say: Lord, they would not hear. For Christ will say in reply: Do you not know that I commanded you to salt, and diligently warned you to do it; ought you not to have feared my word more than them? This ought in all conscience to alarm us. For here you hear the sentence that he pronounces upon all such salt that has lost its savor, and says:

13

Verse 13b

"IT IS THENCEFORTH GOOD FOR NOTHING, BUT TO BE
CAST OUT AND TO BE TRODDEN UNDER FOOT OF MEN."

That is as much as to say: They shall not have a good time of it even here
upon earth, but shall be completely rejected by Christ as those who no
longer belong to him, and shall never be his preachers nor belong to
Christendom, wholly cast out and robbed of all fellowship in heaven and
with all saints; although they may retain the name, and are held in high
honor by the people as the best preachers and holiest people upon earth;
as was the case in the papacy at the time when it was the most pious and
holy, (not as now, when it has grown to be a worldly imperialism and a spiritual devils' government,) when the pope himself preached and ruled the
churches, and had everything admirably arranged, and brought under settled rules and regulations, (as St. Gregory did, and some before and after
him,) which all the world held to be the best government, and the holiest
form of worship that could be established upon earth, and yet it was all
of no account.

For there was no salt there, by which this should have been brought to
the test of the word of God, and should have been rebuked, as being our
own self-devised holiness; but all the world praised and sanctioned it, and
thus gave encouragement to those who were arrogantly presumptuous and
trusted in it, as if they were leading a truly blessed life and were a holy

class; as it also praises and exalts St. Gregory himself, so that, although he was a holy man (as I regard him) yet he accomplished no good by his teaching, and yet made so fair a show that no one can find fault with it, so that, if they could now bring back matters and restore them to what they were, nobody would dare say a word against it, or he would have to be called the vilest heretic that ever was.

This is now one part of the warning, namely, if the salt have lost its savor it is no longer of any use. The other part sounds still more terrible, when he pronounces the sentence upon it, that we are to let it be "cast out and trodden under foot of men." If the true salt, that is the true interpretation of Scripture, has disappeared, by which the whole world should be rebuked, and which should let nothing avail but only simple faith in Christ, then it is all over, and all our teaching and rebuking does no more good. For God has already rejected and damned both the teaching and the living, the master and the pupil.

In short, if this point concerning Christ be not insisted upon, that we are justified and saved through him alone, and if we do not hold all else, aside from him as damned, all resistance and restraint is at an end, yes, there is no measure or limit of all heresy and error, of all sects and parties, when everybody invents and scatters abroad something peculiar of his own; as used to be the case among us under the Pope, when no monk could have a dream without dragging it into the pulpit, and making a special divine service out of it, and no lies were so shameful that they were not accepted, if only any one ventured to take them into the pulpit; until at last things went so far that not only Christ was lost, but God besides, and they themselves believed hardly a single article of the faith any more, so that I may say that in a hundred years there were few Popes that believed a single article; just as it is now in German countries, among those with whom the article concerning Christ has disappeared and one factious party and error after the other has arisen: when one denies the sacrament, another baptism and other articles, and many become altogether Epicurean, who believe nothing at all, just like the Popes and their cardinals at Rome, and so at last become nothing but swine and kine, and die like these.

Therefore, I have always exhorted, just as Christ here does, that the salt remain salt, and lose not its savor, that is, that we urgently insist upon the principal article of the faith. For if this be neglected, not one part can rightly remain, and all is lost; there is no faith or understanding any more, so that no one can give right instruction or advice. In short, one must let everybody trample upon him, that is (as above said,) no bacchanalian or jackass is so contemptible, but that if he can only invent something new, everybody will run after him and believe it. For what have not the abominable monks hitherto dared brazenfacedly to preach, and beguile the people with their brotherhoods, little prayers, rosaries, yes, with their scabby hoods, that they put upon the dead, and therewith promise them heaven? What is that else, than to let every body trample upon you, and be at the mercy of every preacher of lies? This comes from the devil's getting possession of the heart and totally ruining it with his rotten, damnable doctrines and superstition, so that Christ is gone, and the knowledge of him is lost.

For if I cling to this, that Christ alone is my righteousness and holiness, no monk will ever persuade or mislead me by his hood, rosary, this or that work and childish human notion. For through faith I am a judge of all imaginable conditions and ways of living, so that I can condemn everything that offers to show me anything else that is to avail before God. But if I neglect this, and let the treasure go, and am instructed to seek elsewhere and otherwise to be pious, to conciliate God and atone for sin, then I am already prepared for all sorts of snares and nets of the devil, and to let myself be led as he pleases; then presently comes some one who preaches to me: If you want to be pious and serve God, then put on a hood, pray daily so many rosaries, burn so many little candles to St. Anna: then I fall in with this like a blind man and everybody's fool and prisoner, and do everything I am told, so completely that I cannot defend myself from even the most trifling mistake.

See, Christ has himself here foretold this, and given warning that so it would be; and no one has ever lived who knew just how to be on his guard against it. And if we are not now wide awake, and do not take good care that we firmly hold this article, then it will happen to us also, that we hold no article properly and purely, nor cease to err and create factious parties until it is all over, and no preaching or teaching will be of use any more, but we shall stay swine and kine; as it is, alas! already among the great mass, because of our despising the gospel and being ungrateful for it.

14

Verses 14 and 15

YE ARE THE LIGHT OF THE WORLD. A CITY THAT IS SET ON
A HILL CANNOT BE HID. NEITHER DO MEN LIGHT A CANDLE
AND PUT IT UNDER A BUSHEL, BUT ON A CANDLE-STICK,
AND IT GIVETH LIGHT UNTO ALL THAT ARE IN THE HOUSE.

This is the other part of the office which he commits to the dear apostles;
that they are to be called, and to be a light of the world, namely to instruct
souls and point them to eternal life; by this he subjects the whole world to
the apostles, that it is to be and must be enlightened through them, and
concludes that it all, with everything that it can do, is nothing but darkness and blindness. For if it without this had a light that could enlighten
it, (as it indeed thinks it has,) why did he need the apostles for this? Now
see, if this is not a high, excellent office, and an honor above all honor, that
everybody in the world, whether called kings, princes, lords, learned men,
wise men, holy men, must sit down, and the apostles stand up, and all must
let their wisdom, holiness, etc., be rebuked and condemned, as those who
do not know what to teach or how to live, or how they are off with God.

But here comes master Pope with his ugly bishops, who want to be called
the vicegerents of Christ, and of the apostles; who undertake to master the
word of Christ, and depreciate the apostles, where they drivel that it was
not enough that the apostles preached, and that the Holy Ghost sent forth
light through them, but we must hear and heed the councils of the holy

fathers, and the ordinances of the Popes, who have taught much more and better. But we are to know that Christ is not such a juggler who talks with half words; but, because he calls them a light of the world, their teaching alone must avail and be sufficient to enlighten all the world, so that one needs no other light; yes, that what is apart from their teaching is nothing but darkness. Although they may shine long with their lantern, it is after all nothing but mere laws devised by men concerning external things which without their help everybody understands, and could easily himself discover and make so that one ought in fact to call them not lux mundi [light of the world,] but lex Dei [law of God], as those who undertake to govern God himself and his Christendom with their laws, just as if they were much better than the apostles. They obscure thus the light of the apostles with their blind doctrine, with which they cannot properly rebuke or instruct any man's conscience; as we see in all the books of the Pope, and of all the universities, and so they cannot be called either salt or light. For when they do their best, they rebuke the gross, external things that have already been condemned by secular law and the light of reason. But the really hard knots and principal things, as unbelief, false sanctity, they take no notice of, yes, are themselves in them over head and ears. Therefore their teaching is sheer nonsense, and besides darkness and blindness, not to be able to see anything higher to salt and to enlighten than how one is to eat flesh or fish, to dress and behave this or that way.

Therefore, it surely is and remains the office of the apostles alone both to rebuke aright the real internal vices, and again to heal, comfort and cheer up all poor distressed consciences, and allow no one to go unrebuked in wrong-doing or uninstructed and unencouraged in what is good. Therefore Christ also here appoints and consecrates them as preachers, that we shall and must hear them alone, and admit no other factious spirits whom the devil brings in alongside of them, who claim to be the salt and light, yes, even to lord it over Christ, and scream out, the doctrine of faith amounts to nothing, one must aim higher, and otherwise afflict one's self, so that one suffers and mortifies himself; which, if one looks at it on all sides, is nothing but being taught about our own doing, and yet never amounts to showing what is unbelief and rebuking the real arrogant vices that are sticking in that same doctrine, with which they set themselves up as salt and light; they do not stop with the calling and command which he here gives to the apostles and says: Ye shall be the light; at this alone we aim, that we may be sure of this, and confidently say, that Christ has consecrated us to this, and has made it the duty of Christians to salt and shine by virtue of our office and by divine command.

For this is also for this reason necessary, because Christ means that this office shall be exercised not secretly or in only one place, but openly, throughout the world; and he shows them plainly enough, what they have to expect from the world, when he says: "a city that is set on a hill cannot be hid. Neither do men light a candle and set it under a bushel," etc. That is as much as to say: He who wants to be a light must see to it that he do not creep into a corner, but stand forth publicly and be not afraid. For so it goes, as we said before, that those who are called to be apostles, and shine, do not like to come to the front, allow themselves to be frightened off by threats, danger, persecution, or are befooled with friendship, favor, honor and worldly good, so that they do not come forward and open their mouths, but creep into corners, hide behind the hills, and shut up their whistles.

So it is with our clergy who sit in office; and they are ordered to stand up before Christendom and publicly shine with their teaching; but they hide it under the bench, yes, have become worse than that, for they are the very ones that persecute the word, and want to put out the light, and only stir up against it emperors, kings and the whole world; at the same time they sit in the house and want to rule alone the church, have possession of pulpit, baptism, sacrament, and everything that belongs to the calling and office. But this is what the apostles predicted, that shepherds should become wolves, and Antichrist should sit in the temple of God, and exalt himself above everything that is called God and is worshipped.

In contrast with these are the other factious spirits, who have no calling to this office, who might well remain at home in the corner; they want to push themselves in everywhere and be the only ones to shine, so that everybody must hear them and look to them. But these, too, seek only thereby their own honor, and they preach only so long as the people hang on to them and they need fear no danger. But if they were to stand as true preachers, to whom the office is entrusted, and steadily shine in public, letting no wind or weather frighten or silence them, they would soon disappear and let nobody be found at home. So the dear office of the ministry has to be treated on both sides, that either those neglect it who should exercise it, or those want to exercise it who have not been called to it; and so it is never properly attended to, except when Christ provides such persons as he here describes and has prepared beforehand, as above.

He means now here to say: If you wish to be my preachers, you must be really prepared to take your place publicly and stand up before the world, as upon a high mountain, that you may be readily seen and openly heard, concealing nothing or hiding it under the bench, that you ought to preach, neither keeping silence or speaking out of love to any one; but, as you are the light, shining openly and free, without regard to honor or shame, wealth or poverty, hatred or favor, death or life; and know that you are serving me, who has appointed you to be the light. Such would then be the right kind of people, who do not let themselves be bent to the one side or to the other; as Psalm 45 says concerning the office of the ministry: "The sceptre of thy kingdom is a right sceptre. Thou lovest righteousness and hatest wickedness," etc.

This is the virtue and glory of the gospel and its preachers. For all other teachings are free from danger, they all preach what people like to hear and what is agreeable to reason, they need not fear that any one will persecute them. But this teaching is everywhere opposed, because it will come to the front and show that the light and teaching of the world is of no account; then they try in every way to obscure for us this light, and push it into a corner, or throw it under a bushel, so that we may drop our teaching, or recant and let ourselves be bent and interpreted as they may please. But we will not let ourselves be driven from our position, but will continue to be a city upon a hill, and the light upon the candlestick in the house. For he who has made us the light will surely keep us as such. Therefore he now concludes:

15

Verse 16

LET YOUR LIGHT SO SHINE BEFORE MEN THAT
THEY MAY SEE YOUR GOOD WORKS AND GLORIFY
YOUR FATHER WHICH IS IN HEAVEN.

See how earnestly he urges the exhortation, which he would have no need
to do, if there were not great danger and occasion for it; and it is as much
as to say: They will try to obscure your light, and will not endure it; but
only be bold and in good heart against them, so that you may accomplish
only this much, that you do not creep under the bushel, but perform honestly the duties of your office, then I will see to it that they shall not thus
obscure it. For this is certain, so long as a Christian preacher stands in his
lot and does his duty, and can despise the world's abuse and persecution,
the office too must remain, and the gospel cannot fall, because there are
still those remaining who hold to it; as there must be some abiding evermore, even to the last day.

That is to say, however: "That they may see your good works and glorify
your Father which is in heaven," is spoken after the manner of St. Matthew,
who is in the habit of speaking in this way of works. For he, together with
the other two evangelists, Mark and Luke, does not in his gospel treat so
fully and profoundly upon the great subject of Christ as St. John and St.
Paul. Therefore they speak and exhort much about good works; as indeed
both should in Christendom be insisted upon, yet each in proportion to its

nature and dignity: that one should first and most of all hold forth faith and
Christ, and afterwards inculcate works. Since now the evangelist John has
most thoroughly and powerfully discussed the main topic, and is rightly
therefore regarded as the highest and foremost evangelist: Matthew, Luke
and Mark have treated and strongly urged the other side, so that it should
not be forgotten; so that in this matter they are better than John, and he
again in the other.

But you must not look at what is said and taught about works in such a
way as to separate faith from them, as they are docked by our blind teachers: but always connect them with faith, so that they are incorporated with
it, spring from faith and move with it, and are praised and called good
because of it; as I have often taught. So also here, when he says: that they
may see your good works, you must not regard them as mere trifling works,
without faith, as the good works of our clergy have hitherto been; but as
such works that faith performs, and that cannot be done without faith. For
by good works here he means the practicing, illustrating and confessing
the teaching concerning Christ, and suffering for doing it. For he speaks of
those works with which we shine. But shining is the proper office of faith
or teaching, whereby we help others also to believe.

Therefore it is works of the highest and best character, just those from
which it must necessarily follow, as he here says, that our heavenly Father
is honored and praised. For this teaching or preaching takes from us all the
glamour of holiness, and says, there is nothing good in us whereof we can
boast. And besides, it interests the conscience, how it is to deal with God,
exhibits to it the grace and mercy of God, and the entire Christ: that is, it
truly reveals and praises God, which is also the true sacrifice and worship.
These works are to be the first and most important, that are followed also
by those that are called works of love, in daily life and outward treatment
of our neighbor; these shine also, but only in so far as they are begun and
carried on in faith.

Now you can yourself conclude that St. Matthew here is not to be understood concerning the common works which every one is to do towards
his neighbor, from love, of which he speaks in Matt. 25; but chiefly of the
true Christian work, namely correct teaching, insisting upon faith and

showing how to strengthen and keep it, whereby we testify that we are true Christians. For the others are not so reliable, since even sham Christians can bedeck and hide themselves under great, beautiful works of love. But to teach and confess Christ truly is not possible without faith; as St. Paul says, 1 Cor. 12:3: "No one can call Jesus Lord except by the Holy Ghost." For no sham Christian or factious spirit can understand this doctrine; how much less can he properly preach and confess it, although he uses the words and echoes them, and yet does not adhere to them or let them be clear?— preaching always in such a way that one sees he does not understand it, smears his slobber over it, by which he steals the honor from Christ and appropriates it to himself.

For this alone is the surest work of a true Christian, if he so praises and preaches Christ that the people learn this, how they are nothing and Christ is everything. In short, it is such a work that is done not with reference to one or two, when it remains hidden as other works; but publicly before the whole world to shine and let itself be seen, and alone for this reason is also persecuted. (For other works they can very well endure.) Therefore it is properly called such a work by which our Father is recognized and praised. This the other less important works cannot attain to, that have to do only with our fellow-men, and belong to the second table of the law. These have to do with the first three great commandments that refer to God's honor, name and word; and besides they must be well tested and purified by persecution and suffering, that they may endure; also be defamed before the world that they may remain free from the desire of personal honor, and from arrogance, and be so much the more praised before God, as his honor and praise are thereby assailed [i. e. by works courting self-praise, personal honor, etc.]. Therefore, too, they stand most securely, so that God the more vigorously defends them, and makes them effective over against the violent persecutions of the world. Therefore we should give these works the decided preference as by far the most important, and afterward perform the others also as between ourselves and our fellow-men, that so both may have their due—that we first of all constantly teach and insist upon faith, and then live accordingly, and thus everything that we do is of faith; as I have always taught.

16

Verse 17

THINK NOT THAT I AM COME TO DESTROY THE LAW OR THE PROPHETS; I AM NOT COME TO DESTROY, BUT TO FULFILL.

Because Christ the Lord entrusted and strongly commended the office to the apostles, he now goes further and himself begins both to salt and to shine as an example for them, that they may know what they are to preach; and attacks both the teaching and the life of the Jews, to rebuke and to reform their wrong notions and doings; although here, as I have said, he does not treat of the great principal doctrine of faith; but first he begins below, and rightly explains and extols the law, which was greatly obscured and perverted by their Pharisees and Scribes. For that is also a very important matter, that one should make the teaching of God's commands clear and set them forth correctly.

But it is a sharp, unendurable salt, that he attacks and condemns these people as neither teaching nor living aright, and finds fault with them in everything, who were yet the very best and holiest, who were daily teaching the commands of God, and were exercising themselves in holy worship, etc., so that no one could rebuke them; he gave them thereby occasion to fiercely exclaim against him, and to accuse him of wishing to undermine and destroy the law which God had given, etc.: just as the Pope and his crowd cry out against us, and denounce us as heretics who forbid the doing of good works. So he foresaw very well that he would be thus charged, and that his teaching would be interpreted in this way. Therefore he anticipates with a preface and explanation that it is not his intention to undermine the law; but that he is here for the very purpose of rightly teaching and confirming it against those who would weaken it by their teaching.

For there was surely need of such a statement, on account of the high reputation that they had, and in view of the excellent show that they knew how to make and dress up, that they alone were the people of God, that they had so many prophets and holy fathers, that whoever ventured to rebuke them would have to hear at once: Who art thou, that thou wilt be alone wise and blame everybody, as though our fathers and we have all been in error, who have the word of God and preach it? Just as the whole world is now howling at us, and saying we condemn the holy fathers and the whole Church that surely cannot err, because it is ruled by the Holy Ghost, etc. Because thou art blaming our doctrine and life, this is a sign that thou condemnest both the law and the prophets, the fathers and the whole people.

To this now Christ replies: No, I will surely not destroy the law or the prophets, but I hold them in honor and insist upon their observance more earnestly and diligently than you do; yes, so earnestly that heaven and earth shall pass away before I will allow a letter or the smallest tittle to perish or to have been written in vain; yes, I will still further say, that whosoever despises the very least commandment or teaches otherwise, he shall on account of this very smallest thing in the kingdom of heaven be rejected, although he rightly kept all the rest. Therefore we agree upon this point, that we are strictly to teach and observe Moses and the prophets; but the point now is, since we both are required to and wish to teach the law (as also now both parties, viz. the Pope together with the other crowds, and we appeal to the same Scriptures, exalt at the same time the one gospel and word of God), that one may be sure which side rightly holds and interprets the Scriptures or the laws of God, or which does not. About this there is dispute. Here I must salt and rebuke. For the Jews with their glosses have perverted and corrupted the law: and I have come to set things right again; just as we have had to attack the preachings of the Pope, that have corrupted for us the Scriptures with their stench and filth.

He does not thereby deny that they are the people of God, and have the law, the fathers and the prophets; just as we do not deny or condemn the Christians, baptism, gospel, that were under the Pope, but we say, it is the right baptism, gospel, etc., that we have. But we fight against accepting what they have daubed over them, and approving of the way in which they interpret and pervert them, and have defiled the pure doctrine with their nasty and maggoty, yes devilish appendage of their hoods, tonsures, indulgences, purgatory, sacrificial masses, etc. Here we have to salt and work, that we may clear out this stench and make things clean. So it appears that just those who are really destroying the law and the Scriptures adorn themselves with the beautiful name of the Scriptures, the gospel, the Christian Church, etc., and, under this pretence, bring in their maggots, and have so corrupted the church as to rob it of its value; and then they make an ado about us, that we are assailing the Christian Church, the holy fathers, good works, etc.

He now says: I am not come to destroy the law, but to fulfill it; that is, I will not bring another or a new law, but will take the Scriptures that you have and properly extol them, and explain them in such a way that you may know how we are to demean ourselves. For the Gospel or the preaching of Christ does not bring a new doctrine which neutralizes or changes the law; but just that (as St. Paul says) which was promised before in the Scriptures and by the prophets. We accept. therefore, from those who are with us the very same Scriptures, baptism, sacraments, etc., which they have, and do not wish to propose anything new or better. But this we do for the sole purpose that the same may be rightly preached and treated, and that whatever does not accord with it may be taken out of the way.

St. Augustine explains the word "fulfill" in two ways; first, that fulfilling the law means when one adds to the law what it lacks; and secondly, when one fulfills it by working and living. But the first explanation is wrong. For the law is in itself so rich and perfect that one need add nothing to it. For the apostles themselves had to prove the gospel and the preaching concerning Christ out of the Old Testament. Therefore no one, not even Christ himself, can improve the law. For what can be devised or taught higher than the teaching of the first commandment: Thou shalt love God with all thy heart, etc.? He does this, however, that he gives in addition to the law and the doctrine his grace and Spirit, so that one may do and fulfill what the law demands; but that does not mean adding anything to the law. And so he is here not speaking about that, but of the fulfilling that is done by teaching; just as he defines destroying, not as acting against the law by works, but as, detracting from the law by teaching.

Therefore we have the same truth here that St. Paul utters in Rom. 3:31: "Do we then make void the law through faith? God forbid; yea, we establish the law," namely, that he does not mean to bring another doctrine, as though the former one were no longer to avail; but he means to preach and extol the same properly, to show the real kernel and meaning of it, that they may learn what the law is and demands, over against the glosses of the Pharisees, which they have inserted, and have preached only the shells or husks of it. Just as we may say to our papistic friends: we do not wish to abolish your gospel or preach it differently, but to clean it off and polish it, as a mirror that is dimmed and soiled by your filth, so that nothing more than the name of the gospel is left, but no one could rightly see anything in it: so the Jewish teachers kept the text of the law, but with their additions so corrupted it that no correct understanding or use of it could remain.

17

Verse 18

FOR VERILY I SAY UNTO YOU, TILL HEAVEN AND
EARTH PASS, ONE JOT OR TITTLE SHALL IN NO WISE
PASS FROM THE LAW, TILL ALL BE FULFILLED.

That is, I insist upon it, that it must all be taught and held pure and entire, and not the least part of it be done away; whereby he shows that he found it far otherwise, namely, that both doctrine and life had not been rightly conducted. Therefore he must (as here follows) take in hand both of these and thoroughly salt them, that there may be a purification. So also must we teach that we do not allow a letter to be detached from the gospel, but say: Everything must be taught, believed and held purely. He thus intimates that he is about to preach a sharp sermon, and will not lie under the charge that he means to destroy the law; but will turn the attack from himself upon them, and prove how they have weakened and destroyed the law, and for this have daubed their glosses over it. Just as our papistic neighbors have done with the gospel and the Scriptures, when they utterly ignored the most important topic, justification by faith; also, they have withheld one form from the sacrament and concealed the words of the sacrament; yes, they have so coarsely misrepresented, that they have preached these commandments which Christ here announces, not as necessary statutes, but as merely good counsels, directly contrary to these words and stipulations, that sooner heaven and earth must pass away than that one of the least of these be not observed. Thereupon he at once passes an earnest sentence upon such preachers, as follows:

18

Verse 19

WHOSOEVER THEREFORE SHALL BREAK ONE OF THESE
LEAST COMMANDMENTS, AND SHALL TEACH MEN SO, HE
SHALL BE CALLED THE LEAST IN THE KINGDOM OF HEAVEN:
BUT WHOSOEVER SHALL DO AND TEACH THEM, THE SAME
SHALL BE CALLED GREAT IN THE KINGDOM OF HEAVEN.

I will be so positive about these (says he) that I not only will not break any
of them; but whoever is a preacher, and annuls or ignores the very smallest part, let him know that he is not a preacher of mine, but is damned and
shall be turned out of heaven. For that he says, he shall be called the least
in the kingdom of heaven, is nothing else than that he shall not be in the
kingdom of heaven; but, as he holds it to be a small matter that he despises
God's command, so shall he also be despised and rejected.

All the preachers of the gospel must also be prepared to make the same
boast before all the world; as we can confidently challenge our opponents
to show us a passage or article of the Scriptures that we suppress or do not
rightly preach. For they themselves had to testify at the Diet of Augsburg
that our confession is purely scriptural, and not opposed to any article of
the faith. But they are making a great ado about this only, that we do not
also hold their peculiar notions that the Councils and Popes have sanctioned, and we are to be damned because we do not like their nasty maggots and rotten human trifles.

Although we have always shown ourselves ready to work with them, and indeed could still do it, if they would allow us the liberty and diversity, that it is not necessary to salvation nor contrary to the gospel, whether one omits anything or shares in it to please them, as any other free, unnecessary thing, that neither helps nor hinders us; as when, for instance, in the carnival season one shares in the mummery. But this they will not admit; and so we cannot do otherwise, nor give up Christ our Saviour (who has shown and bestowed upon us more kindness through his dear suffering and death, than the Pope, Franciscus, Dominicus, or any saint) for the sake of their rotten notions that can benefit or help nobody. If they would grant us this liberty, we would try to observe everything with them that they demand of us, and even better than they do themselves.

But because they are not satisfied with this, but want to compel us to forsake Christ and the pure doctrine which they themselves cannot find fault with, we despise them, as condemned and rejected by Christ, with both their doctrine and life, as those who not only corrupt but absolutely nullify a word or command of God, in that they shamelessly teach that it is not necessary to love God with all the heart; also, that one honors his parents, if he wants to go into a monastery or give to the Church his money with which he might keep his parents; so also, any one may desert his espoused bride and go into a monastery. In short, everything that the Lord here demands according to the command of God, they have declared to be unnecessary, as though this were merely good advice or works of supererogation, etc.

Hence you see what an excellent sort of Christian teachers and holy people they are, who dare to annul and destroy recklessly all the commands of God, and yet want to go scot free, and venture to require it of us, yes, with threats and force try to drive us to hold their human nonsense to be necessary, and, if we do not accept and praise this, they assail us with horrible edicts and all sorts of furious rage. Now calculate for yourself what Christ will say to it, since he here pronounces so severe a sentence, that he shall have no part in his kingdom who breaks one of the least of these commandments, although he teaches and keeps all the rest exactly. Where do you think is the place for them, except in the glowing fire of hell, where it is the deepest? For there never has risen such a shameful people upon earth, who so shamelessly treated the word of God, which they know to be right, and still wish to be held in honor as Christians that are leaders. Therefore beware of them, and let no one be frightened by their damning, persecution and raging. For here we have the consolation that those who teach purely and truly the word of God, and adhere to that, shall be great with Christ in the kingdom of heaven, although that crowd curses them to the bottom of hell.

I omit, however, here to say how the law must be fulfilled, so that no letter or tittle of it pass, etc., whilst we still teach that no man can fulfill it. For I have said that Christ is here speaking particularly not concerning the life, but concerning the doctrine; and he is not discussing the great subject what he is and what he gives to us, namely, that we cannot be justified or saved by the works of the law, but thereby only come to the knowledge of ourselves, how we are not able to fulfill properly a tittle of it of ourselves. And although after we have become Christians by baptism and faith, we do as much as we can, we still can never thereby stand before God; but must always humbly find our way to Christ, who has most purely and perfectly fulfilled it all, and bestows himself with his fulfillment of it upon us, so that through him we may stand before God, and the law cannot hold us guilty or condemn us. So that it is true that all must come to pass and be fulfilled even to the smallest tittle; but only by this one man, of which enough is said elsewhere.

19

Verse 20

FOR I SAY UNTO YOU THAT EXCEPT YOUR
RIGHTEOUSNESS SHALL EXCEED THE RIGHTEOUSNESS
OF THE SCRIBES AND PHARISEES, YE SHALL IN NO
CASE ENTER INTO THE KINGDOM OF HEAVEN.

Here you see how he plunges in and antagonizes not ordinary people, but
the very best in the whole nation, who were the true kernel and quintes-
sence, and shone before the rest like the sun, so that there was no more
highly esteemed class nor more honorable name among the people than
that of the Pharisees and Scribes; and if one wanted to name a holy man,
he would have to name a Pharisee; just as among us the Carthusians or hermits were called: as the disciples of Christ no doubt themselves believed
that there was no greater holiness to be found than among these, and they
least of all expected that he would assail these people. Nor did he venture
at once to mention names, and blame certain persons among them, but
the whole class; and he rebukes also not certain evil practices or sins, but
their righteousness and holy living; so completely, indeed, that he denies
and closes the kingdom of heaven against them, and condemns them at
once to hell fire. Just as if he now said: All priests and monks, and all that
are called spiritual, without exception, are eternally damned to hell, with
all their system, where it is the best. Who could hear or endure such a
sermon? That is now one thing that he acknowledges, that they have a

righteousness, and lead a correct, honorable life; and yet he so completely rejects it, that if it be not better than that, it is already condemned, and all is lost that one can accomplish by it.

Secondly, notice, that he is treating of those who wish to get to heaven, and who seriously think about another life, which the other great rude mass do not regard, nor do they ask about God and his word, to whom everything that we say about the gospel is preached in vain. But these are preached to, that they may know, that such righteousness is false, which one must salt and rebuke, as that with which they deceive both themselves and others, and lead to hell from the right road, and that they may consider, on the other hand, what the true piety is which the law demands; as Christ now presently will show.

20

Verse 21

YE HAVE HEARD THAT IT WAS SAID TO THEM OF OLDEN TIME, THOU SHALT NOT KILL; AND WHOSOEVER SHALL KILL, SHALL BE IN DANGER OF THE JUDGMENT.

Here he takes up several of the Ten Commandments, to explain them properly, and shows how the Pharisees and Scribes gave no further explanation of them and attached no further significance to them than lies in the mere words, as referring to external gross works. So, in the first place, in this fifth commandment they saw nothing more than the word kill, that means strike dead with the hand; and they let the people stop short with that, as if nothing further were here forbidden, and as if besides a convenient shield were provided, so that they would not be guilty of the killing, though one handed over another person to death. So, when they delivered Christ to the heathen Pilate, they would not defile their hands with blood, that they might continue to be pure and holy; and they were so strict, that they would not even go into the palace of the judge; and yet it was they alone who caused his death, and forced Pilate against his will that he had to kill him. Yet they acted as if they were entirely clean and innocent, so that they even blamed the apostles in regard to it, and said: "You intend to bring this man's blood upon us;" as though they should say: It was not we, but the heathen, that killed him. So we read about king Saul in 1 Sam. 18:25. He disliked David, and would gladly have killed him; but as he wanted to be holy, he thought he would not kill him himself, but send him among the Philistines, that he might be killed there, and his hand not be defiled with his blood.

See, that is the beautiful Pharisee-holiness, that can make itself clean, and stay pious, if it only does not slay with its own hand, although the heart is sticking full of wrath, hatred and envy, and secret evil and murderous designs, and the tongue besides full of cursing and blasphemy; just as is the case with the holiness of our papists, who have become real masters in this business; and, that their holiness may not be rebuked nor they be bound by the words of Christ, they have come handsomely to his assistance, and have deduced twelve counsels from his words, that Christ has not commanded all this as necessary, but has left it at the option of every one to be observed as good advice, whoever wishes to merit something special above others; that it is instruction altogether superfluous, that one can easily dispense with.

But if you ask them for what reason they have invented these recommendations, or how they prove them, they say: Why, if one should teach thus that would mean *nimis onerativum legis christianae*, that is, Christian people would be too heavily burdened; as those at Paris have openly and boldly written against me. Yes, truly, a beautiful reason and a grievous burden, that a Christian should be friendly towards his neighbor, and not let him be in need, as every one wishes to be treated. And because they think it too burdensome, it must not be said to have been commanded, but left at every one's option to be done or not as one may choose; but he who cannot or will not do it shall not be burdened with it. Thus we are to twist the mouth of Christ, master his words, and make out of them whatever we please. But he will not allow himself to be deceived in this way, nor will he recall his sentence that he has here pronounced saying: whosoever has not a better piety, shall find heaven shut against him, and be damned, and as follows afterwards, also, he shall be deserving of hell-fire who says to his brother, Thou fool; from which we may easily conclude whether it was recommended or commanded.

And here they have also discovered a little gloss, to help their lies, and thus they say, it was indeed commanded to refrain from anger and spite in the heart, but not from the tokens of wrath, that is, as we say in German, to forgive, but not to forget, and to have the idea that you will not be angry or do anything bad, and yet withhold all kindness from your neighbor and bestow upon him no good word or token of friendship. Here ask of God himself and Christ, why he did not withhold this kindness from those who crucified him, reviled and most shamefully blasphemed him, but prayed for them and said: Father, forgive them, for they know not what they do, although they were the most shameless villains, who deserved the fiercest wrath and punishment. Yes, if he had been angry at us in that way, who were his enemies and practiced all manner of idolatry and ungodliness, he would have had to stay up there in heaven and not shed his blood and die for us, but say after the manner of this little gloss: I will forgive, indeed, but I will not forget. Meanwhile we should all have continued to be the devil's own, and no man could have escaped going to hell. In short, it is absolutely a disgraceful, cursed little gloss, and in fact a sin and a shame, that any one in Christendom has dared to teach this, in the face of such a clear and open text; yet they have daubed all their books full of these lies, and are trying now besides brazenfacedly to defend them. But hereby we are to see and recognize our Pharisees and hyprocrites, with their great sanctity, which they profess with many special works, but at the same time without hesitation transgress the commands of God and also teach others to do the same; as Christ here and elsewhere depicts them.

It is indeed true, that one must be angry, if those do it whose duty it is, and if the anger does not go farther than to rebuke sin and what is evil; as, when one sees another sin, admonishes and warns him, that he may refrain from it, etc. That is a Christian and brotherly, yes, a fatherly anger. For you see in the case of pious parents, that they do not punish their children in such a way that they mean to do them harm or injury, but that badness may be repressed and evil averted; so also the powers that be are to be wrathful and punish. Here it is indeed right that one should have no anger in his heart, and yet must show signs and tokens of anger, since both the word and the fist are rough and sharp, but the heart remains sweet and friendly and knows of no spite. In short, it is the anger of love that wishes harm to no one, but is a friend of the person, whilst hostile to the sin, as even nature may teach every one. But it will not do to abuse this as a shield, and hide and dress up under it spite and envy in the heart against our neighbor; as those knavish saints do and teach.

So Jesus now takes up this command, and means to say this: You have thus heard from the Pharisees how Moses commanded, and of old it was thus taught: Thou shalt not kill, etc. Therewith you tickle yourselves and deck yourselves out, take on airs as those who diligently teach, and observe the laws of God as they are taught from Moses, and were received by them of olden time; you take your stand and insist upon it: There is Moses, he says, Thou shalt not kill. You hold on to that word, and won't let it mean anything else than just as it sounds in the plainest sense, so that the simple-minded must say: "It is true; that's the way it stands in the book;" thus you darken the word with your continual bawling and your foul glosses, so that one does not see what the words really contain and mean. For do you think that he is speaking only of the fist where he says: Thou shalt not kill? What does he mean by *you?* Not only your hand, foot, tongue, or any other single member; but all that you are, body and soul. Just as when I say to any one: You shall not do this; I speak not with the fist, but with the whole person. Yes, even if I should say: Thy fist shall not do it, I mean not the hand alone, but the whole person to whom the hand belongs; for the hand alone would do nothing if the whole body with all its members did not coöperate.

Therefore, Thou shalt not kill, is as much as to say: You may find as many ways to kill as you have members of the body, by your hand, tongue, heart, by signs and gestures, by angrily looking at any one, by begrudging him his life, by your eyes or even by your ears—if you don't like to hear him spoken of, that all means killing. For then your heart and all there is about you is so disposed that you would be glad if he were already dead, and although meanwhile your hand is quiet, your tongue is silent, your eyes and ears are muffled, yet your heart is full of murder and manslaughter.

21

Verse 22

BUT I SAY UNTO YOU, THAT WHOSOEVER IS ANGRY
WITH HIS BROTHER SHALL BE IN DANGER OF THE
JUDGMENT; AND WHOSOEVER SHALL SAY TO HIS
BROTHER, RACA, SHALL BE IN DANGER OF THE
COUNCIL; BUT WHOSOEVER SHALL SAY: THOU
FOOL, SHALL BE IN DANGER OF HELL FIRE.

Behold, this is the true light, that shows the true meaning of this commandment, and that puts to shame their foul gloss, as a dark lantern in contrast
with the bright sun, and it now shines with such a different appearance,
that they are presently amazed and say, That is teaching with authority, and
not as their scribes. Although this explanation is clear enough, and elsewhere often treated of, we must yet here for the sake of the text expand the
words a little. In the first place he says: He who is angry with his brother
is in danger of the judgment; that is, he has merited the same punishment
that is inflicted upon a murderer, namely, that he should be condemned to
death. For he repeats the very words that stand in the text, Lev. 24:17 (which
he now himself has quoted): He that killeth any man shall surely be put
to death. Because now he who is angry with his brother comes under the
same sentence, he is also properly called a murderer. In the second and
third statement: Whosoever saith to his brother, Raca, or, Thou fool, is in
danger of the council and of hell fire, he means the same thing as to be in
danger of the judgment, namely, that he is in danger of being put to death.

But he mentions three particulars, to show how the punishment becomes greater and more severe the more the sin continues and reveals itself. For he speaks as in a process before the court, when a criminal is to be punished. As namely, when one has committed murder, he is in danger of the judgment, that is, he is brought before the court, indicted, and a charge is brought against him, as one who has caused death. That is the first grade or step towards death; yet the sentence has not yet been passed, so that he still may have room to vindicate himself and be acquitted. Secondly, when however the sentence has been passed that he is to die, then he is in danger of the council, so that a consultation is held concerning him, what kind of punishment is to be meted out to him; then he is again nearer to death, so that he cannot escape. Thirdly, when the sentence of death has now been passed, and all has been determined upon, he is handed over to the executioner, that he may take him away and perform his official duty. So he indicates by these steps, how one sinks deeper and deeper into punishment; just as he who is to be executed draws steadily nearer and nearer to death. Therefore, it is as if it were said: He who is angry in heart is already deserving of death before God; but he who goes further and says: Raca, or, Thou fool, has already had sentence pronounced upon him, etc. In short, he is already damned to hell-fire who is angry with his brother. But he who says Raca, deserves to go still deeper into hell; still deeper, however, he who kills also with words and fist. So the punishment and condemnation is entirely one and the same, and yet the same is heavier and more severe as the sin progresses and breaks out more fiercely.

As to the meaning of Raca, we are told that it signifies all sorts of indications that show our anger against our neighbor: as when one neither speaks to or looks at him; or when one is pleased and secretly rejoices when it goes ill with him; or where one in any way shows that he would be really glad if his neighbor would be utterly ruined; as there are now many of these poisonous, wretched creatures, that array themselves most bitterly against us, both publicly and by secret and treacherous practices, as those who would most gladly hear that we were all exterminated, and yet they pose as holy Christian people.

The other phrase: Thou fool, means not only the various indications [above mentioned] but all the words that come from a bad, poisonous heart, that is hostile to its neighbor. Otherwise, if they come from a kind, motherly heart, there is no sin. For one may indeed rebuke and scold with words, as St. Paul calls his Galatians fools, and Christ says to his disciples: O fools, and slow of heart to believe; yes, not only this, but we must also be angry and wear a stern and forbidding exterior. For this is all a godly anger and vexation at the wrong, not at the person, but for the benefit of our neighbor. In short, it is a necessary anger, that cannot be dispensed with in any house, in any city and government, yes, in any pulpit. For should father, mother, judge and preacher haul in mouth and fist, and neither rebuke nor restrain the evil, government and Christianity and everything would go to destruction through the wickedness of the world. So that the meaning here is: hate the cause, yet love the person; as the jurists very well say, if they only would make the right use of it.

22

Verses 23 and 24

THEREFORE, IF THOU BRING THY GIFT TO THE ALTAR,
AND THERE REMEMBEREST THAT THY BROTHER HATH
AUGHT AGAINST THEE, LEAVE THERE THY GIFT BEFORE
THE ALTAR, AND GO THY WAY; FIRST BE RECONCILED TO
THY BROTHER, AND THEN COME AND OFFER THY GIFT.

He makes a long sermon over this command, which looks indeed like an
easy text, but the vice [here rebuked] is very wide-spread and common,
especially among high, mighty, wise people, as at the courts of kings, lords
and princes, and those who are anything, or can accomplish anything upon
earth, they are most deeply involved in it, and yet must not be blamed with
it. For it wears a very specious appearance, and nothing can dress itself up
so handsomely and adorn itself with the appearance of sanctity, wherewith many people deceive themselves and others; and they do not see how
they are at heart hostile to their neighbor, or cherish a secret spite against
him, and nevertheless want to be pious, serve God, and, as he here says, go
to the altar and bring a sacrifice, supposing that it is all right with them.

   This is the way of it; they put on a handsome appearance and stand
under the cover of what is called *zelus justitiae* [a zeal for justice,] a virtue
that loves justice and is indignant at evil and cannot tolerate it; just as the
sword and ruling authority are appointed to administer righteousness and
punish wickedness; as also father and mother, master and mistress, must

become angry and punish. Here comes now the pious villain, puts on his little robe and says he does it out of love for righteousness, and has good and reasonable cause for what he does: as now princes and others are brimfull of poison, hatred and envy against our people, live on in this spirit, make no conscience of it, and the whole thing is nothing but "indulgences" and "relics." For they cover themselves with the beautiful excuse, that they say they are hostile to heresy, and they make a great virtue out of it, a holy zeal and a love for the truth; and there is at bottom nothing but a shameful, poisonous hatred and spite, that cannot otherwise show and gratify itself.

For I know, and may well say, that all our opponents (except our dear lord the Emperor, personally, who has not been correctly informed about us,) neither have nor know any reason why they should hate and be hostile to us, except mere envy and mischief. For they make no charge against us of any wrong-doing, that we are scamps or scoundrels, or have injured them in any way; they know too, and have had to confess it, that our doctrine is the exact truth; yet they are so full of poison that they would bear with the world full of nothing but desperate villains rather than with us and ours.

So there are many excellent, honorable, learned and otherwise upright people, who are so filled with anger, envy and hatred, and are so embittered by it, that they are unconscious of it, and are fully satisfied that they are doing it by virtue of their office or for the sake of righteousness. For their excuse is too plausible, and so delusive that no one dare accuse them of being anything else than upright, pious people. So their hearts at last become hardened, they strengthen and harden themselves in the poisonous vice, and sin against the Holy Ghost. For it is a two-fold wickedness; first that the heart is full of anger, hatred and envy; secondly, that it is not acknowledged to be sin or evil, but is to be called virtue, which is equivalent to smiting God on the mouth and making him out a liar.

Notice, for this reason Christ warns so diligently that every one be specially careful at this point lest he be deceived by this hypocrisy and false appearance. For no one believes how such a simple statement can be so far-reaching and affect such great people. For by these words, as he says: "If thou bring thy gift to the altar" he shows clearly that he is speaking of those who serve God, and claim to be the true children of God, and are reputed to be the best of all. What is wrong with them, then? Nothing, except that their heart is sticking full of hatred and envy. Dear friend, of what account is it that you are incessantly fasting and praying, giving all your money for God's sake, and castigating yourself to death, and doing ever so many good works, more than all the Carthusians, whilst at the same time you ignore the command of God that he wishes to be obeyed? That you make no conscience of reviling and calumniating others, and yet wish to present a great sacrifice? Just as if one had caused war and murder, and had shed much blood, and afterward paid a thousand ducats for having masses said for those who were killed; or if some one had stolen a great sum of money, and then would give alms for God's sake. Thus they deceive God (yes, themselves) with the pretty pretence, that he must now regard them as genuine living saints.

Therefore he says now: Do you wish to serve God and present an offering, and have you injured any one, or do you cherish anger against your neighbor? then know at once that God will not accept your offering, but lay it right down, and drop everything and go first of all and be reconciled with your brother. By this he means now all works that one can do to serve or praise God (for in those days there was no better work than to offer sacrifice); and he rejects it entirely, and commands that it be dropped at once, unless your heart first assures you that you are reconciled with your neighbor and do not know of cherishing any ill-will. If this be done, then come (says he), and offer thy gift. This he adds, so that no one should think that he wishes to reject or despise such a gift. For it was not an evil act, but one ordered and commanded by God; but that is evil, and utterly spoils it all, that they disregard the higher commands of God and despise them. That is making an abuse of sacrifices against your neighbor.

There is also an abuse in regard to this matter that is of more consequence—that one seeks thereby to be saved, to atone for sin, and to rely upon it and have confidence before God; of this we treat elsewhere. In itself it is a good work; just as all other works of public worship, as praying and fasting, are not to be despised or neglected, where their intention and use are proper, namely, that one does not do them thereby to merit heaven, and when the heart is all right towards our neighbor, and thus both faith and love are pure and right. But if thou prayest and fastest, and yet along with this speakest evil of thy neighbor, defamest and slanderest people, thy mouth indeed speaks holy words and eats nothing; but it meanwhile pollutes and defiles itself with thy neighbor, against the command of God.

Therefore he rebukes and forbids such fasting in Is. 58:3, wherewith they mortified their bodies and made pretence of great devotion, and he says: Behold in the day of your fast ye find pleasure, and exact all your labors. Ye fast for strife and debate, and to smite with the fist of wickedness: ye shall not fast as ye do this day, to make your voice to be heard on high, etc. And he further teaches how we are to fast properly: Is not this the fast that I have chosen? to loose the bands of wickedness, to undo the heavy burdens and to let the oppressed go free, etc. Break thy bread to the hungry, and when thou seest the naked, cover him, etc. Here you see how he is chiefly concerned about our love for our neighbor.

Verses 25 and 26

AGREE WITH THINE ADVERSARY QUICKLY, WHILE
THOU ART IN THE WAY WITH HIM; LEST AT ANY TIME
THE ADVERSARY DELIVER THEE TO THE JUDGE, AND
THE JUDGE DELIVER THEE TO THE OFFICER, AND THOU
BE CAST INTO PRISON. VERILY, I SAY UNTO THEE,
THOU SHALT BY NO MEANS COME OUT THENCE, TILL
THOU HAST PAID THE UTTERMOST FARTHING.

In the previous text he preached to him who had injured his neighbor or
was angry at him: but here he tells how he is to act who is injured; and he
carries out the figure that he had introduced, namely the usual course taken
before a court, when two parties are opposed to one another, one accusing,
the other being accused, and the judge pronouncing sentence and punishing the guilty party; and he means only to say that he who injures another
should peaceably become reconciled with him; that the other, however,
should consent to be reconciled and cheerfully forgive. This is now also a
fine point, and here many can very nicely cover over and adorn their scoundrelism, by saying that they will gladly forgive, but not forget. For there is
ever the pretence at hand, of which I have spoken, that anger against the
wrong is reasonable, and they think they are acting with good reason, and
all is right and proper.

Therefore he warns here again, and shows that in this commandment
not only is wrath forbidden, but it is also commanded that we are cheerfully to forgive and forget the harm that has been done to us: as God has
done with us, and still does, when he forgives sin, that he blots it out of the
record altogether and remembers it no more; yet not so that one must or
can in such measure forget it, that one dared never think of it again; but in
such a way that you can have just as friendly a heart towards your neighbor
as before he injured you. But if the stump remains in your heart, so that
you are not as friendly and kind towards him as before, then it cannot be
said that you have forgotten, not even that you have heartily forgiven, and

you are still the knave who comes before the altar with his gift and means to serve God, whilst his heart is yet sticking full of anger, envy and hatred. But very few people pay regard to this; they all wear the beautiful mask, they do not see how their heart stands in relation to this command, which in short tolerates no wrath or ill-will against one's neighbor.

It is true, as above said, that anger there must and shall be; but take care that it be properly applied, and remember that thou art commanded not to be angry on thine own account; but for the sake of thine office and of God, and that thou must not confound the two, thy person and office. For thine own person thou must not cherish anger against any one, however badly thou art injured; but where thine office requires it, there must thou be angry, even though no harm has been done to thy person. Thus a pious judge is angry at a criminal to whom he wishes no harm for his own person's sake, and whom he would rather leave unpunished, and his wrath proceeds from a heart in which there is nothing but love towards his neighbor, and it is only the evil deed that is to be punished that must bear the wrath. But if thy brother has done something against thee and angered thee, and asks thy forgiveness, and ceases to do evil; then the anger also must subside. Whence comes then the secret spite that thou nevertheless art still cherishing in thy heart, when the cause and occasion of the anger is gone, and instead thereof other acts appear showing that the man is converted and has become a totally different man, and has become a new tree, with new fruits, who now loves and honors thee supremely, so that he blames and rebukes himself on thy account? Thou must before God and all the world be a desperate man, if thou dost not again show thyself thus towards him and heartily forgive him, so that the sentence is properly pronounced against thee that is threatened here.

24

Verses 27 through 30

YE HAVE HEARD THAT IT WAS SAID TO THEM OF OLD
TIME, THOU SHALT NOT COMMIT ADULTERY: BUT I SAY
UNTO YOU, THAT WHOSOEVER LOOKETH ON A WOMAN
TO LUST AFTER HER HATH COMMITTED ADULTERY
WITH HER ALREADY IN HIS HEART. AND IF THY RIGHT
EYE OFFEND THEE, PLUCK IT OUT AND CAST IT FROM
THEE: FOR IT IS PROFITABLE FOR THEE THAT ONE OF
THY MEMBERS SHOULD PERISH, AND NOT THAT THY
WHOLE BODY SHOULD BE CAST INTO HELL. AND IF THY
RIGHT HAND OFFEND THEE, CUT IT OFF AND CAST IT
FROM THEE: FOR IT IS PROFITABLE FOR THEE THAT
ONE OF THY MEMBERS SHOULD PERISH AND NOT THAT
THY WHOLE BODY SHOULD BE CAST INTO HELL.

This is a bit of salt against the teaching of the Pharisees; he treats in it of
two things—first of adultery, then of cutting off. Concerning adultery, they
had given the literal meaning to the fifth commandment, and taught thus:
There is nothing more forbidden than the real act of adultery; and they
did not regard it as a sin if they were at heart inflamed with lust and evil
desire towards another, and also outwardly revealed this with ugly words
and immodest gestures, and this did no harm to their sanctity if they only
did otherwise good works, diligently sacrificed and prayed, etc. That was
not teaching the commands of God, but perverting them; it was not making

the people pious, but only worse; it was giving room and permission for all sorts of sin and unchastity. But here you hear a different master, who shows their sanctity to be sin and shame, and throws true light upon this commandment, and decides that adultery is committed also with eyes, ears, mouth, yes most of all with the heart; as when one looks at a woman, or sports with her, yes thinks of her lustfully.

Now see how matters must have stood among this people, and what kind of people Christ had to deal with, since not only the great, common crowd, but those who stood above other people and ought to teach and control them, not only permit such things, but do them themselves, and increase the occasion for adultery, and yet wish to be counted pious if they only do not actually commit adultery; although it is easy to calculate how pious and chaste people can be for works' sake, if so much allowance be made, and they can carry it so far as to have their heart full of eager lust, that also reveals itself by all sorts of signs, words and gestures towards each other. What else can then follow but the act itself, if opportunity offers? Or, how is he therefore so much the more pious, although he cannot perform the deed that he would like to accomplish and is unceasingly lusting after it in his heart? Just as a wretch can wish to see his master dead, although he is lying in prison, and would like to kill him himself, if he could only get at him: are we therefore not to call him a murderer, or even to count him pious?

But do you say: If that be true, that also with a look adultery can be committed, what are we then to do? Men and women must live together and have daily intercourse. Or are we to run out of the world, or punch out ears and eyes, and have our heart torn out? Answer: Christ does not here forbid that we are to live together, eat, drink, yes, even laugh and be merry; that is all still free of harm, if only the one feature be wanting, that means, to lust after her. It is true, the Jews try to help themselves out in this way, by saying there is no sin, if one loves another with thoughts and signs; just as they do not regard it as sin to be angry with a neighbor and be hostile to him at heart; so that one must not condemn the whole nation and so many holy people, as if they were all murderers and adulterers. Therefore they must apologize for these commandments, that one is not to interpret them so strictly; but, as our learned men have said: These may be good counsels for the perfect, but nobody is bound by them; and they have gone so far in this matter that there has been great disputing and doubting, whether bad conduct with a whore, outside of marriage, is even a sin; and it is in fact now in Italy among respectable people counted an honor, so that one almost regards those as holy who go no farther than this. Again, however, there are those who have narrowed it down altogether too much, and want to be so very holy, that they forbid even looking at any one, and have taught that all association of male and female persons is to be avoided. Hence come the excellent saints that have run away from the world into the wilderness and into monasteries, so that they may shut themselves off from all seeing and hearing, from all dealing and fellowship with the world.

But Christ states the opposite of both these extremes; he will not let the command of God be so twisted; and such counsel be given in the matter as to give a loose rein to unchastity and villainy. For he says in plain and clear words that he who looks at a woman with evil desire is an adulterer, and sentences him besides to hell-fire, when he says it is better that one should put out his eye than that the whole body should be cast into hell. And he also does not want such saints as run away from mankind. For if that were to be the rule, the ten commandments would nowhere be needed. For if I am in the wilderness, separated from everybody else, no one can thank me for not committing adultery, murdering and stealing; and I still may think meanwhile that I am holy and have violated none of the ten commandments, which however have been given by God for the very reason that he may teach us how we are to live aright in the world with reference to our neighbor.

For we are not so made that we are to run away from one another, but are to live together and share both good and evil. For as we are men, we must also help to bear all sorts of human misfortunes and the curse that has fallen upon us, and so prepare ourselves that we can live among bad people, so that every one may there prove his holiness and not let himself be made impatient, so that he flees away. For we must live upon earth among thorns and thistles, in a state of affairs that abounds in temptation, opposition and trouble. And you have not helped yourself in the least though you have run away from the multitude, and yet carry along with you the same bad companion, that is the lust and evil passion that adheres to flesh and blood. For you surely cannot deny your father and mother, though you are alone and locked up, nor can you throw away your flesh and blood from you and let it lie. The command is not to lift your foot and run away; but abide in your lot, bravely to stand and contend against all manner of temptation, and patiently to force your way through and conquer.

Therefore Christ is a true Master, who teaches you not to run away from people, nor to change your place; but to lay hands upon yourself, and cast from you the eye or the hand that offends you, that is, to remove the occasion of sinning, which is the evil lust and desire that sticks in yourself and comes out of your heart. If this be out of the way, you can easily without sin be among the people and have intercourse with everybody. Therefore he says plainly (as above said): If thou lookest upon a woman to lust after her, thou hast committed adultery with her in thy heart. He does not forbid your looking at her; for he is speaking to those who must live in the world among the people, as the whole previous teaching of this chapter and also that which follows abundantly shows. But he means that we are to separate from each other the looking and the lusting.

You may look, indeed, at any woman or man; but only be careful that there be no lusting. For to this end God has ordained that every one should have his own wife or her own husband, so that every one may properly gratify both lust and desire. If you do not go beyond this you have his sanction, and he adds his blessing to it, and is satisfied with it, as his ordinance and creature. But if you go beyond this, and are not satisfied with what God has given you, but go lusting and gaping after others, then you have already gone too far, and have confounded the two, so that the looking is spoiled by the lusting.

This is also the chief cause of adultery, that is always apt to happen when one does not regard God's word in reference to his wife, as that which God gives him and blesses, but at the same time he fixes his gaze upon another woman; then soon the heart goes after the eyes, so that lust also and desire are added, which I ought to have for my wife alone. Aside from this, flesh and blood is overcurious, so that it is soon discontented with and tired of that which it has, is gaping after something else, and the devil adds his promptings, so that one sees nothing in his wife but what is faulty and fails to see what is good and praiseworthy. Hence it comes to pass that every other woman is more beautiful and better in my eyes than my own wife; yes, many a one who has a really beautiful, pious wife, allows himself to be so blinded, that he dislikes her, and attaches himself to an ugly, shameful piece.

Therefore this would be the true art and strongest safeguard against this sin (as I have elsewhere more fully explained, of marriage and wedded life), if every one would learn rightly to regard his spouse according to the word of God, which is the most precious treasure and beautiful ornament that one can find in a man or woman, and would mirror himself in it; then he would love and esteem his spouse as a divine gift and treasure, and would think thus if he sees another (even if she were prettier than his own): Is she pretty? well, she is not so very pretty, and if she were the prettiest on earth, I have at home a more beautiful ornament in my wife that God has given me, and has adorned with his word above all others, even though she be not beautiful in body, or be otherwise defective. For if I look at all the women in the world, I find no one of whom I can boast as I can of mine with a good conscience: This one God has bestowed upon me and placed within my arms, and I know that he and all angels are heartily pleased if I cling to her with love and fidelity. Why should I then despise this precious divine gift, and devote myself to another, in whom I find no such treasure and ornament?

See, I could easily look at all women, and talk with them, laugh and be merry in such a way that still there should be no lust and desire on my part, and I would not let any one seem to be so beautiful or desirable to me, that I would act contrary to God's word and command; and though I was tempted by flesh and blood, yet I did not need to consent, nor allow myself to be overcome, but I had to contend bravely against it and conquer through the word of God, and to live in the world in such a way that no one's wickedness could make me wicked, and no enticement could make me an adulterer. But because one does not see or regard this word of God, it has easily happened, that one becomes tired of his spouse and averse to her, and prefers another and cannot resist the lust and desire. For he does not know the art, that he can rightly regard his spouse according to the beauty and ornament with which God has clothed her for him; he sees no further than according to the eyes, as his wife appears to him ill-shaped or faulty, and another prettier and better. So you understand when looking at a woman is sin, or is not sin, namely, that one is not to look at another as every one is to look at his wife.

Yet we are not here to span the bow too tightly, as if one were to be damned because, when tempted, he feels that this lust and desire towards another begins to arise. For I have often said that it is profitable to live in flesh and blood without sinful, evil inclination, not only in this matter, but also against every commandment. Therefore moralists have made this distinction, with which I concur: that an evil thought, without assent, is not a mortal sin. It is not possible, if some one has offended you, that your heart should not feel, or be moved, and begin to heave to take vengeance. But that is not yet criminal, if it only does not determine and proceed to do harm, but resists this inclination. So also in this case; it is not possible to prevent the devil from shooting into the heart evil thoughts and lust. But then take care that thou dost not allow such arrows to stick there and grow fast, but tear them out and throw them away, and do as long ago was taught by one of the ancients, who said: "I cannot prevent a bird from flying over my head; but I can easily prevent it from making a nest in my hair, or biting off my nose." Thus it is not in our power to prevent this or some other temptation, so that thoughts do not occur to us: if we only stop with their occurring to us, so that we do not admit them, although they knock for admittance, and prevent their taking root, lest they might lead to consent and a purpose to sin. But nevertheless it is still sin, but it is included in the common forgiveness, because we cannot live in the flesh without committing many sins, and every one must have his devil; as also St. Paul complains about the sin (Rom. 7:17) that dwells in him, and says, that he finds in his flesh no good thing, etc.

That, however, some have here raised the question, and pointedly asked whether it is sinful for a man to desire to marry a woman or for a woman to desire to marry a man, is silly, and both questions are contrary to Scripture and to nature. For when should people marry, if they would not have desire and love for one another? Yes, that is the reason why God has given this eager desire to bride and bridegroom, otherwise every one would flee from and avoid marriage. Thus he has also commanded in the Scriptures, that both, man and woman, should love each other, and he shows that he is greatly pleased when husband and wife are well adapted to each other. Therefore this desire and love must surely not be lacking, and it is very fortunate and agreeable if it only lasts a long while. For without this, trouble comes, both *from the flesh* that one soon becomes tired of this state, and is unwilling to bear the discomfort that comes with it; and also *from the devil*, who cannot bear to see two married people treating each other with true affection, and does not rest until he gives occasion to impatience, strife, hatred and bitterness between them; so that it is an art not alone necessary, but also difficult, and peculiar to Christians, to love one's wife or husband properly, so that one may bear the faults of the other and all sorts of carnal misfortune. At first it all goes very well, so that for love (as it is said) they are ready to eat each other up; but when the novelty is over, then comes the devil with satiety, and tries to rob you too much of desire in this direction, and excite it too much in another.

Let this suffice for the topic of lust and desire. But what are we to say about the way Christ spans the bow when he says that we are to pluck out the eye and cut off the hand if it offends us? Are we then to cripple ourselves, make ourselves lame and blind? Then we would have to take our own life, and every one become a self murderer. For if we must throw away everything that offends us, we would have first of all to tear out our heart. But what else would that be than to destroy all nature and the creatures of God. Answer: here you see clearly that Christ in this chapter is speaking not at all of mere worldly affairs, and that all such expressions that occur here and there in the Gospel (such as to deny one's self, hate one's soul, forsake everything, etc.,) do not belong at all to the sphere of secular affairs or the civil government, nor are to be understood according to the statutes of the old Saxons, as the jurists call them, to pluck out eyes, to cut off the hand, and such like; or how could this life and civil government endure? But he is speaking here of spiritual life and spiritual affairs, in which one does not externally, corporeally, and in the sight of the world, throw away his eye or his hand, deny himself and forsake all things, but in his heart and in God's sight. For he is not teaching how to use the fist or the sword, or to control life and property, but only the heart and conscience before God; therefore we are not at all to apply his words in the sense of the legal terms or those of secular government.

In this way he speaks also in Matt. 19:12, about castrating, where he alludes to three kinds of castrated ones or eunuchs. The first and second are such as are eunuchs naturally or are made such by the hands of men; these the world and the jurists call castrated. But the third kind are such as have made themselves eunuchs for the kingdom of heaven's sake; these are called castrated, not externally, in their body, but in heart or spiritually; not in a worldly sense or manner, but (as he says) for heaven's sake. For with worldly matters he has nothing to do. Thus also here, we are spiritually to tear out eyes, hand, heart, and let everything go, that it may not offend us; and yet live in this world, where we cannot do without any of these things.

This is now what is here meant: If thou feelest that thou art looking at a woman with an evil desire, then tear out that same eye or sight (as being forbidden by God) not of the body, but of the heart, from which lustful desire comes; then thou hast rightly plucked it out. For if the evil desire is out of the heart, then the eye will not sin, nor offend thee, and thou lookest now upon that woman with the same bodily eyes, but without desire; thou wilt be just as if thou hadst not seen her. For the eye of which Christ speaks, which was there before, and is called the eye of lust or desire, is no longer there, although the bodily eye remains uninjured. Thus he speaks also about the castrated. If the heart has resolved to live chastely without marriage (if it has grace) then it has made itself a eunuch for the kingdom of heaven's sake, and does not need to injure any member of the body. In short, it is such a castrating and plucking out that neither a fist nor a hangman can do, but the word of God in the heart.

Therefore those are fools who transfer these and similar sayings from the spiritual to the secular sphere, as if Christ had taught what was contrary to secular rule, yes, contrary to the natural order of things. Therefore some have made such fools of themselves that, through impatience and despair of being able to fight against flesh and blood, they have gone so far as to help [i. e. castrate?] themselves, so that the bishops in the councils had to forbid the practice. That all comes of a misunderstanding, that they do not distinguish between the ruling and doctrine of Christ and of the world; they abide by the gross conception of castration, so that they think no further than how the world designates and understands it in its sphere: whilst Christ himself excludes this understanding of it, and takes it away, and distinguishes those who are castrated by nature or by human hands (whether by their own or those of others,) and contrasts them with those who are castrated neither by men's hands nor by nature; whereby he clearly shows that he is speaking alone of spiritual castration, since the body with all its members is entire and uninjured, and yet has not sexual desire as others have, which cannot be cut out of flesh and blood, even though one were to rob himself of his natural members: as they say themselves, that such eunuchs or castrated persons have more desire for or love to women than any others; therefore also great kings (or queens) have preferred such persons as chamberlains, on account of the great fidelity and love they have for women.

But it appears also, that Christ often on other occasions used this expression: "If thine eye, or hand, or foot, offend thee." For they are applied elsewhere in the gospel, also to other matters, in such a way that he used it as a common saying, and applied it as a common comparison to all kinds of sin, that one should not yield to the occasion and inclination to sin; here, however, it is significantly applied to a particular case, namely, to adultery, so that the command is to pluck out the eye that is about to offend us by evil desire: for adultery is commonly occasioned by looking, and comes into the heart through the eyes, if one does not resist the temptation. Thus he employs the same words with reference to another mode of giving offence, (Matt. 18:8 sq.) so that he calls it an offending eye or hand, if a preacher and teacher, or a lord and tyrant, seeks to mislead thee from the truth and true doctrine; and he bids thee to tear it out and cast it from thee, so that one may say: Thou art it is true my eye or hand, my master or ruler; but if thou wishest to turn me from the truth to false faith, or to compel me to do evil, I will not follow thee, etc.

25

Verses 31 and 32

IT HATH BEEN SAID, WHOSOEVER SHALL PUT
AWAY HIS WIFE, LET HIM GIVE HER A WRITING
OF DIVORCEMENT: BUT I SAY UNTO YOU, THAT
WHOSOEVER SHALL PUT AWAY HIS WIFE, SAVING
FOR THE CAUSE OF FORNICATION, CAUSETH HER TO
COMMIT ADULTERY: AND WHOSOEVER SHALL MARRY
HER THAT IS DIVORCED COMMITTETH ADULTERY.

Here we see clearly how they wrested this commandment, giving room
and liberty enough to violate it, and yet not counting their conduct sinful,
if they only did not make too glaring an exhibition of it by open adultery;
for they were permitted, if one disliked his wife and wanted to be rid of
her, and had become fond of another woman, that he might leave her and
court another that better pleased him; and, although the latter had another
husband, they could easily induce him to dismiss his wife, so that he had
to put her away, and yet she should not be said to be taken by violence.
Thus it was also a small matter among them, whether one had had sexual
intercourse with another woman, so that he thereby took her to wife; as
they at any rate wanted to have more than one wife; and they had indeed
brought things to such a pass that every one without qualms of conscience
acted in the matter of marriage and divorce just as he pleased. Therefore,
Jesus takes up also this matter of divorce, rebukes and condemns their
knavery and abuse of the permitted divorce, to instruct their consciences

how one is properly to proceed in this matter, so that one does not go too far and act contrary to the commandment. He touches upon it here, however, only in a few words; for afterwards, in the nineteenth chapter, he discusses it more at large.

How are we now, however, to proceed in matters pertaining to marriage and divorce? I have said that we are to leave this in the hands of the jurists, and committed to the secular government, because marriage is quite a secular, external thing, as wife, child, house and home, and other things that belong to the authority of the government, as this is altogether subject to the reason, Genesis 1. Therefore, what the civil authority and wise people determine and ordain in reference to this matter according to right and reason, with that we should be content. For also Christ does not here appoint or ordain anything as a jurist or ruler, in external matters; but only as a preacher he instructs the consciences so that we rightly use the law concerning divorce, not for knavery and personal wantonness, contrary to the command of God. Therefore we will not here go any further than to see how the matter stood among them, and how those should conduct themselves who wish to be Christians; for with those who are not Christians we have nothing to do (as those who must be governed not with the Gospel but with compulsion and punishment), so that we may keep our office pure, and not grasp after more than is committed to us.

In Deuteronomy 24:1 and 4 we read: "When a man hath taken a wife and married her, and it come to pass that she find no favor in his eyes, because he hath found some uncleanness in her; then let him write her a bill of divorcement, and give it in her hand," etc.; but a prohibition is at once appended to this, that the same man (if he afterwards would like to have her again) "may not take her again to be his wife," etc. Now, this law they soon learned, and bravely abused, so that every one easily discarded and dismissed his wife, when he was tired of her, and longed for another (though Moses allowed such dismissal only when he found "some uncleanness in her" on account of which they could not well remain together); and they took such liberties in this matter that they themselves saw that their custom was blameworthy and quite too wanton, and they therefore asked Christ, Matt. 19:3: "Is it lawful for a man to put away his wife for every cause?" He gives them an answer, too, and reads them a sharp text besides, which they had never heard before, and concludes just as here, that both he who gives the bill of divorcement (except for fornication), and marries another, commits adultery, and decides that she also commits adultery who marries another. (For otherwise she could not commit adultery, if she remained unmarried.) Thereby he not only rebukes them for acting wantonly in the matter of divorcement, but teaches that they should not practice divorcement at all, or, if they do, both parties should remain unmarried, and concludes that divorcing is always a cause of adultery.

To their question, "Why did Moses then allow such divorcement?" he answers: "Because of the hardness of your hearts Moses suffered you to put away your wives." Not that it was commendable or well done; but that you are such vile and rude people, that it is better to allow this than that you do worse, cause misery or murder, or live together in perpetual hatred, discord and enmity: as it yet might even be advisable (if the temporal authorities should so order it), on account of some queer, self-willed, stubborn people, who are never satisfied with anything, and are not at all adapted for married life, that they should be allowed to separate from one another. For government cannot otherwise be carried on; on account of the badness of the people one must often yield something, though it be not well done, lest something worse may happen.

Thus it is now settled, that those who want to be Christians are not to be divorced, but each to retain his or her spouse, and bear and experience good and evil with the same, although he or she may be strange, peculiar and faulty; or, if there be a divorce, that the parties remain unmarried; and that it will not do to make a free thing out of marriage, as if it were in our power to do with it, changing and exchanging, as we please; but it is just as Jesus says: "What God has joined together let not man put asunder."

For trouble here is owing solely to the fact that men do not regard marriage according to God's word as his work and ordinance, do not pay regard to his will, that he has given to every one his spouse, to keep her, and to endure for his sake the discomforts that married life brings with it; they regard it as nothing else than a mere human, secular affair, with which God has nothing to do. Therefore one soon becomes tired of it, and if it does not go as we wish, we soon begin to separate and change. Then God never-theless so orders it, that we thereby make it no better; as it then generally happens, if one wants to change and improve matters, and no one wants to carry his cross, but have everything perfectly convenient and without discomfort, that he gets an exchange in which he finds twice or ten times more discomfort, not alone in this matter but in all others.

For it cannot be otherwise upon earth; there must daily much inconve-nience and discomfort occur in every house, city and country; and there is no condition upon earth in which one must not have much to endure that is painful, both from those that belong to him, as wife, child, servants, subjects, and externally from neighbors and all kinds of accidental mis-haps. When now one sees and feels this, he is soon tired of his condition and discontented with it, or breaks out with impatience, scolding and curs-ing; and if he cannot avoid or get rid of this annoyance, he will change his condition, thinks every one's condition and state better than his own, and when he has been long changing about he finds he has been going farther and faring worse. For to change is soon and easily done; but to improve is doubtful and rare. This was the case, too, with the Jews in their marriage changings and divorces.

Therefore in this matter we ought to do as we have always taught and exhorted: If one wants to undertake anything that he wishes to be blessed and successful, also in temporal affairs, as in marrying, remaining at home, accepting a position, etc., that he appeal to God and seek counsel from him who is to give it, and whose it is. For it is not a trifling gift of God, if one gets a pious, tolerably good wife: why should you not then pray to him that he may cause it to turn out well? For the first eager and curious desire will not accomplish this, or give permanence if he does not add his blessing and give success, and help to bear the occasional discomfort. Therefore, those who do not do this, but rush into things of their own accord, as if they needed no help from God, and do not learn to adapt themselves to circumstances, they deservedly realize in them a real purgatory and hell-ish torment, without the devil's help; and because they bear no trouble with patience, but have selected just what suited them best, and want to set aside and ignore the article that is called forgiveness of sin; they have as a reward a restless, impatient heart, and so must suffer double misfortune and get no thanks for it. But we have said enough of this elsewhere.

But you ask: Is there then no reason for which there may be separation and divorce between man and wife? Answer: Christ states here and in Matthew 19:9, only this one, which is called adultery, and he quotes it from the law of Moses, which punishes adultery with death. Since now death alone dissolves marriages and releases from the obligation, an adulterer is already divorced not by man but by God himself, and not only cut loose from his spouse, but from this life. For by adultery he has divorced himself from his wife, and has dissolved the marriage, which he has no right to do; and he has thereby made himself worthy of death, in such a way that he is already dead before God, although the judge does not take his life. Because now God here divorces, the other party is fully released, so that he or she is not bound to keep the spouse that has proved unfaithful, however much he or she may desire it.

For we do not order or forbid this divorcing, but we ask the government to act in this matter, and we submit to what the secular authorities ordain in regard to it. Yet, our advice would be to such as claim to be Christians, that it would be much better to exhort and urge both parties to remain together, and that the innocent party should become reconciled to the guilty (if humbled and reformed) and exercise forgiveness in Christian love; unless no improvement could be hoped for, or the guilty person who had been pardoned and restored to favor persisted in abusing this kindness, and still continued in leading a public, loose life, and took it for granted that one must continue to spare and forgive him. In such case I would not advise or order that mercy should be shown, but would rather help to have such a person scourged or imprisoned. For to make a misstep once is still to be forgiven, but to sin presuming upon mercy and forgiveness is not to be endured. For, as before said, we know already that it is not right to compel one to take back again a public whore or adulterer, if he is unwilling to do it, or out of disgust cannot do it. For we read of Joseph, Matt. 1:18 sq., that although he was a pious man, yet he was not willing "to take unto him Mary his espoused wife" (when he saw that she was pregnant); and was praised because "he was minded to put her away privily," and not lodge complaint against her and have her executed, as he might well have done.

In addition to this cause of divorce there is still another: if one of a married couple forsakes the other, as when one through sheer petulance deserts the other. So, if a heathen woman were married to a Christian, or, as now sometimes happens, that one of the parties is evangelical and the other not (concerning which Paul speaks in 1 Cor. 7:13), whether in such a case divorce would be right? There Paul concludes: If the one party is willing to remain, the other should not break the engagement; although they are not of one faith, the faith should not dissolve the marriage tie. But if it happens that the other party absolutely will not remain, then let him or her depart; and thou art not under any obligation to follow. But if a fellow deserts his wife without her knowledge or consent, forsakes house, home, wife and child, stays away two or three years, or as long as he pleases (as now often happens), and when he has run his riotous course and squandered his substance and wants to come home again and take his old place, that the other party must be under obligation to wait for him as long as he chooses, and then take up with him again such a fellow ought not only to be forbidden house and home, but should be banished from the country, and the other party, if the renegade has been summoned and long enough waited for, should be heartily pronounced free.

For such a one is much worse than a heathen and unbeliever, and is less to be endured than a miserable adulterer, who, though he once fell, can still reform again and be faithful as before to his wife; but this one treats marriage just as he pleases, does not feel himself under any obligation to abide as husband and father with wife and children and perform his duty toward them, but holds himself sure of a safe reception if the notion takes him to return. But this is the state of the case: He who wishes to have wife and child must stay with them, share with them good and evil, as long as he lives; or if he will not, that we teach him that he must do it or be entirely separated from wife, house and home. But where these causes do not exist, their other defects and faults are not to be counted a hindrance or lead to a divorce, such as quarrels or other mishaps. But if parties are divorced (says St. Paul), then let them on both sides remain unmarried.

Let this suffice for what is said on this subject in the text, for I have else-where written enough about it. The chief safeguard against such divorce and other domestic trouble is (as I have said) that every one learn to bear with patience common faults and mishaps in his condition and surround-ings, and to overlook them in his wife, and be assured that we cannot have everything just right as we would have it. Why you cannot have it other-wise or better in your own body, and must put up with all sorts of filth and disagreeableness that it daily causes you; so that if you were to throw away everything that is unclean about it, you would have to begin with the belly that nourishes you and has to keep you alive.

If now you can endure this in your body, so that it makes a stench for you before you are aware of it, or begins to suppurate and ulcerate, so that there is no purity in your skin, and you make due allowance for all this; yes, you show all the more care and love for it by waiting upon it, washing it, enduring and helping where anything is wanting; why should you not do it here in the case of your own spouse whom God has given you, in whom you have a still greater treasure and whom you have more cause to love? For there ought to be such love among Christians as that of each member of the body towards every other (as St. Paul often remarks), when one kindly regards the faults of another, himself sympathizes with them, endures and removes them, and does all he can to help his neighbor. Therefore, our prin-cipal duty is nothing else than simple forgiveness of sin, both in ourselves and toward others; so that, as Christ in his kingdom without intermission is bearing with and forgiving all manner of faults, so also we among our-selves bear and forgive in all conditions and in all things. May God allot to him who will not do this, that he may never have rest, and make his single misfortune or plague ten times worse.

26

Verses 33 through 37

AGAIN, YE HAVE HEARD THAT IT HATH BEEN SAID BY
THEM OF OLD TIME, THOU SHALT NOT FORSWEAR
THYSELF, BUT SHALT PERFORM UNTO THE LORD THINE
OATHS: BUT I SAY UNTO YOU, SWEAR NOT AT ALL;
NEITHER BY HEAVEN, FOR IT IS GOD'S THRONE: NOR
BY THE EARTH, FOR IT IS HIS FOOTSTOOL; NEITHER BY
JERUSALEM, FOR IT IS THE CITY OF THE GREAT KING.
NEITHER SHALT THOU SWEAR BY THY HEAD, BECAUSE
THOU CANST NOT MAKE ONE HAIR BLACK OR WHITE. BUT
LET YOUR COMMUNICATION BE YEA, YEA; NAY, NAY; FOR
WHATEVER IS MORE THAN THESE COMETH OF EVIL.

This text has been spun out with many glosses, and many a queer notion and error has been drawn from it, so that many great doctors have been worried about it, and could not become reconciled to the blunt prohibition here that we are to "Swear not at all," but "let your communication be Yea, yea, and Nay, nay." So that some have stretched their conscience so tightly, that one doubts whether one ought to take a solemn oath not to avenge himself when he is set free from prison, or whether we are by an oath to make peace and a treaty with the Turks or unbelievers, etc. Now we cannot deny that Christ himself and St. Paul often took an oath; besides, it is said, in the Scriptures, that those are praised who swear by his name; so that also here we must make a distinction, so that we rightly understand the text.

But we have been told sufficiently, that Christ does not wish here to interfere with the secular authority and ordinance, nor to detract at all from the powers that be; but he is preaching here only for the individual Christians, how they are to conduct themselves in their ordinary life. Therefore we are to regard the swearing as forbidden in exactly the same sense as above the killing and the looking upon or desiring a woman. Killing is right, and yet it is also wrong; to desire a man or a woman is sin, and it is not sin; but in this way, that we rightly distinguish both, namely, that it is said to you and to me: if you kill, you do wrong; if you look at a woman to desire her, you do wrong. But to a judge he says: If you do not punish and kill, you shall yourself be punished; likewise to a married man or woman: If you do not cleave to your spouse, you do wrong. So both are right, that one is to kill and not to kill, to be and not to be with a woman; namely, that you do not be wrathful or kill, or look lovingly upon a woman, unless you are specially authorized by God's word or command to do so. If you are wrathful, however, when God commands you, or if you have a wife according to the word of God, then each is right; for what God says and commands is a very different thing from when you do it of your own accord.

As you have understood that, so understand this also; that the prohibition here is, "Swear not at all," just as he has entirely forbidden killing, so that there may be no wrath in the heart; in like manner, that we shall keep so aloof from man and woman as not to be looking at them, or thinking upon them to desire them. And it would be a dangerous sermon if we were to apply it to the exercise of governmental authority or to married life, and were to say to the judge, Thou shalt not become indignant, or give practical proof of wrath; or to a wedded pair, Thou shalt not look upon or love thy wife or husband: but we must turn about here and teach the opposite, saying: Thou judge shalt be angry and punish; and every one shall have and love his spouse. How then does Christ say one must desire no woman, and have no wrath in his heart? Answer, as said above, he is speaking of the woman that God has not given you, and of the wrath that is not demanded of you, that you are not to have. But if it is demanded of you, then it is no longer yours, but it is God's wrath, and no longer your desire, but that which is given and ordained by God; for you have God's word for it that you shall love your spouse and not desire any other. Thus also in regard to swearing; we must see to it, if we have God's word for it or not.

That he here insists so much upon the prohibition, that he does also in opposition to their false teachers, who preached in this way, that taking an oath and swearing, although done needlessly and without the word of God, was not sin; yes, they had made a distinction (as Christ here shows) how one might swear freely, and what oaths should be valid or not; as, that one might readily swear by heaven, or by Jerusalem, or by his head; that those were little oaths, and did not have much validity, if only the name of God were not invoked; they had indeed at last carried it so far that a mere yea or nay was of no account, and they held that it mattered nothing if they did not do anything which they had not sworn to do; just as they had taught in regard to killing, that one should not consider a secret anger and spite as sin; the same also, if one were hostile to his wife, had no desire for her or love for her, but had desire for another and proved this by looking at her and sporting with her, and by other signs.

Against such impure saints he began to preach, and says: If you do not become different and more pious you will not enter the kingdom of heaven. The matter of swearing must not be treated as you are doing, who make it right and valid where and when you choose; but the command is, You are not to swear at all, neither by the temple, nor by Jerusalem, nor by your head, as little as by God himself; but let your dealings with each other be yea and nay, and abide by that. For that is an abuse of the name of God, if one to the yea or nay adds oaths and swearing, as if a mere yea and nay were not valid or binding unless the name of God were added. There is also a further abuse, that people swear so thoughtlessly, as is now so commonly done, when they use the name of God with almost every word. That must all be strictly forbidden; as also cursing that is done in God's name, if it must not be done.

For cursing is just like swearing, both being good and bad. For we read in Scripture that often holy people have cursed; thus, Noah curses his one son, Ham, and the patriarch Jacob pronounced an evil blessing and a curse upon his three sons, Reuben, Levi and Simeon, also Moses against Korah; yes, Christ himself bitterly curses in the psalter his Judas, and in the Gospel the false teachers; and Paul, Gal. 1:9, curses all teachers who preach otherwise (even if it were an angel from heaven), that they shall be anathema, that is, condemned and cursed by God; as if we should say: Let God oppose them and totally destroy them, and give them no mercy or good fortune. So the time may come when one must curse, or do wrong. Thus, that we should now ask God's blessing upon pope, bishops and princes and wish them success, whilst they with malicious schemes and wicked plottings are seeking to shed the blood of pious people and to throw Germany into confusion; *that* Christians should not do, but should and must say in regard to it: Dear Lord, curse, and hurl all their scheming to the bottom of hell. Hence, no one can rightly pray the Lord's prayer without implying a curse. For, when he prays: Hallowed be thy name, thy kingdom come, thy will be done, etc., he must gather up in a mass everything that is antagonistic, and say: Cursed, execrated, disgraced be all other names, and rent asunder and destroyed be all kingdoms that are opposed to thee, gone to ruin be all hostile schemes, wisdom and purposes, etc.

This, however, is the distinction: Of himself no one is to curse or swear, unless he has God's word for it, that he must curse or swear. For, as above said, where it is done in accordance with the word of God, then it is all right to swear, to be angry, to desire one's wife, etc. But it is in accordance with the word of God, if he orders me to do it by virtue of my office and on his account, or demands it through those who are in office. Thus, that we may understand it by an illustration, if it should happen that thou art imprisoned, and in the hands of the authorities, and they would demand of thee an oath not to seek for vengeance against them; or, if a prince demands an oath of allegiance; or a judge demands an oath from a witness; then it is your duty to take the oath. For there stands the word, that thou shalt obey the powers that be. For God has so ordained and established government, that one must be under obligations to another, so that all questionable matters may be adjusted, decided and settled by the use of the oath, as the epistle to the Hebrews teaches.

But do you say: Yes, but here stands a different word, that Christ says: Thou shalt not swear. Answer, as above said concerning killing and being angry: Thou, *thou* shalt not do it, as for thyself. Here, however, it is not thou that swearest, but the judge who orders thee to do it, and it amounts to the same thing as if he did it himself, and thou art now the mouth of the judge. Now Christ here neither commands nor forbids anything to the government, but lets it take its own course as it is bound to do; but he forbids you to swear of your own account, arbitrarily or from habit; just as he forbids to draw the sword, yet does not thereby prevent your being obedient to the government, if your prince had need of your services, or would summon you to go to war; for then you are bound to enter heartily into the work of the war, and it is no longer your hand or sword, but that of the government; and you are not doing it yourself, but your prince, to whom God has committed it. Thus we speak also in similar cases. As, if it should come to pass, that we would make a treaty and concord with our enemies or the Turks, then the emperor and princes could both give and take an oath, although the Turk swears by the devil or his Mahomet, whom he regards and worships as his God, but we worship our Lord Christ and swear by him. Thus you have now a cause, for which it is right to swear, namely, the necessity of taking an oath from obedience to the government, to confirm the truth or to endure things for the sake of peace and harmony.

The other reason is love, though it be not demanded by the powers that be, but is done out of kindness to a neighbor, etc., just as also love is wrathful and rebukes, when it sees a neighbor sin or go astray; as Christ teaches in Matt. 18:15. For it cannot laugh at this or praise what is evil. Thus I may very well show love to the wife of another man, if she be in need or distress, that I may help her out of it; that is not a carnal, forbidden love, but one that is Christian, brotherly, that springs not from my own lust or indiscretion, but because of my neighbor's need; and it has the sanction of God's word, which says: "Thou shalt love thy neighbor as thyself."

Accordingly, if I see any one in spiritual need and danger, weak in faith, or conscientiously fearful, or seriously doubting, and so forth, then I am not alone to comfort, but to asseverate besides to strengthen his conscience by saying: As sure as God lives and Christ died, so surely this is the truth and the word of God. There an oath is so needful that we cannot do without it. For by that the true doctrine is established, the erring and timid conscience is instructed and comforted, and delivered from the devil. Therefore in such a case you may swear just as hard as you can. Thus Christ and Paul swore, and called God to witness. Thus an oath is suited to every threatening or promise that a Christian preacher preaches, both in alarming hardened sinners and comforting the timid.

In the same way, if one is to vindicate his neighbor or rescue his honor in opposition to bad, malicious tongues, one may also say: Before the dear God you are wrongly accusing him, etc. For this is to use God's name aright, to the honor of God and the truth, and for our neighbor's benefit and salvation. For in such a case you have the word and command hovering over you, that orders you to love your neighbor, to rebuke the disorderly, to comfort the sad, etc.; and because it is commanded it cannot be wrong, yes, it even urges you to swear, and you do wrong if you neglect to do it.

In short, if you have the word of God [on your side], then may God give you grace right away to swear, to rebuke, to be angry, and to do all that you can. But whatever is aside from this, not commanded, nor for your neighbor's need or advantage, in that case you should do none of these things. For God wants nothing at all that you do of your own motion, without his sanction, be it what it may, even if one could raise the dead. Much less will he tolerate it, that one should abuse his name, appealing to it when there is no need or occasion for it, or that one daily at home and every where else use it improperly, as is now done, when men swear with all they say, especially in beerhouses, so that it were well if this were strictly forbidden and punished. Thus you have a proper, clear understanding of this matter, so that one need not vex himself in vain in regard to this text and make a purgatory out of it when there is none.

Now Christ says: I say to you, Swear not at all, neither by heaven, nor by the earth, nor by Jerusalem. Here we see, the city was held in high esteem and honor, so that they swore by it; and he confirms this, and calls it a city of God, and it is elsewhere also called the holy city. It was holy, however, for this reason, that God's word was there, and through that God himself dwelt there; and it was a good custom, and no doubt inaugurated by good people, that the city was so highly esteemed, (as the prophet Isaiah also gloriously praises it), not for its own sake, but on account of the word.

Accordingly we may well call every city holy that has the word of God, and boast that God is really there.

But that he says: Thou shalt not swear by thy head, for thou canst not make one hair white or black, that he says concerning his creature, not concerning the use we make of it: For he does not mean to say that we cannot powder our hair that it may become black or some other color; but that it is not in our power to bring out a hair that is white or black, nor can we prevent it from becoming thus or otherwise. But when it has grown, then we can cut it off altogether or burn it; just as we can to some extent change one created thing by means of another, but we cannot take any part in having it created so or otherwise. Thus he makes our own head a sanctuary, as that which is not of our work or power, but the gift and creature of God.

That he now concludes: "Let your speech be Yea, yea; Nay, nay," etc., that he plainly addresses to such as have no command or occasion to swear. For (as was said) of his own accord no one should swear at all. But when these two features are added, command or necessity, then you are not asked to swear for yourself; for you do it not of your own accord, but on his account who demands it of you, namely, your governmental authority, or the need of your neighbor, or God's command.

27

Verses 38 through 41

YE HAVE HEARD THAT IT HATH BEEN SAID, AN EYE FOR
AN EYE AND A TOOTH FOR A TOOTH: BUT I SAY UNTO
YOU, THAT YE RESIST NOT EVIL: BUT WHOSOEVER
SHALL SMITE THEE ON THY RIGHT CHEEK, TURN TO
HIM THE OTHER ALSO. AND IF ANY MAN WILL SUE
THEE AT THE LAW, AND TAKE AWAY THY COAT, LET
HIM HAVE THY CLOAK ALSO. AND WHOSOEVER SHALL
COMPEL THEE TO GO A MILE, GO WITH HIM TWAIN.
GIVE TO HIM THAT ASKETH THEE, AND FROM THAT
WOULD BORROW OF THEE TURN NOT THOU AWAY.

This text also has been the occasion of much inquiry and error to nearly all
the teachers who have not known how to distinguish rightly between secular and spiritual matters, between the kingdom of Christ and of the world.
For when these two are confounded and not clearly and accurately separated, these matters can never be correctly understood in Christendom,
as I have often said and shown. Now we have thus far heard nothing else
than that Christ directed his teaching against the Pharisees, who were
misleading the people, both by their teaching and their way of living, and
were misinterpreting and perverting God's command in such a way that
the outcome was only sham saints, as it is to this day. For we find always
among the preachers some (if not the majority) such Jewish saints, who
teach nothing more than about sin and piety in external works.

As now in previous passages he rebuked and rejected their teaching and false interpretation, he here also takes up the passage, that stands recorded in the law of Moses, for those to whom was committed governmental authority, and who were to punish with the sword, that they should and had to take eye for eye and tooth for tooth; in such a way, that they sinned just as heavily if they failed to use the commanded sword and punishment, as did the others who seized the sword and took revenge themselves, without command: as in former passages, he who did not dwell and abide with his wife, to whom he had been married, sinned just as much as he who dwelt unmarried with another woman. That they now had perverted and confounded, so that they applied to themselves this text, that was meant only for the authorities, and they interpreted it in such a way, that also every one might take vengeance upon his own responsibility, take eye for eye, etc., just as they had confounded matters in other passages, and applied to themselves the being angry, which belongs to and was enjoined upon the authorities; also they had torn away from its connection with married life the carnal desire; in the same way, too, they had perverted swearing, aside from its proper use in time of need and for purposes of love, to their own trivial habit and other abuses.

Now comes Christ and overturns this perverted, false notion and theory, gives the authorities their due, but teaches his Christians, so distinctly as individuals, aside from official position and authority, how they are to live, personally, that they desire no revenge, and that they be so disposed, if one smites them on one cheek, that they may be ready, if necessary, to turn to him the other also, and not only refrain from taking revenge with the fist, but also in heart, with their thoughts and all their faculties. In short, he calls for a heart that is not impatient, revengeful or disposed to break the peace. This is now a righteousness very different from what they taught and held, and yet they wanted to deck themselves out with texts from Moses, that one might readily avenge himself and offer resistance, if he were violently attacked, because it stands in the text: An eye for an eye, a tooth for a tooth, etc.

Now many people have stumbled at this saying, and not only the Jews, but even Christians, have stumbled at it. For it seemed to them too strict and hard, that one must not resist evil at all, since we must have law and punishment among us; and some have quoted in opposition the example of Christ, John 18:23, when he was smitten on the one cheek, before the priest Annas, and yet did not offer the other, but asserted his innocence and rebuked the servant of the priest, which seems in violation of this text. Therefore they said that it was not necessary to turn the other cheek to the smiter, and they came to the relief of the text in this way, that it is enough that one is ready at heart to offer also the other; which may not be untruthfully said, but was not rightly understood. For they suppose that to offer the other cheek to the smiter means that one must say to him: See, thou hast this cheek too, and smite me again; or that we are to throw the cloak to him who wants to take the coat. If that were the meaning, then we would have to give up at last house and home, wife and child. Therefore we say that here no more is intended than that every Christian is taught that he must be willing and patient to suffer whatever is necessary, and not seek revenge or strike back.

But still the question and dispute here remain, whether one is to suffer all sorts of things from everybody, and in no case make any resistance; also if we are not to contend or complain before the court, or to claim or demand one's own. For if this were absolutely forbidden, there would be a strange state of affairs, so that one would have to submit to everybody's caprice and insolence, and no one could be safe from another, or keep anything, and at last there would thus be no government at all.

To answer this, thou must always observe this main point, that Christ is preaching for his Christians alone, and means to teach them what kind of people they are to be, in contrast with the carnal notions and thoughts which then were still cleaving to the apostles, who supposed that he would establish a new government and empire, and give them places in it, so that they might rule as lords, and bring into subjection to them their enemies and the evil world; as indeed flesh and blood always wishes and seeks in the gospel that it may have its rule, honor and advantage, and have nothing to suffer; after this, too, the pope has hankered, and has come to rule in such a way that his establishment has become a mere secular government, and one so dreaded that the whole world has to be subject to him.

So we now see, too, that all the world is seeking its own in the gospel [is selfishly using the gospel], and thus so many sects and parties arise, that aim at nothing else than how they can push themselves forward and make masters of themselves, and crush out others; as Münzer began with his peasants, and as others have shown who imitated his example. And even real Christians are tempted in the same way, when they see things going so badly in the world, even in their own sphere, so that they feel like laying hold and managing things. But it ought not to be so, and no one should think that God wants to let us govern and rule with secular law and punishment; but the deportment of Christians should be totally different from this, so that they have nothing to do with such things or even to care about them, but should let those to whom such things are committed care for the division of property, trading, punishing, protecting, etc., and be content with their disposal of them; as Christ teaches: Give to Caesar the things which are Caesar's. For we are transferred to a different, higher sphere, which is a divine, eternal kingdom, where we need none of the things that belong to the world, but every one is in Christ a lord for himself, both over devil and world, as has been told elsewhere.

Those now who are part of this same secular administration, must necessarily have control of right and punishment, and observe the distinction of rank, of persons, dispose of and divide property, so that all things are well-ordered, and every one may know what he is to do and have; and no one should interfere in the office of another, nor impose upon another, or take what belongs to him. For these things we have lawyers, who are to teach this and manage such matters. But the gospel has nothing to do with such things, but teaches how the heart is to stand related to God; and in all such matters it should be so disposed that it remains pure, and does not stumble upon a false righteousness. This distinction mark and observe carefully, as being the very foundation principle in accordance with which we can easily answer such questions, so that you may see what Christ is speaking about, and who are the people to whom he is preaching, namely, concerning spiritual matters and life, and for his Christians, how they are to live before God and in the world, and conduct themselves so that their heart may cleave to God, and have no concern about worldly government, authority, power, punishment, anger, revenge, etc.

If now one asks whether a Christian is to go to law, or defend himself, etc., then answer simply: No. For a Christian is such a person who has nothing to do with such worldly affairs and law, and belongs to such a kingdom or government in which the only current rule is, as we pray: Forgive us our debts as we forgive our debtors. Here there should be nothing but mutual love and service, even towards those who do not love us, but are hostile to us, and do us harm and injury, etc. Therefore he says to such that they shall not resist evil, and even not seek revenge, but that they should turn the other cheek to him who strikes them, etc.

And then there is another question, whether a Christian may be a man in a secular position and conduct the office and work of a ruler or judge, in such a way that the two persons or two kinds of office are joined in one man, and he thus be a Christian and a prince, judge, lord, servant, maid, which are merely worldly persons, for they belong to the sphere of the world. To this we answer: Yes. For God has Himself ordained and appointed this worldly sphere and these distinctions, and has besides confirmed and praised them by his word. For otherwise this life could not endure, and we are included in them, yes, born in them, before we became Christians. Therefore we must remain in them, too, as long as we are here upon earth; but only so far as our outward, worldly life and condition are concerned.

Therefore it is not indeed possible to ignore these secular relations, for a Christian must be some kind of a worldly person, because he, at least as to body and property, is under the emperor; but as to his own person, according to his spiritual life, he is only under Christ, and not under the authority of the emperor or of any man. And yet externally he is subject to and under obligations to him, in so far as he is in a civil position or office, has house and home, wife and child; for all such things are of the emperor. Therefore he must necessarily do what he commands him, and what is required by such an external life, and does wrong, if he should have house, wife, child, servants, and would not nourish or protect them, if necessary; and it would not suffice for him to say that he was a Christian, and had to forsake everything or let it be taken from him, etc.; but he must be told: You are now under the control of the emperor, where you do not count as a Christian, but as a father, lord, prince, etc. A Christian you are, as to your own person, but as to your servant you are another person, and are bound to protect him.

See, we are now speaking of a Christian *in relation*, not of him as a Christian, but as bound in this life to another person, whom he has under or over him, or also alongside of him, as lord, lady, wife, child, neighbor, etc., when one is bound to defend, shield and protect another, if he can. Therefore it would not be right to teach here to turn the other cheek and to throw away the cloak after the coat. For that would be just playing the fool, as was said of a cranky saint, who allowed the lice to nibble at him, and would not kill any of them on account of this text, asserting that one must suffer and not resist evil.

Are you a prince, judge, lord, lady, etc., and do you have people under you, and want to know what is becoming in you? Then you do not need to inquire of Christ, but consult the law of the emperor or of your state, which will soon tell you how you are to conduct yourself towards your inferiors and protect them. What kind of a foolish mother would she be, who would not defend her child against a wolf or a dog and deliver it, and then say: A Christian must not defend himself? Ought we not to teach her by a good flogging, and say: Are you a mother? then do a mother's duty, that is committed to you, and which Christ has not abrogated, but much rather confirmed.

Thus we read of many holy martyrs, who under infidel emperors and lords have gone forth to war, when summoned, and in all good conscience have struck right and left and killed, just as others, so that in this respect there was no difference between Christians and heathen; and yet they did nothing contrary to this text. For they did it not as Christians, for their own person, but as obedient members and subjects, under obligation to secular person and authority. But if you are free and not obligated to such secular authority, then you have here a different rule, as a different person.

Therefore only learn the difference between the two persons that a Christian must carry at the same time upon earth, because he lives among other people and must use the goods of the world and of the emperor, just as well as the heathen. For he has the same blood and flesh that he must maintain, not through the spiritual authority but through the land and soil that belongs to the emperor, etc., until he is bodily removed altogether out of this life into another. If now this is properly distinguished, just how far the personality of the Christian and that of the man of the world extends, you can nicely explain all these sayings and apply them properly where they belong, so that one may not mix and confound them together as the pope has done with his teaching and ruling.

This is now what we have to say of the person who is obligated toward other persons under secular rule, which is called that of father, mother, lord and lady, etc. But how is it, if only your own person is concerned, so that injury or injustice is done to yourself, whether it is proper then to oppose this with violence and defend one's self? Answer: No. For here even the principles of the world and of the emperor themselves teach: Striking back provokes quarrels, and he who strikes back invokes injury. For by so doing he becomes obnoxious to judicial authority and loses his right; just as in other cases, as when some one robs or steals from you, you have no right to steal or rob from him and forcibly to take anything from him. But we are generally disposed to avenge ourselves quickly, before one has time to look about himself. But this ought not so to be.

But if you are not willing or able to endure it, then you may go before the judge with him and there maintain your cause. For he allows it to happen that you in the ordinary way demand and take your rights, but so that you are careful not to have a revengeful heart. So a judge may properly punish and put to death, and yet he is forbidden thereby to have hatred or a spirit of vengeance in his heart; as it often happens, that one abuses his office to gratify his own caprice. If now, however, this does not occur, and you simply seek to protect and maintain yourself properly against violence and abuse, not to avenge yourself or injure your neighbor, then you do no wrong; for when the heart is pure then all is right and well done. But there is danger here, for the reason that the world, along with flesh and blood, is evil, and it always seeks its own, and nevertheless wears a plausible appearance and conceals the scoundrel.

So it is not forbidden to go to law and lodge complaint against injustice, violence, etc., if only the heart be not faulty, but equally patient as before, and one is doing it only to maintain what is right and not give place to what is wrong, and from sincere love for righteousness; as I gave an illustration above from the case of Joseph, the holy, who complained of his brothers to their father, when they had done something wrong and an evil report had gone abroad about them; and he is praised for this, for he did it not out of an evil heart, that he wanted to betray them, or wanted to create strife, as they regarded it, and in consequence became hostile to him; but he did it out of a friendly, brotherly heart, for their good. For he did not like to see that they should be the objects of an evil report, so that it could not be said that he sought revenge or meant harm, but did it for their good, and suffered in consequence of their blaming him with mischief.

This we read, too, in the Gospel, Matt. 18, in the parable of the servant to whom his lord forgave all his debt, and he was not willing to forgive his fellow-servant a small debt, that the other servants were very sorry, and told this to their master, not because they were revengeful or glad of his misfortune, but kept fist, heart and mouth quiet, so that they did not swear, or carry slanderous reports to others, but brought the matter before their master, whose business it was to punish, and they sought what was right, but with a truly Christian heart, as those who were under obligation to their master to be true to him; for so it should necessarily be, whether in a house or in a city: if a pious, faithful servant or subject sees another do wrong or injury to his master, that he report it to him and shield him from harm; in like manner, a pious citizen, if he see violence and harm done to his neighbor, that he help and defend him. These are all secular transactions which Christ has not forbidden, but rather sanctioned.

For it must surely not be that we are to give room and occasion for every one's caprice, and submit to it in silence and do nothing about it, if we can in the usual way succeed in defencing ourselves; although, otherwise, we must necessarily suffer, if injustice and violence are done to us. For we must not sanction what is wrong, but give witness to the truth, and may properly appeal to the law, against violence and outrage; as Christ himself before the high-priest Annas made his appeal to justice, and yet, notwithstanding, submitted to be smitten, and offered not only the other cheek, but his whole body.

Behold, you have thus an excellent, clear statement as to how you are to proceed in both these cases, so that we have no need of the prolix and dangerous glosses that used to be sought after; but, so that we keep things apart, and do not mix them, in order that each may move in its own sphere and yet both be effective, namely, in such a way that a Christian may, without sin, carry on all kinds of worldly business, but not as a Christian, but as a worldly person, and yet his heart remain pure in his Christianity, as Christ demands; which the world cannot do, but it abuses all worldly ordinances and law, yes, all creatures, contrary to the command of God.

Thus, if a Christian goes to war, or sits and acts as a judge, and punishes or sues his neighbor, this he does not as a Christian, but as a warrior, judge, jurist, etc.; but retains nevertheless a Christian heart, desiring to harm no one, and sorry that an evil must befall his neighbor; and he lives thus at the same time as a Christian towards everybody, who suffers all sorts of things, for his own person in the world, and yet along with this also, as a worldly person, holds fast, uses and does everything that the law of the land, or city, or family demands. In short, a Christian, as a Christian, lives for none of those things that one sees in him, in this outward life. For all this belongs to the government of the emperor; which Christ does not mean to overthrow, nor to teach that we are to run away from it, and to leave the world or one's office or place in society; but we are to make use of this rule and established order, and remain under our obligation to it, and yet inwardly live under another rule that has nothing whatever to do with that one, also does not hinder it, but readily endures its presence alongside.

Thus we now approach the text with this distinction [in view] and make all these various applications of it, namely, that a Christian is not to resist any evil; again, that a worldly person is to oppose all evil, so far as his official position calls for it. How the head of a family is not to allow his servants to oppose him or to abuse each other, etc., so also a Christian is not to have a dispute with any one, but to give up both coat and cloak when they are taken from him. But a worldly person is to protect and defend himself by appealing to law, if he can, against violence and outrage. In short, in the kingdom of Christ the law demands the enduring of everything, forgiving and repaying good with evil. Again, under the rule of the Emperor we should endure no wrong, but guard against evil and punish it, and help to defend and maintain the right, as each one's office or position demands.

But if you say: Yes, still Christ says here in plain words: Resist not evil, that sounds so distinct, as if it were absolutely forbidden? Answer: Yes, but see to whom he says this. For he does not say there is to be no resisting of evil, for that would be a downright overturning of all rule and authority; but thus he speaks: You, you shall not do it. What are these *You?* They are the disciples of Christ whom he is teaching how they are to live as to themselves, aside from the worldly government. For to be Christians is a different thing (as has been sufficiently stated), from holding and executing a worldly office or calling. Therefore he means to say: Let him who is clothed with worldly authority resist evil, execute justice, punish, etc., as the jurists and the laws teach; to you, however, as my disciples, whom I teach, not how you are to regulate yourselves outwardly, but how you are to live before God, I say: You shall not resist evil, but suffer all sorts of things, and have a pure, friendly heart towards those who do to you wrong or violence; and if some one takes your coat, that you do not seek revenge, but rather let him take your cloak also, if you cannot prevent it, etc.

He states two ways by which one suffers wrong, or has his own taken from him. In the first place, through mere violence and outrage, as when one is smitten on the mouth, or openly robbed, without any warrant of law; that means, to strike upon the one cheek. Secondly, if it is not open violence, but is done under the semblance and with help of the law; as when one seeks an occasion against you before the law, as if he had a claim upon you, so that he may compel you to give up your own. That Christ calls taking your coat by law, when one denies your right to your own, and you must both innocently suffer injustice and besides be held guilty as if you were in the wrong, etc.; not that you suffer injury or violence by the law, which is appointed to defend the pious: but, that scamps and scoundrels are sitting as judges and in office, whose business it is to execute justice, and yet, if one cannot get at you with violence, they turn and twist the law, and make an ill use of it according to their caprice; just as the world artfully and daily does, so that now nothing is so common as to make right wrong, and right out of wrong, by all sorts of sudden expedients and queer tricks.

Most frequently, however, this happens to pious Christians, to whom the world is at any rate hostile, and takes pleasure in tormenting. Therefore Christ tells them of it beforehand, that they must expect this in the world, and must submit to suffering, especially if it happens because they are Christians, that is, on account of the gospel and the spiritual government, so that on its account they expect abuse, and let everything take its course. For we must at all events suffer, since as single persons we cannot do anything or defend ourselves against the authorities if they set themselves against us. Otherwise, if this be not the case, and you can defend and protect yourself by means of the law, so that justice is done to you or yours, then you do right, and ought to do it.

28

Verse 42

GIVE TO HIM THAT ASKETH THEE, AND FROM HIM THAT WOULD BORROW OF THEE TURN NOT THOU AWAY.

He indicates three things that Christians are to endure in temporal things: that they allow things to be taken from them, that they suffer willingly and freely give. Here they (the scribes) taught no further than the law of the world and of the Emperor reaches, which does not bid you to give your own to another, nor to allow it to be taken from you; but it teaches you how to manage and deal with your property, so that you get an equivalent for it by buying, selling, exchanging, etc. Now Christ has nothing to say about this, but lets things take their course, as reason teaches, how one is to divide property, to trade, etc. But he shows what a Christian ought to have, over and above all this, namely, these three things, that he allows things to be taken from him, either by violence or with the semblance of right; also, that he cheerfully gives, and also cheerfully lends.

Therefore, we must here again distinguish between secular law and the teaching of Christ. According to secular law you may properly use your possessions, trade with them, buy and sell; as we read of the holy patriarchs, that they dealt with money and property, like other people, just as it must indeed be if we will live among the people, nourish wife and children, etc. For this all belongs to such a life, so that the belly can claim its own, and it is just as necessary as eating and drinking.

But over and above this, Christ teaches you, that in all these things you should nevertheless be ready gladly to let things be taken from you, to do good, or to give, and also to suffer, if you can, and to endure violence, not alone with your property, but also with your life, as has been explained under the previous text; and all this especially for the sake of the Lord Christ, if one tries to get at you because of the gospel, so that in that case you are ready to give up not only your coat but your cloak also, not only property and honor, but also your very life. For in such a case there can be no doubt, and a different case, indeed, can not easily occur. For in other cases, which belong to worldly affairs and government, you have judges and law, if injustice or violence be done to you, that you can appeal to and find help. But if you cannot secure justice or protection, then you must suffer; just as those even must suffer who are not Christians.

But here we must see to it, that we do not give knaves and rogues a chance to take advantage of the doctrine and assert: The Christians must suffer in every way, therefore we may confidently encroach upon their property, take and steal it; and a Christian must submit to sit there with all that he has before every desperate scoundrel, so that everything is open before him, and one must give or lend to him as much as he wants, and not demand it again, etc.; as the wretched, renegade Emperor Julian made merry over this text, and took from the Christians whatever he wanted, saying that he wanted to pay them in their own coin. No, my dear fellow, that's not the way. It is indeed true, that Christians are to be ready to endure all manner of suffering; but if you come before the judge, or fall into the hands of the hangman, then look out for what he will make you suffer. A Christian must expect to suffer what is done to him by you and every one else; but it is not his duty to allow free play for your caprice, if he can prevent it by an appeal to the law and by the help of the authorities. And although the authorities may not be willing to protect him, or even may themselves act with violence, he is not on that account to ignore the treatment as if he sanctioned it.

So also here, although he ought to lend and give to every one that asks him; yet if he knows that he is a scoundrel, it is not his duty to give to him. For Christ does not require me to give my own to every knave, and withhold it from my own and others, who need it, whom I am besides bound to help, and then myself be in want and a burden to others. For he does not say that we are to give and to lend to everybody, but to him who asks us, as the one who is in need, etc., not to the one who capriciously wants to force something from us, as those who already have enough, or who want to feed themselves without work by imposing on other people. Therefore we ought to see to it and know what sort of people we may have in any place, who may be poor and without property, or who are not [in this condition], and not encourage every scamp or tramp who has no need and could very well provide for himself. For there is plenty of such trash now roaming about the country, who want to avail themselves of this teaching, and under its sanction revel upon the property of others, and squander everything, and so wander from one place to another. We ought to turn such fellows over to the constable, and let them be taught something else, that they must not deceive pious people with their crankiness.

St. Paul teaches this in 2 Cor. 8:13, where he himself is asking for a contribution from the Corinthians for the poor Christians in the famine, so that it should not be given with the intention that the others should have ease and they should have trouble, that is, that they should have trouble and labor, and themselves suffer want, so that the others should be put in good humor by their gifts; and in 2 Thess. 3:6, he commands the Christians that they shall withdraw from such as walk unworthily; but each one is to work quietly, eat his own bread and not be a burden to others; and concludes that he who will not work shall also not eat. Therefore, he who can work shall know that this is God's command, that he do something to provide for himself and not be burdensome to others. For there are still enough of those who need it, so that we besides have enough to lend and give, as the Scriptures say, Deut. 15:11: The poor shall never cease out of the land. For we are, therefore, not to lend and give in such a way, that we fling our gifts away into the wind, and do not see to whom we give them; but we are first to open our eyes, who he is, whether he is *petens*, (as Christ says,) that is, whether he is in need, and is properly asking, or whether it is a deceiver or a scamp.

In this case you must act as a worldly person, so that you may be prudent as you are living among the people, and may know the poor, and see what kind of people you are dealing with, and to whom you should or should not give. If you then see that it is an honest seeker, open your hand and lend to him, if he can repay you again. But if he cannot, then bestow it upon him and square the account; as there are pious people who would gladly work and provide for themselves, with wife and children, and yet they cannot succeed, but now and then get into debt and trouble; for such every town should have its commom treasury and alms, and church officers who should find out who these people are, and how they live, etc., so that one does not encourage lazy tramps or burden the community.

29

Verses 43 through 48

YE HAVE HEARD THAT IT HATH BEEN SAID, THOU SHALT LOVE THY NEIGHBOR AND HATE THINE ENEMY. BUT I SAY UNTO YOU, LOVE YOUR ENEMIES, BLESS THEM THAT CURSE YOU, DO GOOD TO THEM THAT HATE YOU, AND PRAY FOR THEM THAT DESPITEFULLY USE YOU, AND PERSECUTE YOU; THAT YE MAY BE THE CHILDREN OF YOUR FATHER WHICH IS IN HEAVEN: FOR HE MAKETH HIS SUN TO RISE ON THE EVIL AND ON THE GOOD, AND SENDETH RAIN ON THE JUST AND ON THE UNJUST. FOR IF YE LOVE THEM WHICH LOVE YOU, WHAT REWARD HAVE YE? DO NOT EVEN THE PUBLICANS THE SAME? AND IF YE SALUTE YOUR BRETHREN ONLY, WHAT DO YE MORE THAN OTHERS? DO NOT EVEN THE PUBLICANS SO? BE YE THEREFORE PERFECT, EVEN AS YOUR FATHER WHICH IS IN HEAVEN IS PERFECT.

This saying, which Christ here quotes, does not stand in any one place in the Old Testament, but here and there in Deuteronomy, concerning their enemies, the heathen around them, as Moab, Ammon, Amalek; and, although it is not expressly said that they shall hate their enemies, yet it follows from these statements, as he says in Deut. 23:6, that they are never to show any favor to the Ammonites and Moabites, and their other enemies, also never to congratulate them or wish them success. This was indeed making a liberal grant to the Jews and opening a wide door for them, and they made good use of it too. But just as in other matters, so they failed also rightly to understand this, but carried it too far and abused it to gratify their own caprice. Therefore Christ explains it differently, and shows them the right meaning of the law, which they ignored, and gave prominence to such sayings as seemed to sound in their favor, so that they might therewith find support for their crookedness.

Here mark again the distinction: in the first place, that he is speaking only of what Christians, as Christians, are to do, especially for the sake of the gospel and of their Christianity. Thus, if some one hates me, envies, slanders or persecutes me for the sake of Christ and of the kingdom of heaven, I am not to hate, persecute, slander and curse him in return, but to love, benefit, bless and pray for him. For a Christian is a man who knows no hatred or animosity at all against any one, has no anger or revenge in his heart, but simply love, mildness and beneficence; just like our Lord Christ and our heavenly Father himself is, whom he here too takes as his pattern.

Now the question arises: What are we to say to this, that in the Scriptures we often read that holy people cursed their enemies, and even Christ and his apostles did the same? Is that loving and blessing one's enemies? Or, how can I love the pope, whom I daily revile and curse, and with good reason, too? The simple answer is: I have often said, the office of the ministry is not our office, but God's. But what is God's, that we do not do, but he himself, through his word and office as his own gift and business (or creature) [Geschäft, in some copies, Geschöpffe.] Now it is written, John 16:8, that it is the office and work of the Holy Spirit to reprove the world; but if he is to reprove it, he must not act the hypocrite or flatterer and say what it likes to hear; but he must rebuke and roughly assail it; as Christ denounces woe upon his Pharisees and Paul says to Elymas, Acts 13:10: "O, full of all subtilty and all mischief, thou child of the devil," etc.; and Stephen, Acts 7:51–53, reads the high-priests a hard, sharp lesson; and especially St. Paul, Gal. 1:8, heaps it all in one denunciation and calls all those anathema, that is interdicted and accursed, and consigned to the bottom of hell, who do not teach the pure doctrine of faith.

See, thus does the word of God call the whole world to account, roughly seizes both lords and princes, and everybody else; it denounces and curses their whole way of living, which it is not becoming for you or me to do, unless it is our official duty. David was right in proceeding thus in the second psalm, and telling all kings and lords to consider and humble themselves and submit to the doctrine concerning Christ, to be rebuked and taught better, or they should be summarily damned and given over to the devil. I would not dare to do that; but God's word moves in this way, thunders and lightens, and storms against great mighty mountains, and strikes in, so that it smokes; it dashes to pieces everything that is great, proud, disobedient, as is said in Ps. 29:3; and again, it sprinkles, and moistens, plants and strengthens what is weak and sickly, as poor parched plants.

If now any one wants to rush in, snapping and snarling with cursing and scolding, not as a teacher and preacher, who has been entrusted with the administration of God's word, he does wrong. But he who has been entrusted with this office must execute it; and he also does wrong if he neglects it, or through fear does not open his mouth, and rebuke what is to be rebuked without regard to persons; as we must now say to our bishops that they are tyrants and scoundrels, who act openly with all injustice and caprice against God and the right. For this I do not of myself, but in view of my office; otherwise, as to my own person, I must not wish any evil to any person upon earth, but on the other hand wish well and speak and act kindly to everybody. For I am not in this way hostile to the pope, bishops and all the enemies that persecute us and so greatly torment us. I do not at all begrudge them any of the temporal goods, power and honor that God gives them, indeed would gladly help them to keep them, yes, would even besides be much more glad if they were as rich also in spiritual goods as we are, and had no want; and it would be our heart's joy if we could by the sacrifice of our very life bring them to this, and snatch and save them from their blindness and from the power of the devil.

But as they positively will not have this, nor can endure or accept anything good that we offer them, we must also let them go their way, and say: If it has to be that one or the other must perish, God's word and the kingdom of Christ, or the pope and all his crowd, then let him rather go to the bottom of hell, in the name of his god, the devil, so that only God's word may remain. If I must bless and praise, or curse and damn one of the two, then I will bless God's word and curse them, with all that they have. For I must place the word of God above everything else, and hazard body and life, the favor of the world, goods, honor, and every precious thing, so that I may keep that and cling to Christ, as my highest treasure in heaven and on earth. For one of these two things must take place, that either the word of God may abide, and they fall in with it; or, if they will not accept of mercy and goodness and all happiness, then they must not suppress it [the word of God].

Thus a Christian can easily accommodate himself to the situation, so that he may properly conduct himself towards both enemies and friends, and love, bless, etc., every one, so far as his neighbor's person is concerned; but yet, along with this, so far as God and his word are concerned, that he do not suffer these to be encroached upon; but he must place this above and before everything else, and make everything bend to it, without regarding any one, friend or foe, inasmuch as this is not our cause, nor our neighbors', but God's, and him it is our duty to obey, before everything else. Therefore I say to my worst enemies: So far as my person is concerned, I will most gladly help you and do everything good for you, although you are my enemy and are doing me nothing but harm; but so far as God's word is concerned, there you are not to expect any friendship or love, if you ask me to do something against that, even if you were my nearest, best friend; but, if you will not endure this, I will pray for and bless you in such a fashion that God may dash you down to the ground [in some copies, "that God may oppose you and bring you to shame."] I will gladly serve you; but not to the end that you may overturn the word of God; you never can bring me to give you for such a purpose as that even a drink of water. In short, men we are to love and serve; but God above everything else: so that, if we are called upon to hinder or thwart these, then there is no more place for love or service. For the command is: Thou shalt love thine enemy and do him good; but to God's enemies I must also be an enemy, so that I do not with them run counter to God.

Thus he has refuted this position too, against the foolish notion of the Jews, who gave a false interpretation to the Scriptures, as if they were allowed to be hostile to their enemies; and he so explained the law, that they were to have no enemy at all against whom they should be hostile; although Moses had said that they should not have and make any friendship with certain strange heathens, whom not they but God himself had specially designated as his enemies. But that they should themselves regard as enemies whomsoever they would, and curse, persecute and torment them, that was not the intention of Moses. For Solomon also, who rightly understood and explained Moses, speaks thus: If thine enemy hunger, feed him; if he is athirst, give him to drink; which saying St. Paul also quotes, Rom. 12:20. For to hate one's enemy is a trait of an ordinary person and belongs to an office of divine appointment; but the command: Love thy neighbor as thyself, applies to the whole community and to each individual particularly.

But see how high he places the standard, that he not only rebukes those who do evil to their enemies, but also denies the piety of those who fail to do them good when they need it. For he says first: Love your enemies. But to love means, to have a good heart and cherish the best wishes, with cordial sympathy, and be especially amiable towards every one, and not mock at his misery or misfortune.

He means also that we are to show the same feeling by our words, when he says: Bless them that curse you, etc., so that we are not to utter an evil word against them, even if they most violently abuse, slander, revile and curse us, but to speak to them kindly and wish them well. Hence comes that beautiful, Christian expression, employed by some pious people, when they hear that some one has done them wrong, or played some ugly trick upon them—they say: May God forgive them! as though moved by compassionate sympathy, and not desiring anything else than that no harm may come to them from God on account of it. That means a good tongue against other evil tongues, so that both heart and mouth show nothing but love.

Then, in the third place, he means that this [loving] heart should be shown also by deeds, and all kinds of friendly acts, saying: Do good to them that hate you. But this is a very rare virtue, and such a doctrine as does not at all suit the world, and it is quite impossible for nature to return nothing but good for all sorts of evil, and not be overcome by malice and shameful ingratitude; but to overcome evil with good, as St. Paul says. Therefore he had before stated that he who would be a disciple of Christ and get to heaven must have another and better righteousness than that of the Pharisees and Jewish saints.

The fourth topic, however: "Pray for those that despitefully use you and persecute you," bears more directly upon our doctrine and faith, than upon our person and life. For that they persecute us, this happens on account of God's word, they claiming that they are right and we are wrong. When this is the case it is our duty to pray and commend the matter to God, because we have no one upon earth to whom we can appeal for vindication. And since we see that those who persecute us are running counter not to us, but to God himself, and are interfering with his kingdom, and are doing the greatest harm not to us, but to him himself, and have become obnoxious to his wrath and condemnation; we should rather have pity on them, and pray for them, that they may be brought out of their blindness and fearful doom. For no one can do us any harm, unless he has first done it to a far greater Lord, namely the high Majesty in heaven.

Yet this also only in so far as it is done aside from official responsibility and does not interfere with this, so that we, as I have always said, carefully distinguish the teaching which relates in general to each single person, from the teaching which belongs to those who are in office, whether spiritual or temporal, whose work it is to punish and withstand the evil. Therefore, even though they be in themselves kind, yet right and punishment, as their official work, must run their course; and it would not be right for them to neglect this, as through compassion, for this would be to help, strengthen and encourage the evil; as if I should say to our enemies, the pope, bishops, princes, and whoever they may be, who persecute and trample upon the gospel and the poor people that adhere to it: Dear sirs, may the dear God reward you, you are pious people and holy fathers, etc.; or if I were to keep silence, and worship them, or kiss their feet. No, dear brother, the right thing for me to say is: I am a preacher, who must have teeth in his head, must bite and salt, and tell them the truth; and, if they will not hear, I must excommunicate them, shut up heaven against them, consign them to the fire of hell, and turn them over to the devil, in God's name, etc.

Whosoever now has this office, to rebuke, to revile, etc., let him do it; but aside from the office, let every one follow this teaching, not to revile or curse, but to act in a kind and friendly manner, although others may act badly, and thus divert the punishing from yourself and turn it over to those whose office it is. For the evil doer will be apt to find his judge who will not spare him, even if you do not avenge yourself or seek to do it. For God will not suffer any wrong to go unpunished, but will himself take vengeance upon our enemies, and will send home to them what their treatment of us has merited; as he himself says: Vengeance is mine, I will repay; accordingly St. Paul exhorts Christians, Rom. 12:19: "Avenge not yourselves, but rather give place unto the wrath of God;" by which words he not only teaches, but also comforts, as if he would say: Do not assume to take vengeance upon one another, to curse and wish evil to each other; for whosoever does you harm or injury, he is interfering with an office that is not his, assuming to punish or injure you without orders, yes, contrary to the command of God. If now you do also the same, then you interfere with the office of God, and sin just as greatly against him, as he has done against you.

Therefore restrain your fist, and give place to his wrath and punishing, and let him attend to it, who will not let it be unavenged, and who punishes more severely than you would desire. For he has not assailed you, but much rather God himself, and has already fallen under his displeasure; he cannot escape from him, as no one has ever yet escaped him. Why then will you be angry, since God's wrath, which is immeasurably greater and more severe than the wrath and punishing of the whole world, has already fastened upon him, and has already taken greater vengeance than you could do; and besides, he has not done you the tenth part of the harm that he has done to God? Why then do you wish to curse heavily and take vengeance, since you see that he is lying under this severe condemnation, so that you should rather have pity on his misery, and pray for him, that he may escape from it and reform, etc.

And to confirm and impress this teaching he presents two examples: first, when he says: That ye may be the children of your Father which is in heaven; for he lets his sun rise on the evil and the good, and sends rain upon the just and upon the unjust; as though he should say: If you want to be called true children of your Father in heaven, then let his example move you so that you also live and act as he does. He causes his sun to rise daily, and sends rain both upon the pious and the evil. Here he has in a few words included all the earthly benefits that God bestows upon the world, when he mentions these two things, the sun and rain. For if these, or even one of them, were wanting, the whole world would long since have become waste, and have perished. If the sun did not daily rise, one could never work, but all animals, along with all trees, vegetables and grass would perish from frost. Hence the sun alone conveys the blessing of which the world is full, and which it cannot pay for, so that all, both animals and man, can seek their nourishment, and it bestows also heat and warmth, so that everything remains alive, grows, increases, and does not perish. In short, it is not possible to enumerate what benefits God bestows every hour and moment through the sun. Yes, where is the man that acknowledges this, or is thankful for it?

But, although God gives, produces and preserves everything through the sun, yet we must have the rain also. For if the sun were constantly shining, everything at last would dry up and pine away for heat, and no fodder or grain could grow for man or beast. Therefore he has tempered it with the rain, so that it can revive, and retain its moisture and strength. There are now embraced in these two the four things that belong to life, which the philosophers call the *primas qualitates*, cold, warm, dry and moist, so that there must not be one without the other. For if there were nothing but cold, or again nothing but heat, there could be no life. Now the sun brings two of these, heat and dryness; the rain also brings two, so that it is cold and moist. Thus God gives to the whole world daily most abundantly and gratuitously, to his enemies as well as to his friends, life, with all that is needed for its use and advantage. Yes, he causes it to rain the most in a waste, wild forest and ocean, where it is of no use at all, and gives only scant showers where pious people live. Yes, he gives the best kingdoms, countries, people, money and goods to the worst scoundrels; to the pious, however, hardly bread enough to eat.

Since now God everywhere in the wide world displays to us these illustrations, just as if he wished thereby to exhort us and to say to us: If you do not know what kind of a person I am, and how I am doing good to you, ask the sun and moon and rain about it, and everything that is cold, wet, warm or dry; then you will see not only innumerable benefits that I am displaying to my Christians, but also much more to the wicked, who show me no gratitude, but reward me by persecuting most shamefully my Son, and pious Christians; so, that you must be ashamed to look at the sun, that is daily proclaiming this to you, ashamed even to look at a little flower or the leaf of a tree. For it stands written upon all leaves and grass, and there is no little bird, yes, no trifling fruit, no berry, no little grain, so minute that does not show this to you and say: For whom do I yield my fruit or berry? For the vilest miscreants and scoundrels upon earth. What charge do you then bring against yourself, for having no love at all towards God, or benevolence toward your neighbor, and for not showing at least some kindness to others, since he is doing you so much good, without ceasing, by means of all his creatures?

Now there is surely no man upon earth who suffers the hundredth part as much from bad fellows as He must daily suffer, not alone by this, that men abuse his goods and all his creatures for purposes of sin and shame; but much more, that the very ones who have the most of these goods, as kings, lords and princes, are as hostile to him and his word as to the devil himself, so that they would gladly destroy it at once, if they could; they rage and storm against it with all manner of abuse, cursing, reviling, and besides with actual violence, so that there is no one upon earth to whom more hatred and envy, along with all sorts of knavery and trickery, are shown than to his Christians. Well, this is what he has to endure daily from the whole world; yet he is so good, and daily causes the sun to shine, and lets those enjoy his blessings abundantly who rather deserve not to have a blade of grass or a moment of sunshine; but they merit rather that he should rain upon them incessantly nothing but hellish fire, and hurl upon them thunderbolts, hail, spears and bullets. But he must be called a very good Father who bestows upon such desperate scoundrels so much property, land, people, fruits and good weather, and allows them to lord it in every way over his domain, so that sun and moon and all creatures must serve them, and allow themselves to be abused in the interest of all their caprice and wickedness against God. If now we wish to be children of this Father, we ought to let these striking examples move us to live accordingly.

The other illustration is taken from the evil fellows and murderers among themselves. They also understand the art of clinging together and treating each other well; yes, they make common cause with one another, and yet their whole aim is to injure other people, to rob and murder, and this alone for the sake of temporal, uncertain advantage. Therefore you ought surely to be ashamed (he means to say), who are called Christians and God's children, and want to get to heaven, and have such a good, faithful Father, who promises and gives you everything good; and yet you are no better than robbers and murderers, and are like all bad fellows upon earth. For there never have been any so bad as not to observe kindness and friendship towards one another; how could they otherwise get along? For even the devils in hell cannot antagonize each other, or their kingdom would soon be destroyed; as Christ himself says.

See, now, how good are you, if you are friendly and gracious only towards your friends? You are just about as good as thieves and rogues, whores and scoundrels, yes, as the devil himself. Yet you act loftily, are secure, and think you are all right, and can take on splendid and boastful airs as if you were an angel; as our factious spirits now boast of the great love that they have for each other, so that one must see from this that the Holy Ghost is with them. But what is it that they do? They love their own riotous rabble; along with that they are full of deadly and murderous hatred against us, who have never done them any harm; so that we can see very well what sort of a spirit they have, and yet they can very well boast that they have as much love as scamps, scoundrels and murderers, as much indeed as the devils towards each other. After this fashion no man upon earth would be wicked. For there is no one so desperately bad that he does not need to have somebody for a friend; how else could he live among people, if he were snarling and snapping at everybody? If now you wanted to conclude here: He loves his friends, therefore he is good and holy; then you must make at last the devil, and all his, good and pious.

Therefore Christ here means to conclude against the Pharisaic saints, that what they teach about love, etc., is all knavery; and he teaches them to turn the page and look at the Scriptures aright, if they want to be the people of God, so that they might see and show love towards their enemies. Thereby they could prove that they had a true love, and were God's children, as he shows his love to enemies and the ungrateful. For Moses himself also plainly said this, as in Exod. 23:4, 5: "If thou meet thine enemy's ox or his ass going astray, thou shalt surely bring it back to him again;" also, "If thou see the ass of him that hateth thee lying under his burden, thou shalt surely help him up again," etc. Here they should have found that they were under obligation to love their enemies, if they had rightly looked at the text, and had not merely glanced at it, as our blind teachers skim over the surface of the Scriptures. For since he here commands them to restore and help up an ass or an ox that belongs to an enemy: he means that they should so much the more do it when the enemy himself is in danger of person, property, wife, child, etc.; and it amounts to this: Thou shalt not desire thy neighbor's injury, but prevent it, and, if thou canst, help him and promote his advantage. Thereby you can at last move him, and by kindness overcome and soften him, so that he cannot but love you, because he sees and experiences nothing evil, but only love and pure goodness in your treatment of him.

Thus Christ now ends this chapter with this teaching and these illustrations, and says: Therefore be ye perfect, as your Father in heaven is perfect. Here our sophists have indulged in many dreams about perfection, and have applied everything to their orders and classes, as if pastors and monks alone were in the state of perfection, and one higher than the other: the bishops higher than the others, and the pope the highest of all. In this way this word is snatched away entirely from the ordinary class of Christians, as if they could not be called or be perfect. But you hear that Christ is not here talking to bishops, monks and nuns; but in general to all Christians who are his disciples and who wish to be called the children of God, not like the publicans and base fellows, such as the Pharisees and our ecclesiastics are.

But how are they to be perfect? Answer, briefly, for elsewhere I have treated of it more fully: We are not to be or become perfect, so as not to have any sin, as they dream about perfection; but to be perfect means, here and everywhere also in Scripture, that in the first place the doctrine [that we hold] be entirely correct and perfect, and then that the life also be directed and move accordingly; as here this doctrine is that we are to love not only those who do good to us, but also our enemies. He now who teaches this, and lives according to this teaching, he teaches and lives perfectly.

But the teaching and life of the Jews were both imperfect and wrong, for they taught to love only their friends, and they also lived accordingly. For that is a partial and divided, and only half a love. But he demands a whole, round, undivided love, so that one loves and benefits his enemy, as well as his friend. Thus I am called a real perfect man, one who has and holds the doctrine in its entirety. If, however, the life does not fully accord with this, as indeed it cannot, since flesh and blood constantly hinder, that does not detract from the perfection: only so that we strive after it, and daily move forward in it, in such a way that the spirit is master over the flesh, and holds it in check, keeps it under and restrains it, so that it does not have an opportunity to act contrary to this teaching; in such a way, that I let love move in the true middle way, uniformly toward everybody, so that it excludes no one. Then I have the true Christian perfection, that holds its place in no special offices or classes; but it is and is to be common to all Christians, and forms and fashions itself according to the example of the Heavenly Father, who does not part and parcel out his love and kind deeds, but lets all men upon earth enjoy them alike, through sun and rain, none excluded, good or bad.

Part II: The Sixth Chapter of St. Matthew

30

Verses 1 through 4

TAKE HEED THAT YOU DO NOT YOUR ALMS BEFORE MEN,
TO BE SEEN OF THEM: OTHERWISE YE HAVE NO REWARD
OF YOUR FATHER WHICH IS IN HEAVEN. THEREFORE,
WHEN THOU DOEST THINE ALMS, DO NOT SOUND A
TRUMPET BEFORE THEE, AS THE HYPOCRITES DO IN THE
SYNAGOGUES AND IN THE STREETS, THAT THEY MAY HAVE
GLORY OF MEN. VERILY I SAY UNTO YOU, THEY HAVE THEIR
REWARD. BUT WHEN THOU DOEST ALMS, LET NOT THY
LEFT HAND KNOW WHAT THY RIGHT HAND DOETH; THAT
THINE ALMS MAY BE IN SECRET, AND THY FATHER WHICH
SEETH IN SECRET HIMSELF SHALL REWARD THEE OPENLY.

Hitherto the Lord Christ was rebuking the false teachings and interpretations of Scripture, by which the people had been led only to avoid sinning with the fist, the heart meanwhile remaining internally entirely impure; and he showed and clearly exhibited the true meaning of the Scriptures and of the law. Now he assails their way of living, after denouncing their teaching, and rebukes their good works, and shows that they have nothing good, neither in doctrine nor works, although they were daily teaching and doing good works, as holy people, so that they were regarded as the best kernel of the whole Jewish people, and as the holiest on earth, and the whole world had to look to them as its mirror and pattern, according to which they should live: as we have hitherto known how to look for the true doctrine and life nowhere else than among our spiritual pastors and monks; and yet these are now rebuked by the Gospel, so that every one sees that they have neither taught nor lived aright, but have misled and deceived themselves and the people.

Now it is truly a mortifying preaching that comes into the world in such a way as to let these holy people have no claim to anything right or good; whereby it will merit to be opposed and not tolerated in the world. But the Holy Ghost does not shrink on this account, but goes on, as it is his office, wherever he comes, to rebuke both; as indeed both need to be rebuked. For this is true, where the teaching is not right, there it is impossible that the life, which must be directed and controlled by it, should be right and good; but what one does in accordance with it, those are bye-paths and deviations, and so much the worse because at the same time there remains the semblance and the notion that it is the true, divine teaching which points and leads towards heaven, and the works have the name of being good, and yet they look no further than to the fist: as they supposed it was enough, and well done, if they only did the works, gave many alms, fasted and prayed, no matter how their heart stood towards God; and besides they were defiled by the shameful trait that they were doing it all only to be seen by the people and get honor and glory by it from the people; for that reason Christ here rebukes and utterly rejects it.

And first of all he rebukes their alms, which is still the best among all external works. For it means nothing else than to help the poor and needy; and it embraces not only giving a piece of bread to a beggar before the door, but all sorts of kind deeds and all good works done to a neighbor. For the little word *alms* is taken from the Greek word □□□□μ□□□□□, which means *mercy;* as we also generally call them works of mercy. Whence also the Scriptures praise these works above all others, even those done towards God, as sacrificing, praying, etc.; as Christ himself says through the prophet Hosea: I have delight in mercy and not in sacrifice. So also in Is. 58, he finds fault with their grieving him by fasting and scourging their bodies, and demands these works, that they are to do good to the poor, to feed the hungry, to clothe the naked, etc. How does it then happen, that he here rebukes the Pharisees on account of such a good work? Answer:

He does not rebuke the work, but their purpose and aim in doing it. For the deed would be in itself good, but it is spoiled by their smearing their filth over it, because they seek only their own glory and honor before the people by it, and do it not for the sake of God or their neighbor. Therefore he pronounces a short, sharp judgment, that all such alms, however great, many and costly they may be, are in vain and of no account.

But who believes that this vice and fault is so common in the world, and especially in the case of the best, and how few there are of those who without this seeking for worldly honor or favor are doing good works? Take all the alms given in the whole papacy, and count up as many as you can find, that are not given with this intention. Yes, the world will never get to understand what it really means to give alms. For we are all inclined that way, if the people would not begin to praise us, or to show us honor, gratitude or favor, every one would soon draw back his hand. For if the pope had said to the princes and founders [of monasteries, etc.]: Gentlemen, I will not give you a penny for all your foundations and alms, etc., what do you suppose they would have given for churches and other institutions? They would not have had a stone hauled or laid in position; as we now see, because we teach correctly and exhort to these works, so that we are to give for God's sake, from a pure, simple heart, without any seeking for our own honor or merit, etc., now nobody wants to give a cent. But hitherto, when they had praise and honor for doing it, it snowed with alms, endowments and wills; and yet this had something to do with it, that men believed they were meriting heaven thereby; nevertheless, that was not the real reason, but it was just what Christ here says, that it was a great thing in the eyes of the people, and was praised. Otherwise they would not have cared for it, so as to do it for the sake of God and the kingdom of heaven.

This we can readily understand by the fact, as said above, that if we persuade and urge the people most earnestly to perform such good works, and represent it in the most attractive way that we can, as something heartily pleasing to God, along with all the angels in heaven, and that God will reward it a hundred fold: still nobody will touch it. What is the defect in our plea? Simply this, that one is no longer to get for it praise and honor, gratitude and praise before the world. Because the head is cut off, the body will not follow any more. But if the head were to become alive again, then things would soon move on again as they used to do, when this was the way it went. If a rich prince gave so much to a monastery, then they all came and said: *Deo gratias!* and they promised to merit it [God's favor] with their prayers and divine worship. That had to be proclaimed in all pulpits, and all the world had to say: O, that is a splendid deed! That is the way it was done everywhere in all the papacy; although there may have been a few whom God found honest. See, this is a sure indication that this was done only so as to merit thereby gratitude, honor and praise.

In addition to this you have also this evidence, that these saints soon become angry and withhold their gifts, if they experience ingratitude or contempt. For if they did not do it for the reason mentioned, they would not become angry at this, or for that reason cease, but they would continue and say: I did not begin it for that purpose, and for this reason I will not cease; but for God's honor and pleasure I will do it, even though no one gives me a good word for it. But if you come scratching along after this fashion: I have done so much for him, and it is forgotten already, and there's no grati-tude in the people, etc., I would gladly take out my heart and give it to some one; but since I see that it has to be lost, and he shows himself so ungrate-ful, and all my labor and trouble go for nothing, I'll let him have hell fire before I give him a cent or a crust of bread; see, there the scamp peeps out, and you show by your own words why you are doing it, namely, that people are to worship and celebrate you, and honor you as a god; as we now see in the case of some great miserly bishops, how they can rage and scold, if one is not always thanking them, or saying what they like to hear, so that they even insult princes and lords with it, and want to blame everybody.

See, this is the shameful perversion of good works, and the common fault in all the world, that nobody does anything good without such a design. For the world cannot get out of the crazy notion, nor tolerate and overcome ingratitude. That is where the monks come from, who ran off into the wilderness, because they were too weak to endure this, that they should be in the world, help and do good to everybody, and get as their reward nothing but contempt, harm, disgrace and ingratitude. But what devil tells you to do a good work with the expectation of meriting the honor and favor of the world, which is uncertain and can soon fall away and be changed, and not to have a better object in view, namely God, for then it cannot be lost, as he will richly repay you, both now and hereafter? And you are served exactly right; since you are such a rogue, and aim at nothing else than to be worshipped by the people, and make a god of yourself; he can very well let the world and the devil deal with you, so as to take your godhead from you and throw it into the dirt, where it ought to lie. For, as you try to sit on God's throne and appropriate the honor that belongs to him, he very properly hurls you down again, so that complete disgrace is all the thanks you get for the stolen honor.

Therefore, it is a miserable business, as to the world [in its relation to alms-giving]: whether it is professedly pious or wicked, in either case it is worthless. For it will either be an open devil, with evil works; or it will be God himself, with good works. It is intolerable, in either case. Therefore no one can do a good work unless he is a Christian. For if he does it as a man, then he does it not for the honor of God, but of himself and for his own benefit; or, if he pretends it is for God's honor, this is a malodorous lie.

Thus Christ now means to teach how one is rightly to give alms, and says: If thou givest alms, do not have a trumpet sounded before thee, and have it loudly reported, so that a whole town must know it and talk about it; just as among us, when a charitable distribution is made, all the bells are rung; but, if you give alms, do it so that your left hand does not know what your right hand does. That is just what St. Paul says in Rom. 12:8 and elsewhere: He that giveth, let him do it with simplicity. But to give with simplicity means that one does not seek thereby his own honor, favor, gratitude, or reward, and is not influenced by any one, whether he be unthankful or not; but he gives away freely what he wishes to give; just as God gives daily, and causes his sun to shine, regardless of the thankful or unthankful, just as if he saw nobody. That is a simple heart and intention, which neither seeks nor desires anything else than only God's will and honor.

These simple alms we do not find among the worldly. For their giving is of such a character, that the right hand gives, but the left hand takes That is called—givers, takers—as the children mockingly call each other; yes, given in such a way that one takes ten times as much in place of what he

gives, as, where one gives a drop of water and takes a cask of wine. For the
world gives in such a way that it will have the honor that is immeasurably
greater than all money and property, and buys thee with a trifle, so that
it may have in thee a perpetual captive, with body and life, and whatever
thou hast, yes, and God himself besides.

Therefore says Christ: If thou givest alms with the right hand, take care
that thou dost not seek to take more with thy left hand; but hold it behind
thee, and do not let it know anything about it; so that it means given with
simplicity, and not taken, or given in such a way that one must owe thee
ten times as much, and celebrate and worship thee as an idol; as our young
squires now do—if they have served some with a ducat or two, they want
to have him so bought and under such obligations to them, that he must let
everything be gold that they say and do, and dare not say a word to them
except what they like to hear. My good friend, if you can sell your bits at
that rate, you are not a poor tradesman, by any means.

Therefore let every one know how to guard against this vice, and watch
himself closely that he be not also found among these. For there are but
few people that are aware of it, and it deceives also even those who suppose
they are very pious and full of good works and are yet in this way twice as
bad as others; thus God is specially hostile to this vice, and can less endure
it than that one should openly rob his neighbor and do him wrong, than to
give in this way, and so shamefully spoil the good work, so that you make
of yourself an idol, and you more securely bind and hold your neighbor
than any one else. But that is the way it goes; where the true doctrine lies
prostrate, and yet everybody professes great piety, there these good works
follow, that have nothing but a vain show, and do twice as much harm as
open evil works.

But some one may say: What is to come of it, that he says that alms are
to be secret? Is it objectionable for one to let it be proclaimed and shown
to those who are to take and receive it? Answer: No; you must see what
Christ has in view, for he is looking at the heart and intention, namely, if
it is given or bestowed so that honor and glory are sought by it, then it is
of no value before God, although many poor may thereby be helped. But to
give alms in secret means where the heart does not expose itself, or seek

honor and name from it; but is so disposed that it gives away freely, without regarding whether it may have any show or praise before the people; yes, if besides it is despised and abused by everybody, thus it is called secret and done alone before God, even though it takes place openly before all the world. For it is covered over by this simplicity of the heart that does not inquire or care about the issue, let God decide, let come from it gratitude or ingratitude, good or evil. For thus I do not see it, though others may see it; thus I and others in our preacher's office must do, so that we do not concern ourselves whether we thereby please the people or not; yes, must rather expect for it contempt, ingratitude, persecution, and all sorts of misfortune. For every good work must expect this, and by it be tried and proved, that it may endure and be found upright; which is not the case with the other hypocritical sham work.

In short, he who means to be a Christian must not want to do, or omit any good work, out of regard for others, but only in order to serve God with his office, calling, money, goods, or whatever he has or can do, and honor him so far as he can, although he may never merit any thanks thereby upon earth. For it is also impossible that a pious man should be here rewarded for the very smallest work that he does, even if he were crowned with gold and received a whole kingdom. Therefore he should look for nothing more than getting his bread and butter for it, and expect no reward from the world, that is not worthy to recompense a good work, or indeed to recognize and honor a real Christian; and if it even knows him, it is not so good as to thank him. Because, therefore, it is not undertaken out of regard for the world, it ought not to be omitted on its account; but it should be commended to God, who will abundantly reward it; not secretly, but openly, before the whole world and all angels.

If we do not so understand and feel in this matter, we cannot perform any really good work; but we become impatient, discontented, and allow ourselves to be overcome by the shameful ingratitude of the world, so that thereby this good work is ruined and lost; and it then appears that we meant to do it not for God's sake, but for the sake of the people. And as for myself, I would long ago have given the world its walking papers and let it go to the devil, rather than let it hear a word from me. But it is no concern of hers, but of our dear Father in heaven; out of love for him, and for his praise and honor, we will preach and do good, because all else in the world is hostile to him and most shamefully despises and reviles him, and does all it can to oppose and vex him; and we take our comfort from the fact that he yet lives if all the world perishes; and because he has declared and promised that he will properly recompense and reward it, he surely will not lie to us. Then try it, and you will find that it will not fail you. This, at first, in a general way, is what we have to say in regard to almsgiving and all other good works, how a Christian is to be disposed in heart in regard to them, etc.

31

Verses 5 and 6

AND WHEN THOU PRAYEST, THOU SHALT NOT BE AS THE
HYPOCRITES ARE; FOR THEY LOVE TO PRAY STANDING
IN THE SYNAGOGUES AND IN THE CORNERS OF THE
STREETS, THAT THEY MAY BE SEEN OF MEN. VERILY I
SAY UNTO YOU, THEY HAVE THEIR REWARD. BUT THOU,
WHEN THOU PRAYEST, ENTER INTO THY CLOSET, AND
WHEN THOU HAST SHUT THY DOOR, PRAY TO THY
FATHER WHICH IS IN SECRET; AND THY FATHER WHICH
SEETH IN SECRET SHALL REWARD THEE OPENLY.

Along with almsgiving, or doing good to our neighbor, it is also our Christian duty to pray. For, just as the necessities of the present life demand that we do good to our neighbor and sympathize with him in his need (for that is why we live together upon earth, so that one may serve and help the other); so, because we are daily exposed in this life to all manner of danger and need, that we cannot avoid or turn aside, we must also ever call upon God and seek for help, both for ourselves and every one else.

But as proper almsgiving is a rare thing in the world, not only because of the common robbing and stealing that abound in the world, as no one does good to his neighbor, and everybody scratches on his own dung-pile, and does not ask how his neighbor gets along; but also because if they do a good deed, they seek only their own interests thereby; so that thus the world is nothing else than a set of robbers and thieves, both on the right and left, both bodily and spiritually, both in bad works and good; just so now is praying a rare thing, that no one does but Christians, and yet it was such a common thing in the world, especially among the Jews, as Christ here shows, in synagogues and at the corners of the streets, and now in so many churches, monasteries, nunneries, etc., muttering and bawling day and night with singing and reading, so that the world is everywhere full of it, and there is no lack of this work, and yet taken altogether it is not worth a cent.

For since Christ here rebukes and rejects all their praying, who were nevertheless so diligently practicing it, only that they might be seen of men and get glory; how much more is the praying of our ecclesiastics to be condemned, who seek nothing else thereby than that they may fill their bellies, and not one of them would say a *pater noster* if he did not get pay for it. And when they have done their best, they have mumbled over a bag-full of words, or intoned them, without heart, sense or faith, just like bells or organs; they have gotten thereby the honor and glory of being the only ones that pray; but that the others, as occupied with worldly affairs, cannot pray or serve God, and they must pray in our stead, so that we may make lords of them by our money and goods.

But how necessary prayer is, is not to be told here; we ought indeed ourselves to feel this, since we live in flesh and blood that are full of all sorts of evil tendencies; besides, we have the world around us and against us, that causes us much misery and affliction, and manifold trouble; and in addition the devil is everywhere around us, who originates innumerable sects, parties and heresies, and drives us to unbelief, despair, etc., so that there is no end to this, and we have no rest, because we are surrounded by these enemies who do not cease until they have stricken us down, for we as single poor men are much too weak for so many enemies. Therefore God says in the prophet Zechariah 12:10, that he will give to his own "the spirit of grace and of supplication," wherewith they may be sustained during their present exposure, and guard and defend themselves against the evil, harmful spirit. Therefore it is the special work of Christians, who have the Spirit of God, that they be not weary and idle, but pray without ceasing, as Christ elsewhere teaches.

But now comes the test, that it be a genuine prayer and not a hypocritical one, as theirs was, and ours has hitherto been. Therefore Christ begins by teaching them how to pray aright, and shows how they are to go about it, namely, that they should not stand and pray openly upon the streets, but should pray at home, alone, in their chamber, in secret, etc.: that is, that they should first of all lay aside the false desire to pray for the sake of the appearance and reputation, or anything of that kind. Not that we are forbidden to pray upon the street or openly; for a Christian is not bound to any place, and may pray anywhere, upon the street, in the field, or in church; but merely, that it must not be done with reference to the people, to get honor and profit from it, just as he forbids sounding a trumpet or bells at alms-giving—not for that reason, but he rebukes the addition and the false motive with these words: that they may be seen of men.

Thus it is also not commanded as necessary that we must go into a closet and shut the door; although it is suitable for one to be alone when he wishes to pray, as he can pour out his prayer to God free and unhindered, and use words and gestures that he could not in the presence of others. For although prayer can take place in the heart without any word or outward indication, yet this helps to stir up and enkindle the spirit; but the heart should, aside from this, be praying almost without intermission. For a Christian (as above said) has the spirit of supplication always present within him, so that his heart is perpetually engaged in supplication and prayer to God, whether he is eating, drinking, laboring, etc. For his whole life is devoted to the dissemination of the name, honor, and kingdom of God, so that whatever he does must contribute to this.

But yet (I say) in addition to this we must also pray outwardly; both individually, that each person use a benediction or a Lord's Prayer, or the Creed, or a psalm, in the morning, in the evening, at table, and when he has time, and collectively, when they come together, handle the word of God, and thereupon thank him and call upon him in view of the common need. This has to be done openly, and time and place are set apart for this purpose, when the people assemble; this is a precious method of prayer, and a strong defence against the devil and his wiles, for then the whole Christian community combines with one accord, and the more earnest the effort, the sooner the prayer is heard, and the more efficient it is: as it is even now doing much good, averting and hindering many artifices of the devil, that he would otherwise employ through his agents, so that surely what is now left secure, both in ecclesiastical and secular affairs, is preserved through prayer.

But what are the needful elements and characteristics for constituting a real prayer, I have often elsewhere said and treated of, namely, to repeat in a word, that we are urged to it, first, by the command of God, who has strictly enjoined it upon us to pray; then, his promise, in which he assures that he will hear us; thirdly, our contemplation of our need and misery, which so oppresses and burdens us that we greatly need to carry this straight to God, and pour it out before him, as he has commanded; fourthly, that we upon this word and promise of God pray with true faith, in full confidence that he will hear and help us; and all this in the name of Christ, through whom our prayer is acceptable to the Father, and for whose sake he gives us every grace and blessing.

This Christ shows also here with the word: Pray to thy Father in secret, etc., and afterwards more distinctly, where he says: Our Father who art in heaven, etc. For this amounts to saying that our prayer is to be addressed to God as to our gracious, kind Father, not as to a tyrant or angry judge, etc. Now no one can do that unless he has the word of God, that he wishes to have us call him Father, and that as a Father he has promised to hear and help us, and that he have this faith in his heart, so that he cheerfully dare call God his Father, and pray with hearty confidence, and rely upon this prayer, as assuredly heard, and await help.

But there were none of these elements in that Pharisaic prayer, for they thought no further than how the work was to be done, so that they might be looked upon as holy people, who like to pray; or like our monks and priests, so that they may fill their belly by it. Yes, they are so far from holding that they ought to pray with such faith, that they have regarded it as a folly and presumption that one should congratulate himself upon the certainty that his prayer is acceptable to God and heard by him; and thus, although they prayed, they counted everything as a pure venture, and thereby grievously angered God by unbelief and abuse of his name, against the first and second commandments.

Therefore learn here that no true prayer can be offered without this faith. Do you, however, feel weak and timid? for flesh and blood always hinder faith, as if you were not worthy or fit and in earnest to pray; or do you doubt whether God has heard you, because you are a sinner? then cling to the word and say: Though I am a sinner and unworthy, yet I have the command of God, that tells me to pray, and his promise that he will graciously hear me, not because of my worthiness, but for the sake of the Lord Christ. By this means you can drive away the thoughts and doubts, and cheerfully kneel down and pray, not regarding your worthiness or unworthiness, but your need and his word upon which he tells you to build; especially since he has placed before you and put into your mouth the words how and what you are to pray for (as follows), so that you joyously send up these prayers through him, and can lay them in his bosom, that he may lay them by his own worthiness before the Father.

32

Verses 7 through 13

BUT WHEN YE PRAY, USE NOT VAIN REPETITIONS, AS THE
HEATHEN DO: FOR THEY THINK THEY SHALL BE HEARD
FOR THEIR MUCH SPEAKING. BE NOT YE THEREFORE
LIKE UNTO THEM: FOR YOUR FATHER KNOWETH WHAT
THINGS YE HAVE NEED OF, BEFORE YE ASK HIM. AFTER
THIS MANNER THEREFORE PRAY YE: OUR FATHER
WHICH ART IN HEAVEN, HALLOWED BE THY NAME.
THY KINGDOM COME. THY WILL BE DONE IN EARTH, AS
IT IS IN HEAVEN. GIVE US THIS DAY OUR DAILY BREAD.
AND FORGIVE US OUR DEBTS, AS WE FORGIVE OUR
DEBTORS; AND LEAD US NOT INTO TEMPTATION, BUT
DELIVER US FROM EVIL: FOR THINE IS THE KINGDOM,
AND THE POWER, AND THE GLORY, FOR EVER. AMEN.

He rebuked above their wrong intention in prayer, as they sought their own
honor and profit among the people even in doing that which was directed
to God alone, calling upon him and beseeching him for help in our need
and temptation. Here he is rebuking this perversion of prayer, that they
suppose it is praying if one uses many words and vain repetitions, and he
calls it a heathenish method, a trifling useless prattle, as of those who suppose they will otherwise not be heard. For he saw very well that this would
be the case, and that such an abuse would continue in Christendom, as it
existed among them already at that time, so that prayer would be made a

mere work, that would be valued in proportion to its size and length, as if thereby it were admirably done, and thus instead of a true prayer there was a mere prattle and babbling, of which the heart knew nothing.

Thus, as we see, it was carried on in monasteries, nunneries and the whole ecclesiastical crowd, that seem to have had nothing else to do in their calling than to weary themselves daily so many hours, and at night besides, with singing and reading their Horas; and the more of this they could do, the holier and greater worship they called it. And yet among them all there was not one that uttered a real prayer from his heart: but they were all filled with the heathenish notion that one must tire God and one's self with crying and muttering, as if he neither could nor would otherwise hear; and they have thereby accomplished nothing else than to waste their time and punish themselves like asses, with their praying.

Therefore they have themselves said that there is no harder work than to pray; and that is in fact true, if you aim to make a work or labor out of your praying, imposing upon your body to read or sing so many hours continuously, so that any day laborer would rather choose to thresh for a whole day, than only to move his mouth for two or three hours one after another, or look straight into a book. In short their prayer was not a sighing or desire of the heart, but a mere force-work of the mouth or tongue: so that if a monk has been reading or muttering his Horas for forty years, he has not prayed from his heart for an hour during all that time. For they never think of presenting their wants before God in their prayers, but they think only that they must do it, and God must regard this trouble and toil.

But the Christian's prayer, which is offered in faith upon the promise of God, and presents before him from the heart its need, that is easy, and occasions no labor. For faith soon tells what it wants, yes, with a sigh that the heart utters and that cannot be reached or uttered in words, as Paul says. The Christian prays, and because he knows that God hears him, he does not need to prate everlastingly. Thus the saints in the Scriptures prayed, as Elijah, Elisha, David and others, with short, but strong and powerful words; as we see in the Psalms, in which there is hardly one that has a prayer of more than five or six verses. Therefore the old fathers have very properly said, there is no use in many long prayers, but they praise the short ejaculatory prayers, in which one lifts a sigh heaven-ward with a word or two; which one can do very often when he is reading, writing, or doing some other work.

But the others, who make only a huge labor out of it, can never pray with satisfaction or with devotion, but they are glad when they are through with their babbling; for it must be so, if one prays without faith and with no feeling of need, thus there can be no heart in it: but if the heart is not in it, and the body is to do the work, then it becomes difficult and vexatious; as we see also in secular labor: he who does anything unwillingly, how difficult and disagreeable it is; but on the contrary, if the heart is cheerful and willing, then it takes no notice of the work. So also it is here; if one is in earnest about it, and takes pleasure in prayer, then he neither knows nor feels any labor or trouble, but looks only at his need, and has finished singing or praying the words before he knows what he is about. In short, one should pray short, but often and strongly; for God does not ask how much and long one has prayed, but how good it is and how it comes from the heart.

Therefore Christ now says: Your Heavenly Father knows what you need before you ask for it; as if he would say: What are you about, that you think to overwhelm him with your long babbling, so that he may give you what you need? You do not need to convince him with words, or instruct him at length; for he knows beforehand better what you need than you do yourselves. Just as if you were to come before a prince or a judge who knew your case better than you could describe it to him, and you would undertake to make a long story to inform him about it, he would rightly laugh at you, or rather be offended at you. Yes, we do not know, says St. Paul, how we are to pray; so that, if he hears us and gives us something, he gives it above what we can understand or hope for. Therefore sometimes he lets us ask for something that he does not soon give, or indeed does not give at all, as knowing very well what we need or what would be useful to us or not; what we ourselves do not see, and at last must ourselves confess that it would not have been good for us if he had given to us in accordance with our prayer. Therefore we need not teach him or prescribe with our long babbling what and how he is to give to us: for he will give in such a way that his name may be hallowed and his kingdom and his will may be advanced and promoted, etc.

But do you say: Why then does he let us pray and present our need, and does not give it to us unasked, since he knows and sees all our need better than we do? He gives surely to the whole world daily so much good freely, as sun, rain, corn, money, body, life, etc., which no one asks or is grateful for; as he knows that they cannot get along for a single day without light, eating and drinking; why does he then tell us to pray for these things? Answer: He does not require it, indeed, for the reason that we are to teach him this with our praying, viz., what he is to give us, but in order that we may acknowledge and confess what kind of blessings he is bestowing upon us, and yet much more he can and will give; so that we by our praying are rather instructing ourselves than him. For thereby I am turned about, that I do not go along like the ungodly that never acknowledge this or offer thanks for it; and my heart is thus turned to him and aroused, so that I praise and thank him, and have recourse to him in time of need and look for help from him; and the effect of all this is that I learn more and more to acknowledge what kind of a God he is; and because I address my supplications to him, he is the more disposed to answer me abundantly. See, this is now a genuine supplicant, not like those other useless talkers, who babble indeed a great deal, but never acknowledge this. But he knows that what he has is the gift of God, and he says from his heart: Lord, I know that I cannot of myself produce or get a piece of my daily bread, or shield myself against any kind of need or misfortune; therefore I will await it and beseech it from thee, as thou dost teach me, and dost promise to give me, as he who is ready with favors regardless of my thoughts, and who anticipates my need.

See, such acknowledgment in prayer is pleasing to God, and is the true, highest and most precious worship which we can render to him; for thereby the honor and gratitude that are due are given to him. This the others do not do, but they seize and devour all the gifts of God, just as hogs; they appropriate one country, city, house, after another; never think of paying any regard to God; want meanwhile to be holy with their great intonations and babbling in the churches. But a Christian heart, that learns out of the

word of God, that we have everything from God and nothing from ourselves, such a heart accepts this in faith and familiarizes itself with it, so
that it can look to him for everything and expect it from him. Thus praying
teaches us, so that we recognize both ourselves and God, and learn what we
need and whence we are to seek for it and get it. Thus there is developed an
excellent, sensible man, who can readily adapt himself to all circumstances.

Christ, having thus rebuked and rejected these false and useless prayers,
proceeds himself to give an excellent brief form, how and what we are to
pray, that embraces all kinds of wants that are to drive us to prayer, so
that we can daily remind ourselves of them in such short words, and no
one may be excused, as though he did not know how or what he is to pray;
and it is a very good practice especially for ordinary people, children and
house servants, to pray the whole of the Lord's prayer daily, morning and
evening and at table, and also at other times, so that one may present to
God in it all our needs in general. Since, however, the Lord's Prayer is sufficiently expounded in the Catechism and elsewhere, I will add no further
comments at present.

It is, however, as has often been said, surely the very best prayer that
was ever uttered upon earth, or that any one could conceive, since God the
Father gave it through his Son, and laid it upon his lips; so that we dare not
doubt that it is extremely pleasing to him. He admonishes us at the very
beginning, both concerning his command and his promise, in the word:
"Our Father," etc., as the one who demands from us this honor, that we are
to ask from him, as a child from its father, and he wants us to have the confidence that he will gladly give us what we need; and this is further also a
part of it, that we glory in being his children through Christ; and thus we
come in accordance with his command and promise, and in the name of
the Lord Christ, and appear before him with all confidence.

Now, the first, second and third petitions refer to the highest benefits
that we receive from him: namely, first, because he is our Father, that he
may have his honor from us, and his name be held in high honor in all the
world. Herewith I gather into one heap all sorts of false belief and worship, the whole of hell, all sin and blasphemy, and pray that he may put a
stop to the abominable belief of the pope, the Turks, the factious spirits

and heretics, all of whom desecrate and abuse his name, or under his name seek their own honor. There are indeed but few words, but their meaning is as wide as the world, against all false doctrine and life. Secondly, after we have his word and true doctrine and worship, that also his kingdom may be and remain in us, that is, that he may control us in this doctrine and life, and thereby protect and preserve us against all the power of the devil and of his kingdom, and that all the kingdoms that rage against it may go to destruction, so that this kingdom may stand. And, thirdly, that not our will, nor that of any man, but alone his will may be done, and that what he thinks and advises may succeed, in opposition to all designs and undertakings of the world and whatever may strive against this will and counsel, even if the whole world masses itself and struggles to maintain its antagonistic cause. These are the three most important topics.

In the other four petitions we find ourselves confronted by the need that daily meets us on our own account, with reference to this poor, weak, temporal life. Therefore we pray, in the first place, that he may give us our daily bread, that is, everything that is needful for the preservation of this life: food, a healthy body, good weather, house, home, wife, child, good government, peace, and that he may preserve us from all manner of calamity, sickness, pestilence, dear times, war, insurrection, etc. Then, that he may forgive us our trespasses, and not regard the shameful misuse of and ingratitude for the blessings which he daily so richly bestows upon us, and that he may not for this reason refuse and deny us these or punish us with the disfavor that we deserve; but graciously forgive us, although we, who are called Christians and his children, do not live as we should. Thirdly, because we are living upon earth, in the midst of all manner of temptation and vexation, where we are assaulted on every side, so that we are hindered, and are tempted not alone outwardly by the world and the devil, but also inwardly by our own flesh, so that we cannot live as we should, nor be able to endure for a day amid so much danger and temptation; we pray therefore that amid this danger and need he may sustain us, so that we are not thereby overcome and ruined. And, finally, that he may at last wholly deliver us from all evil, and when the time comes, that we are to pass out of this life, may grant us a gracious, happy dying hour. Thus we have laid upon his bosom briefly all our bodily and spiritual need, and in a few words have gathered up a world of meaning.

But there is in the text a small appendage that closes the prayer, as with a common grateful confession; which is this: For thine is the kingdom, and the power, and the glory, for ever. These are the proper titles and names that belong to God alone. For these three things he has reserved for himself, that is, to govern, to judge, and to glory. No one has a right to rule or have supremacy except God alone, or those to whom he has entrusted it, through whom as his servants he exercises the control. Likewise no man has a right to judge another, or to be angry and punish, except he who holds the office by divine appointment. For it is not a natural right of men, but one given by God.

These are the two, that he here calls the kingdom, or the sovereignty, so that all authority may be his; and then, the power, that is, the result of the deciding, *exsecutio*, so that he can punish, hold the wicked in subjection and protect the pious. For he who punishes, does it in God's stead, and it is all owing to his power that one handles justice, protects and sustains. Therefore let no one avenge himself or punish, for it is not his office or sphere, and it does not avail; as he says: Vengeance is mine, I will repay; and elsewhere he threatens: He who takes the sword, shall perish by the sword.

So also the glory, or honor, is alone God's own, so that no one may boast of anything, of his wisdom, holiness or ability, except through him and from him. For, that I honor a king or prince and call him Gracious Lord, or bend the knee before him, this is not done on account of his person, but on God's account, as he is sitting in majesty in God's stead. So, when I show honor to father and mother, or to those who are in their stead, I do this not to man, but to the divine office, and I honor God in them; thus, where there is authority and power, to this is due honor and glory.

And thus his kingdom, power and glory prevail in the whole world, so that he alone rules, punishes and is glorified in the divine offices and estates, as father, mother, master, judge, prince, king, emperor, etc., although the devil, through his agents, opposes himself and aims to hold the authority and power, exercise vengeance and punishment and monopolize all the glory. Therefore we pray also especially for his name, his kingdom and his will, as those that alone should avail, and that all other names, kingdoms, power and will may go to destruction; and we thus confess that he is the highest in all these three respects, but the others are his instruments, by which he acts and accomplishes these things.

33

Verses 14 and 15

"FOR IF YE FORGIVE MEN THEIR TRESPASSES, YOUR
HEAVENLY FATHER WILL ALSO FORGIVE YOU. BUT IF
YE FORGIVE NOT MEN THEIR TRESPASSES, NEITHER
WILL YOUR FATHER FORGIVE YOUR TRESPASSES.

That is a remarkable addition, but a very precious one; and any one may
well wonder how he happens to add such an appendix to this particular
petition: Forgive us our trespasses, etc., whilst he might just as well have
added also such a fragment to one of the others, and have said: Give us our
daily bread, as we give to our children; or, Lead us not into temptation, as
we tempt no one; Deliver us from evil, as we rescue and deliver our neighbor; and yet no petition has anything added to it except this one. And it
looks besides as if the forgiveness of sins was gained and merited by our
forgiving: what would then become of our doctrine that forgiveness comes
alone through Christ and is received by faith? Answer to the first: He meant
especially to state this petition in such a way, and to link the forgiveness of
sin to our forgiving, so that hereby he would obligate the Christians to love
each other, and to make this their main and foremost duty, next to faith
and the reception of forgiveness, to be constantly forgiving their neighbor; so that, as we live in faith toward him, so also towards our neighbor in
love, that we do not vex or injure others, but think that we always forgive
although we are injured (as this must often happen in this life); or we are to

know that we are also not forgiven. For if anger and ill-will be present, this spoils the whole prayer, so that one cannot pray or wish any of the former petitions. See, this means the making of a firm and strong bond, by which we are held together, so that we do not become disunited, and create divisions, parties and sects, instead of our coming before God, to pray and get what we need: but we are to forbear with one another through love, and remain of one accord. If this be the case, the Christian man is perfect, as both believing and loving aright. What other faults he may have, these are consumed in the prayer, and all is forgiven and cancelled.

But how does he attach in these words forgiveness to our doing when he says: If you forgive your neighbor, you shall be forgiven, and again, etc.? Does not that make forgiveness depend upon faith? Answer: The forgiveness of sin, as I have often said elsewhere, occurs in two ways; first, through the Gospel and the word of God, which is received internally in the heart before God, through faith; secondly, externally, by works, of which 2 Peter 1:10 says, when he is teaching about good works: Dear brethren, be diligent to make your calling and election sure, etc. Here he means, that we are to make this sure, that we have faith and the forgiveness of sin, that is, that we show the works, so that one may tell the tree by the fruits, and that it may be manifest that it is a good and not an evil tree. For where there is true faith, there assuredly good works will follow. In this way a man is both inwardly and outwardly pious and upright, both before God and man. For this is the result and the fruit, with which I make myself and others sure that I am a true believer; which I cannot otherwise know or see.

So also here the external forgiveness which I practically show is a sure sign that I have the divine forgiveness of my sins. Again, if this is not shown towards my neighbor, then I have a sure proof that I am not forgiven before God, but am still in unbelief. See, this is the twofold forgiveness; one internal in the heart, that clings alone to the word of God; and one external, that breaks forth, and assures us that we have the internal one.

Thus we distinguish works from faith, as an internal and external righteousness; but in such a way that the internal is there first, as the root and stem from which the good works as the fruit must grow; the external, however, their witness, and as Peter says, *certificatio*, an assurance that the other is certainly there. For he who has not the internal righteousness, he does none of the external works. Again, if the external signs and proofs be wanting, I cannot be sure of the former, but am deceiving both myself and others. But if I see and feel that I am gladly forgiving my neighbor, then I can conclude and say: I do not this work naturally, but I feel myself through the grace of God disposed otherwise than before.

This is a short answer to the twaddle of the sophists. But this is also true, that this work, as he here calls it, is not a mere work like others that we do of ourselves; for faith is not thereby overlooked. For he takes this work and plants a promise upon it, so that one might honestly call it a sacrament, thereby to strengthen faith. Just as baptism too is to be regarded as a work that I do, when I baptize or am baptized; but because God's word is associated with it, it is not a mere work, as that which itself avails or effects something: but a divine word and token upon which faith rests. Thus also, our prayer, as our work, would not avail or effect anything; but its efficacy comes from this, that it is done in accordance with his command and promise, so that it may well be regarded as a sacrament, and rather as a divine work than as one of our own.

I say this for this reason, because the sophists look at the works that we do, only by themselves, aside from God's word and promise. Therefore, when they hear and read these passages that refer to works, they must indeed say that man merits this by his doing. But the Scriptures teach thus: that we are not to look to ourselves, but to God's word and promise, and cling to this by faith, so that, if you do a work prompted by the word and promise, then you have a sure proof that God is gracious to you; in such a way that your own work, that God has now taken to himself, is to be to you a sure proof of forgiveness, etc.

Now God has provided various ways, modes and manners, through which we obtain grace and the forgiveness of sins; as, first, baptism and the sacrament; also (as just said) prayer; also absolution; and here our forgiveness; so that we are richly provided for, and can find grace and mercy everywhere. For where would you seek it nearer than with your neighbor, with whom you are daily living, and have daily occasion to practice this forgiveness? For it cannot be that you are not much and often offended: so that we have not only in church or with the priest, but in the midst of our life, a daily sacrament or baptism, one brother with another, and every one at home in his house. For if you take hold of the promise through this work, you have the very thing that you get in baptism. How could God be more richly gracious to us than by hanging about our neck such a common baptism, and binding it to the Lord's prayer, which [baptism] every one realizes in himself when he prays and forgives his neighbor? So that no one has cause to complain or to excuse himself, that he cannot bring himself to it, and it is too high and far off for him, or too heavy and dear, since it is brought home to him and his neighbor, right before his door, yes, put into his bosom.

See, if you look at it, not with reference to the work itself, but with reference to the word which is associated with it, you find it an excellent, precious treasure, so that it is no longer your work but a divine sacrament; and it is a powerful consolation that you can attain to the grace of forgiving your neighbor, although you may not be able to come to other sacraments. This ought to induce you willingly to do this work from the heart, and to be thankful to God that you are worthy of this grace: you ought surely to run after this to the end of the world, and spend all your means for it; as we used to do for the fictitious indulgences. He who will not receive this must be a shameful, cursed man, especially if he hears of and recognizes this grace, and yet remains so crooked and stubborn that he will not forgive, whereby he at once loses both baptism and sacrament and everything else. For they are all linked together, so that he who has one should have them all, or retain none. For he who has been baptized ought also to receive the sacrament; and he who receives the sacrament must also pray; and he who prays must also forgive, etc. If you do not forgive, you have here a fearful sentence, that your sins also shall not be forgiven, although you are among Christians and are enjoying the sacrament and other blessings; but these will be all the more injurious and condemnatory for you.

And that Christ may the more incite us to do this, he has employed kind, friendly words, saying: If ye forgive men their trespasses, etc. He does not say: their wickedness and villainy, or perverseness and vice, etc. For by a trespass he means such a sin as is committed rather through weakness or ignorance than from malice. Why does he thus minimize and reduce the sin of our neighbor—for we often see that many a one sins deliberately, from sheer wickedness and an evil will? He does it for the reason that he wishes to allay your anger, and soften you, that you may willingly forgive, and he is more concerned to make your heart sweet and friendly than to make the sin as great as it is in itself.

For before God it is and must be so great, that it deserves eternal condemnation, and excludes from heaven, even though it be a small sin, and only a fault, if one does not acknowledge, and ask your pardon for it. But he does not mean that the sin should be thus regarded by you and me, whose prerogative it is not to punish sin, but to forgive it; so that you should think thus: Although your neighbor has done something against you through malice, yet he is still misled, taken captive and blinded by the devil. Therefore you ought to be so pious as to rather pity him, who is overcome by the devil, so that it may be called a great, unpardonable sin, on the part of the devil who has put him up to it, but on the part of your neighbor, a failure and fault; as Christ also himself has done toward us, when he prayed on the cross: Father, forgive them, for they know not what they do. That was making our sin small and of little account, which is yet in itself the very greatest that was ever committed on earth. For what greater sin can be committed than most shamefully to torture and kill the only-begotten Son of God?

Yet you must so interpret this error and fault that your neighbor who has sinned against you may acknowledge it, and request forgiveness and desire to reform. For I have elsewhere said that there are two kinds of sin; one that is confessed, which no one should leave unforgiven; the other which is defended—this one none can forgive, for it will not be regarded as sin or accepted as forgiveness. Therefore, also Christ, Matt. 18:18, where he is speaking of forgiveness or the keys, places both side by side, binding and loosing; to show that one cannot absolve the sin which one will not acknowledge to be sin or have forgiven, but must bind it in the depth of hell; but on the other hand, those which are confessed we are to absolve and raise to heaven, etc.

Just as it is with the office of the keys, so is it also with each Christian in regard to his neighbor; who, although he should be ready to forgive every one that injures him, yet, if any one will not acknowledge and refrain from sin, but besides will continue in it, you cannot forgive him; and this not on your account, but on his, because he will not have forgiveness. But so soon as he acknowledges his guilt and asks forgiveness, everything must be granted, and the absolution follow promptly. For since he rebukes himself and forsakes his sins, so that no sin any longer adheres to him, I should the rather pass them by; if he however himself clings to them, and will not forsake them, I cannot take them from him, but must let him lie in them, making for himself out of a pardonable sin an unpardonable one. In short, if he will not recognize himself, we must burden his conscience as heavily as possible and show no mercy, as he will perversely be the devil's own. On the other hand, if he confesses his sin, and seeks your pardon, and you refuse to forgive, then you have laden it upon yourself, so that it will condemn you too.

Thus Christ intends also that the sin be confessed, inasmuch as he still calls it a transgression; he does not mean to deny that it is wrong, or to impose it upon you to sanction it as properly done, or treat it as right or good; only if it have become pardonable, and of so small an account as to be called only a fault, that you then say to your neighbor: Although I cannot praise it, and it is wrong, yet, since you acknowledge your error and your heart is now changed, and you have no ill-will against me, I will also gladly overlook it as a fault and oversight, and will forget my anger.

If you now are thus disposed towards your neighbor, God will also show himself again towards you with a sweet friendly heart, and he will make your great, heavy sin that you have committed against him, and are still committing, of such small account that he calls it only a fault, if you acknowledge it and pray for forgiveness, as he is more inclined to forgive than we can expect him to be. Now you should offer your body and life to God for such a heart, and seek for it to the end of the world; as they used to seek for it in the papacy, and worried themselves for it with many kinds of works. Now there is here such a heart offered to you, presented and given altogether gratuitously, just as baptism, the gospel and all its blessings; and you get more than you with all your works and those of all men could acquire. For here you have the sure promise that cannot belie or deceive you, that all your sins, however many or great they may be, shall be before him as small as human daily weaknesses, which he will not count or remember so far as you have faith in Christ. For just as other sacraments originate in and operate through the Lord Christ; so also, that our prayer is heard and we have certain forgiveness; that we have not deserved it, but all is acquired through him and bestowed upon us; so that he always remains the sole Mediator, through whom we have everything, so that also the forgiveness based upon this work avails alone through him.

So you see now why Christ added this appendage to the prayer, so that he might thereby unite us the more closely together, and preserve his followers in unity of spirit, both in faith and love, so that we do not allow ourselves to be separated on account of any sin or fault, that we may not lose faith and everything else. For it cannot be otherwise than that many offenses will daily occur amongst us in all callings and kinds of business, when we are saying and doing towards one another what one does not like to hear or endure, and give occasion to wrath and contention. For we still have our flesh and blood, that acts after its own fashion, and easily lets slip an evil word, or an angry sign or deed, by which love is wounded, in such a way that there must be much forgiveness among Christians; as we also incessantly need forgiveness from God, and must always cling to the prayer: Forgive us, as we forgive; unless we are such ungodly people, that we always more readily see a mote in our neighbor's eye than the beam in our own, and throw our sins behind us. For, if we should look at ourselves daily from morning till evening, we should find so many cleaving to us that we should forget other people, and be glad that we could engage in prayer.

34

Verses 16 through 18

MOREOVER WHEN YE FAST, BE NOT AS THE HYPOCRITES, OF
A SAD COUNTENANCE: FOR THEY DISFIGURE THEIR FACES,
THAT THEY MAY APPEAR UNTO MEN TO FAST. VERILY, I
SAY UNTO YOU, THEY HAVE THEIR REWARD. BUT THOU,
WHEN THOU FASTEST, ANOINT THY HEAD AND WASH THY
FACE; THAT THOU APPEAR NOT UNTO MEN TO FAST, BUT
UNTO THY FATHER WHICH IS IN SECRET; AND THY FATHER
WHICH SEETH IN SECRET SHALL REWARD THEE OPENLY.

As he rebuked their almsgiving and praying, so does he here rebuke their
fasting. For these are about the three good works that comprehend all the
rest: the first, all kinds of good deeds toward our neighbor; the second, that
we are concerned about all manner of needs, both those of others and our
own, and bring them before God; the third, that we mortify our body. But,
as they had shamefully abused both almsgiving and praying, so that they
thereby sought not God's honor but their own glory; so did they also abuse
and pervert fasting, not to keep their own body under constraint and in
discipline, nor to praise and thank God; but to be seen of men, and have
a name, so that people would have to be astonished, and say: O these are
excellent saints, who do not live like other common people, but go about
in gray coats, hanging their heads, looking sad and pale, etc. If these do
not get to heaven, what will become of the rest of us?

But he does not mean to have fasting in itself rejected or despised, just as little as he rejects almsgiving and praying, but he rather confirms these, and teaches how to use them aright: so he means to properly restore fasting, so that it be rightly used and properly understood, as should be the case with a good work.

It originated among the Jews, when Moses commanded them to fast about fourteen consecutive days, in the autumn, at the feast of expiation. That was the common fast, which they all observed at the same time. In addition the Pharisees had their special fasts, so that they did something more and were counted more holy than others. For that fast was not appointed that they might thereby be seen and observed by others, since it was kept by all the people; and what is common to all, with that no one can specially distinguish himself. Therefore they had to undertake many special fasts, that they might be seen, as much higher and more spiritual than common people; hence they also boast in the gospel against Christ: Why do the disciples of the Pharisees fast so often, and thy disciples do not fast? etc. Besides, they assumed distinguishing attitudes and marks by which it should be known when they were fasting; they disfigured their faces, so that they did not wash or anoint themselves, but looked sad and gloomy, and put on such a wonderful earnestness that men had to talk and sing about it, etc.

Now comes Christ and demolishes this fasting, and teaches the direct contrary, and says: If you wish to fast, then fast in such a way that you do not have a sad countenance; but wash and anoint your face, so that you appear merry and cheerful, as on a holiday, so that no difference is noticeable between your fasting and keeping holiday. For it was customary among the Jews for them to sprinkle their bodies with aromatic water and anoint their heads, so that their whole person was fragrant when they were keeping a holiday or wanted to be cheerful. If you fast in this way, between yourself and your Father alone, then you have fasted rightly, so that it pleases him; but not as if it were forbidden on a fast day to wear poor clothes or go unwashed; but the notion is rejected that it is to be done for the sake of the reputation, and in order to make people open their eyes at your peculiar way of doing it. Indeed we often read of how they fasted, putting on sackcloth and casting ashes on their heads; as in the case of the king of Nineveh and the whole city. But that was another kind of fasting that their need and misery taught them.

Now, we have copied from the Jews our great fasting season, and at first kept fourteen days; then we became holier, and stretched this out to four weeks, until at last it was drawn out to forty days; but, not content with that, we have set apart besides two days in every week throughout the year for fasting, the Friday and Saturday; finally the four golden or compulsory fasts; these were yet all common or general fasts: besides this, the advent season found some special saints who made a fast out of that, aside from what the monks in monasteries observed; and then every one selected some special saints in addition to the general fasts, until the result was that all of this was of no account if each one did not make his own fast.

Now such fasting as this all taken together is not worth a penny. For the primitive fathers may indeed have meant it well and observed the fasts properly; but it soon was overdone and ruined by the filth, so that it was of no account. And it got what it deserved. For as this wonderful multiplication of fasts was mere human trifling, so it soon degenerated into shameful abuse. For I may honestly say that I never saw a genuine fast in the papacy, in what they call fasting. For what kind of a fast is that for me, when they prepare a meal at noon of costly fish, excellently spiced, more and better than for two or three other meals, and the strongest drink besides, and spend an hour or three at it until they have filled their belly full? And that was a common thing and a trifle even among the very strictest monks. But the holy fathers, the bishops, abbots and other prelates got at it in earnest at once with ten and twenty courses, and at night took so much refreshment that several threshers could have fed for three days upon it. It may well be that some prisoners, or poor and sickly people, have had to fast through poverty; but I know of no one who fasted for the sake of devotion, and still less now. But now these, my dear papists, have all become good Lutherans, so that none of them thinks any more about fasting; but meanwhile they let our poor pastors have hunger and trouble and hold a real daily fast in their stead.

Since then this fasting has turned out to be a great deal worse than that of the Jews and Pharisees, who did honestly and truly fast, only that they sought their own honor thereby; but ours under the name of fasting has become a mere feasting, and is no fast, but a mockery of God and of the people; besides having the disgraceful addition of making a distinction in the kinds of food, and forbidding the use of some, so that they call only that fasting if one abstains from the use of meat, but meanwhile have the best fish with excellent condiments and spices and the strongest wine; therefore I have advised, and do still advise, that we trample such fasting under our feet as an abominable mockery of God; so that it vexes me that men should carry on and endure this blasphemy in Christendom, and deceive God with the mask of calling such a life of high living and belly-filling a fast and a good work.

This is now a gross, shameless, disgraceful deception, which does not need the Scriptures for a rebuke, but every peasant, yes a child of seven years, can comprehend and understand. But they have also added the still more disgraceful abuse (which ruins even true fasting), that they sought thereby great merit before God, as thereby to atone for sin and propitiate God; so they impose this fasting as penance in absolution. That is really fasting in the name of all the devils, smiting Christ in the mouth and trampling him under foot: so that so far as abuse is concerned, if something bad must be done, I would sooner allow that one should guzzle to repletion; and I would rather see a gorged sow, if I have to look at filth, than such a saint who fasts most strictly on water and bread.

The teaching and books of all the monks, the papal bulls, all the pulpits, are still full of this abomination, so that they know nothing of any other fasting when they are doing their very best I will say nothing about their magnifying the gross, shameful, lying fasts of which we have spoken, and their thereby establishing and confirming the worship of the saints; and no one has been found to say a word against these abuses. Therefore I still assert that all my life long I never saw in all the papacy a fast that was a truly Christian one; but only disgraceful fasting and feasting, instead of real fasting, and, along with that, sheer idolatry and hypocrisy, whereby

God was insulted and the people deceived. Therefore let us learn here what it means to fast aright.

There are two kinds of fasts that are good and commendable; one may be called a secular or civil fast, ordered by the government, as any other ordinance or command of the authorities, not demanded as a good work or a divine service. For that I would like to see, and would advise and help to bring it about, that the emperor or prince should issue the order that for one or two days in the week no meat should be eaten or sold, as a good useful ordinance for the country, so that everything should not be gobbled up, as is now done, until at last dear times must come and nothing is to be had. After that, I would be glad if at certain times, once a week, or as might be thought best, people did not have a meal in the evening, except a bit of bread and a drink, so that everything is not consumed with incessant gormandizing and swilling, as we Germans do, and that we should learn to live temperately, especially the young, plump, strong people. But that should be an entirely secular matter, subject to the temporal authority.

In addition to this there should be also a general spiritual fast, which we Christians should observe, and it would be a good arrangement to hold a general fast a few days before Easter, Whitsuntide and Christmas, and thus distribute the fasts through the year. But by all means not for the purpose of making an act of worship out of it, to merit something by it, or to propitiate God; but as an external Christian discipline and exercise for the young and simple people, that they may learn to adapt themselves to the times, and to make the needful distinctions throughout the year; as we have hitherto kept the four ember-weeks, that every one was guided by. For we must distinguish and mark off certain times for the rude common crowd, as fast and feast days, for preaching and commemorating the principal events of the life of Christ; in such a way that thereby no special divine service is aimed at, but only a memorial day, whereby one can divide up the whole year and tell what special time it is. So I would have no objection to people fasting on every Friday evening throughout the whole year, setting it apart as a day to be distinctly marked. But such fasting I neither can nor will inaugurate, unless it were beforehand harmoniously agreed upon. See, thus the Christian Church would have plenty of fasting to do, so that they could not blame us for despising and entirely refusing to fast.

But this is also still not the real Christian fasting that Christ has in view, which has special reference to each person in particular, and which, if it is to deserve the name of true Christian fasting, must be done thus, not merely by not eating in the evening, which is only a part of it, and the very least part; but it consists in your disciplining and restraining your body. This relates not only to eating, drinking, sleeping, etc., but also to being idle, indulging in sports, and everything that pleases and pampers the body. True fasting means quitting and refraining from all such things, and solely in order to curb and humiliate the flesh; as the Scriptures inculcate fasting, and call it *affligere animam*, to mortify the body, etc., so that it renounce voluptuousness, high living, pleasure. This was the fasting of the primitive fathers; they ate nothing the whole day, went about sorrowing, and denied the body everything, so far as nature would allow it.

This fasting we now meet with rarely, especially among our spiritual monks and priests. For the Carthusians, who claim to lead the strictest lives, do not practice it, although they make some pretence of doing it, by wearing a dress of haircloth; but they gormandize, nevertheless, and cram their belly full of the best food and drink, and without any care live most luxuriously. No; it does not mean thus to quibble and deceive, but it demands the mortification of the body, and withholding from it all that pleases and gratifies it; and even if they did really fast aright, yet they would still make a devilish abuse of it by basing their holiness upon it and claiming to get something special from God by it, etc. Therefore, we are not to build anything upon it, although our fasting may be of the very best kind. For there may be a secret scoundrel lurking behind it, against faith or love; as also the prophet Isaiah, 58:3, (as quoted above) rebukes the fasting, by which they mortified their bodies, but at the same time cheated and oppressed their debtors, etc. Thus Christ also rejected the fasting of the Pharisees; not that they did not honestly fast, but because they sought thereby their own glory and honor, etc.

Therefore, very much is needed to make fasting a truly good work, and pleasing to God. For he cannot at all endure it that you pay your court to him with your fasting as a great saint, and yet at the same time cherish hatred and wrath against your neighbor, etc.; but if you want to fast properly, bear in mind that you are first to be a pious man, and have both genuine faith and love. For this business has to do not with God or our neighbor, but with our own body, etc. But nobody wants to do this. Therefore, I may well say, that I have never seen any real fasting. For there has been nothing but half and fragmentary fasting, and a miserable deception, when they, for appearance sake, break off a meal, but nevertheless daily tickle the body; except that now in the case of some pious preachers and pastors in the villages and elsewhere, who have to do it from necessity, and besides suffer reproach, ridicule and all manner of annoyance, and get from no one as much as a piece of bread. With these there is neither pleasure, nor show, nor easy times; these are they who wander in the world, whom no one knows, of whom the world is not worthy (as is said in the epistle to the Hebrews, 11:38). But the Carthusian monks and our insurrectionary rabble in their robes of haircloth and their gray coats, at these we are to look with amazement, and say: O, what holy people are these! How hard it is for them to go about so shabbily clothed; and yet they are always guzzling and swilling their belly full.

See, that I call the real fasting of Christians, if one mortifies the whole body and forces it, with all the five senses, to relinquish and do without everything that ministers to its ease, whether this be done willingly or by compulsion, (yet that one gladly assents to this and endures it), whether one eats fish or flesh; but nothing more than sheer need requires, so that the body is not thereby injured or incapacitated, but held under constraint and at work, so that it does not become idle, or lazy and lewd. But such fasting as this I do not presume to require, nor will I impose it upon any one. For every one must here look to himself, and judge his own feelings, for we are not all alike, so that one cannot set up a general rule; but every one, in proportion as he is strong, and feels what his own flesh requires, must in such proportion afflict or relieve it. For the intention here is to antagonize lust and the excitement of the flesh, and not nature itself, and it is not limited by any rule or measure of time or place; but it is to be steadily applied, if necessary, so that we hold the body in check, and habituate it to endure discomfort, if it become necessary to do it; and it is to be used according to the discretion of every one, so that no one may undertake to measure it off by rules, as the pope has done; just as we cannot measure off prayers, but let them be free, if any one's devotion suggests or demands them; nor can we apply it to the almsgiving, to whom, or when, or how much we are to give, as if forced by necessity and law.

This is the extent of the general law for all Christians, and it is commended that every one live temperately, soberly and discreetly, not for a day or a year, but daily and continually, which the Scriptures call *sobrietatem*, living soberly; so that, although they cannot observe all the principal fasts, yet do this much that they are moderate in eating, drinking, sleeping, and in all the needs of the body, that it may minister to what is necessary and not to what is superfluous and capricious, and not live here as if we were only to eat and drink, to dance and be merry. If, however, sometimes through weakness we are guilty of some excess, that will have to be reckoned under the head of forgiveness of sins, as other daily failings.

But first of all see to it that you are in advance pious and a true Christian, and are not thinking to render a service to God through this fasting; but serving God must be simply faith in Christ and love to your neighbor, so that you do just what is your duty. If this be not the case with you, then rather let the fasting alone. For fasting is meant only to be imposed upon the body to cut off outwardly its lust and the occasions for lusting; just as faith does the same inwardly in the heart. Let this be enough said about fasting.

Now we must look also at the words that Christ appends to all of these things, almsgiving, praying and fasting—that they are to be secret, then will our Father, who seeth in secret, reward us openly. For it is a necessary comforting assurance for Christians who do these works uprightly, since in the world their works are maligned and so covered up and concealed that no ungodly person can see them; and even if he sees them, yet with eyes open he does not acknowledge them. Thus, take ourselves for example, what good we do through the grace of God, that no one sees, and the whole world denounces us as those who pray, fast, and despise and forbid all good works, and occasion only misfortune and discord. But how we pray, both openly and secretly, that they are not to see, even if they hear it and are standing alongside, and would like to attack us publicly, as we are helping to keep the peace and do good, etc. For God has so ordained it, as the Scriptures say, that no ungodly person shall see the glory of God, that is, everything that God says and does; as also Isaiah says, 6:10: Make the heart of this people fat, and make their ears heavy, and shut their eyes; lest they see with their eyes, and hear with their ears, and understand with their heart, and convert, etc.

And so it is with us, both in our doctrine and life. For I suppose our gospel is not hidden, in itself, but so noised abroad that they all see and hear it; else they would not so furiously rage against it; yet they cannot see it, and it must be called among them not the gospel, but a damnable heresy. So also they do not see its fruits in us and our good works that we show towards them, as our enemies, and humble ourselves most completely before them, offer them peace and everything that is good, and besides faithfully pray for them: yet they are not worthy to recognize this, but must for this very reason so much the more horribly persecute us. Thus they also do not see our fasting, how our preachers willingly endure hunger and trouble, that they may serve the people, etc. But when they fast along with a good, fat collation, and three or four courses, that is a splendid feat and great holiness; just as our praying must be considered as nothing in contrast with their babbling and howling in the churches.

See, thus, the entire Christian life must be and remain hidden, and cannot attain to any notoriety nor have any show and display before the world. Therefore be satisfied, and do not worry about it, though it be concealed, and indeed covered up and buried, so that no one sees or regards it, and be content that your Father up there in heaven sees it; he has sharp eyes and can see very far off, although it be covered by great, dark clouds, and buried deep in the earth; in such a way that the life of all Christians is intended alone for the eyes of God. For that is at all events the outcome of it all; we may live as we will, and do as well as we can, yet we still cannot please the world, nor do what seems right to it or worthy of praise, and it does not really deserve to be helped and benefited.

Therefore we must also again give it its walking papers and send it home to the devil, and confidently defy it with such rhymes as: "Let the world go, it has a poor show," etc. It is enough that we are acting to please him who sees what we do; and we will neither do nor leave undone anything to please them, God helping us, whether they thank or abuse, are angry or laugh; we will not at any rate make it otherwise than it has always been. Why should we then strive after the honor or gratitude that cannot be obtained? No, we will commend it to the scoundrels that wear rosaries about their necks, are bellowing day and night in the choir, are gormandizing on nothing but fish and stinking oil, etc., and are doing nothing but lost works; these shall gain the honor and glory from the world, as they deserve them both, and they belong together, as cattle and a stable, with the devil behind. For as the works are, so shall also the priests be, that one villain may praise another.

That is one part of the consolation, that we know that the world is not worthy of us; but we have another One in heaven, who beholds us and our works. The other part is, that he says: "Thy Father which seeth in secret shall reward thee openly;" that it will not only be seen, but also rewarded; and not in secret, but openly, that the whole world may see, along with its own perpetual disgrace. Therefore let him dispose of it; he will bring it to light, so that it is not kept in the dark, and [he will do it] on earth and in the presence of the people; as also the thirty-seventh Psalm comfortably teaches: "Commit thy way unto the Lord; trust also in him, and he shall bring it to pass. And he shall bring forth thy righteousness as the light, and thy judgment as the noonday." See how the dear martyrs were so shamefully murdered, and yet they now so shine forth that all the world in contrast is a mere stench. So John Huss before our day was condemned, with unheard of brutality, and his name (as they supposed) was forever obliterated; yet now he shines forth with such honor that his cause and teaching must be praised before the whole world, and the matter of the pope lies in the dirt most ignominiously.

Then let us now be shoveled under and stay hidden; the time will come when God will draw us forth, that our cause must shine before the eyes of all the world, even yet in this life, but still more gloriously at that day when some poor man will step forth with his fruits and good works, and put to shame the whole papacy and the world, so that his cause will be perfect light and clearness, but the other nothing but filth; only so that we cling to the word of Christ, and do not care or be worried about it that we are now befouled and thrown into the dark before the world: but look to him and do everything for his sake. For God's work and word cannot lag behind, but must come forth to the light, however deeply it is covered up and buried; so that I have often myself wondered, when I looked at the papacy, how the devil through the pope's abominations has thrown the dear gospel into a dung-pile and puddle, and covered it up so completely that I thought it would not be possible for the truth ever to come forth again amid such perversions of masses, purgatory and numberless other abominations: yet it had to come forth, just when it lay the deepest, and they were thinking that they had settled the matter for ever.

The same thing happened to Christ himself; when they had put him under ground and supposed they had covered him up so deeply that nobody would ever mention him again, then he blazes forth and shines by his word so brightly that they all had to go under for ever. Therefore we ought also to feel safe, for we have his word, so that our doctrine and works must come to the light and be praised before the eyes of all the world; although now they are concealed; unless God himself must stay in the dark. See, this is the comforting assurance, given to us as an admonition, that we are to exercise ourselves in really good works, and not worry ourselves because they are not observed by the world, for it is too blind; and just as little as it recognizes God, just so little does it recognize his word and works; and it will never come to see how grand a thing it is to be a baptized child, or a Christian who receives the Lord's Supper and gladly hears the word of God; but has to look at it as a mere water-bath, or a bit of bread, and a useless talk. So also it does not see what he is doing who rightly fasts or prays. Therefore we commend it to him who can see it, and hope that he will put to shame the blind, crazy saints, with their pompous, hypocritical display by which they are now darkening the life and works of Christians.

35

Verses 19 through 21

"LAY NOT UP FOR YOURSELVES TREASURES UPON EARTH,
WHERE MOTH AND RUST DOTH CORRUPT, AND WHERE
THIEVES BREAK THROUGH AND STEAL: BUT LAY UP FOR
YOURSELVES TREASURES IN HEAVEN, WHERE THIEVES
DO NOT BREAK THROUGH NOR STEAL: FOR WHERE YOUR
TREASURE IS, THERE WILL YOUR HEART BE ALSO."

He has been thus far rebuking their false interpretations of the ten commandments, and purifying and cleansing the befouled and obscured doctrine; then he taught the nature of real good works in contrast with their
false, pretended good works; in such a way that we may rightly understand
the ten commandments and do really good deeds. Now he begins to warn
against the temptations that beset this doctrine, and continues in this strain
almost until the eighth chapter, and means to set forth the whole matter
most admirably, as a skilled master, who omits nothing that may serve to
keep us in the true doctrine and life.

First of all he takes up the beautiful, great vice that is called avarice. For
these are about the two worst plagues that always make their appearance,
if we preach the gospel and try to live accordingly: first, false preachers,
who corrupt the doctrine; then squire avarice, who hinders right living; as
we see now, since the gospel is preached again, that the people have become
much more avaricious than before, they rake and scrape together as if they
were almost dying from hunger; they formerly groped in blindness, as if

stupefied, listened to the preaching of irresponsible dreamers, and gave by the score what was demanded, so that they neither saw nor knew what was being taken from them; but now, since their eyes are opened, that they know how they ought to live and perform really good works, they watch their pennies so closely, and are as avaricious, as if each one would like to monopolize the treasures of the world: so that I cannot otherwise explain it, or tell whence it comes, except that it must be a temptation from the very devil himself, who always interjects this abominable vice along with the light of the gospel, to hinder it. For the gospel gives us the consolation that we not only are there to live forever, but are also here to have enough to eat, as we read in the eighth Psalm: that Christ is to be a King and Lord over all the world, and have in his hand all sheep and oxen, and all the beasts upon earth, so that he will not let us die of hunger. Now, this we know; and yet we ourselves are much more deeply immersed in avarice and care for daily food than before, and are all the time short of funds and out of pocket, and cannot give for the glory of God the tenth part of what we used to cram down the throat of the devil.

Christ taught the same thing in many other places, and announced it beforehand. As, when he sent out his apostles to preach, his chief care and admonition were that they should beware of these two things, false teaching and avarice; and he strictly charged them that they should take no provision with them on the way, nor be concerned about what they should eat and drink, so that (as above said) the two most injurious things in Christendom, by which it is greatly perverted, are: spiritually, the faith by false doctrine, bodily, the fruits by avarice. Therefore there is need here of preaching and warning, when we have decided upon doctrine and life, that we take due care to adhere to it and not be diverted from it by false interpretations of Scripture; and then to beware of avarice that it do not secretly ensnare and get possession of us, so that we do not aim only at temporal things, to have enough here, as if that were all.

For it is a dangerous, insinuating vice, and can put on an attractive appearance and start beautiful thoughts, so that it even deceives Christians, and no one can be sure of being safe against it. For when they see how ill it goes with them in the world, that is ever imposing upon them, and begrudging them even a bit of bread, so that they for its sake must nearly die of hunger; how the poor preachers are now left to endure trouble and want; they are so tempted that they consider how they may get and accumulate something, so that they may stay in the world, until at last they actually become involved in worldly care and avarice, and through this let their ministerial office fall and lie, and some even let go the gospel altogether.

See, for this reason Christ now begins with many words to preach against the great idol mammon, and paints it in the most detestable colors, so that one should by all means be on his guard against it; and he says, in the first place: Lay not up for yourselves treasures upon earth, where moth and rust doth corrupt, and where thieves break through, etc. Here he gives to the treasures upon earth three burrowers, rust, moths and thieves; these are scandalous watchmen when they are set over treasures. Now God has wisely ordained that where a treasure is there must such fellows be that watch it; just as commonly the sparrows or rats and mice with the corn. For it is not worth anything better, since we do not rightly use money and property, but through sheer avarice scrape it together for ourselves, and no one gives or grants it to another.

But this means not only the moths and rust that devour clothes or iron and brass; nor mice and rats, that can be caught in traps; also, not the mere thieves that secretly empty the coffers, but also the great living moths and public thieves, as the great corrupters and profligates at court, that can empty bins and purse for a prince, and at last strip him of all that he has; so also in cities, not only those who creep into a citizen's house, but who with cunning secrecy suck out the city's resources by usury and extortion in the market and wherever they can; so that, in short, wherever there is money and property there must also moths and thieves be, eager for it; and everything in the world is full of these rats and mice, wherever people live together. For what else than such a rust or moth is an unfaithful counsellor at court, or an officer who does nothing but nibble away at a prince's money or property as long as it lasts? As there are now many of these hypocrites, who with daily, heavy, unnecessary and useless expenses make the princes poor, and who do not care whether a prince is prospering or going to ruin, if they can only be masters of his money and manage things as they please. Thus also, in all towns and villages we find everything full of rats and moths, both great and small, secret and public, as shoemakers, cobblers, tailors, butchers, bakers, brewers and saloon-keepers, and other trades, workmen and day-laborers. Yes, in every house, he who has a lazy, unfaithful servant or maid, what else has he than a weevil, that devours more for him than if he had his floor full of rats and mice? Now see what a fine god mammon is, who has no better protectors and courtiers about him than mere moths and rust, so that if one has been gathering treasures for a long while, yet there must be so much devouring by this kind of hangers-on that no one who ought to enjoy it is glad or takes pleasure in it; and not many treasures of great men and princes have ever been well invested, but they have generally been wasted through wars, or devoured by these miserable cankers, or otherwise uselessly squandered or destroyed. Therefore, those are best off who have not many treasures, for they have not many rats to feed, and need not be afraid of thieves.

How, then, are we to have no treasures at all, and are all hereby condemned who gather treasures upon earth? Surely that cannot be the case. For, if everybody would do as you and I do, to-morrow nobody would have anything in house and home. The lords and princes must acquire and have provision for land and people. For to this end God has created gold and silver and given them mines. Thus we read in the Scriptures that Moses taught the king that he should not have too many horses, too much gold and silver, etc. Thereby he admits that he may gather treasures moderately; as also King Solomon himself boasts [that he has gathered treasures], and the patriarch Joseph gathered so much that he made all Egypt the king's own, with its corn, money, property, cattle, and the very bodies of the people besides, as complete vassals; thus Abraham, too, had many sheep and much gold and silver with which he traded. What shall we say to it then, that he here so clearly forbids us to gather treasures? since he himself (if we wanted to reckon with him) had a fund, because Judas held the bag, and yet there was always a balance on hand, so that they never wanted for anything when he sent forth the disciples, as they themselves said. Why, then, does he here forbid this, and say that they shall take no money, nor scrip, nor shoes with them?

Answer: It has been said above, often enough, that Christ in this sermon teaches a single person or a Christian man; and that a man of the world and a Christian are to be kept quite distinct. For a Christian does not mean a male or female, young or old person, lord, servant, emperor, prince, farmer, citizen, nor anything that is part of the world and may be known by a worldly designation; he has no person or mask, and should neither have nor know anything in the world, but be satisfied with his treasure in heaven. He who does not properly make this distinction cannot rightly understand these sayings; as our sophists and fanatics, who mix and confound these things together.

A prince may very well be a Christian, but as a Christian he is not to rule; and in so far as he rules he is called not a Christian, but a prince. The person is a Christian, but the office or princeship has nothing to do with his Christianity. For, so far as he is a Christian, the gospel teaches him that he is to injure no one, not to punish or take revenge, but to forgive everybody, and to endure whatever injury or injustice is done to him. That is (I say) the lesson of a Christian. But that would not constitute a good government, if you would preach in that way to the prince; but he must speak thus: My Christianity is something between God and myself, that has its own rules, how I am to live with reference to him; but besides this I have in the world another office or rank, that I am a prince. This person does not stand related to God, but the relation is between me and my land and people, etc. In this respect the question is not how you are to live towards God, and what you are to do and suffer for yourself; let that be for your person as a Christian, that has nothing to do with land and people. But your princely person must do none of these things or have anything to do with them; but think how it may manage the government, keep and protect justice and peace, punish the wicked.

See, in this way both ranks or offices are rightly divided, and yet in one person, and so to speak are contradictory, so that one person shall at the same time suffer everything, and not suffer; but in such a way that to each office its own appropriate experience is applied: namely, as said above: If it affects me as a Christian, then I am to endure it; but if it affects me as a secular person, which is not between God and me, but bound to land and people, (whom I am commanded to help and protect, and the sword is placed in my hand for this purpose,) then it is not suffering that is called for, but the opposite. So every man upon earth has two persons: one for himself, bound to no one, but to God alone; aside from that, a secular one, with which he is bound to others; as we must be mixed together in this life, as a husband or householder with wife and child; who, although he is a Christian, must nevertheless not suffer it from those related to him that they practice knavery or reckless behavior in the house, but he must resist and punish wrong-doing, so that they must conduct themselves properly, etc. If you rightly apprehend this difference, then it is easy to understand the teaching of Christ. For he is speaking here, and in all his sermons, not about how a secular person is to do and live; but how you are to live uprightly towards God as a Christian, who has not to concern himself about the world, but only about the life to come.

Thus I say also in regard to this text: My person, that is called a Christian, is not to care for or lay up money; but I am to be heartily devoted to God only. But externally I may and am to use temporal good for my body, and, as to other people, so far as relates to my secular person, I may gather money and treasures; yet not too much, so that I do not make an avaricious belly out of myself, that cares only for itself, and can never be filled. For a secular person must have money, corn and provision for his land, people, or others that belong to him. Thus, if one could rule in such a way as the patriarch Joseph in Egypt, so that all the storehouses and vessels should be full of food, and could manage the country in such a way that all its need would be provided for, from which provision one could help the people, advance to them and distribute among them, if necessary; that would be an excellent treasure and an admirable and Christian use of worldly goods. For what a prince gathers, he gathers not for himself, but as a person belonging to all, yes, as a common father of the whole land. For we must not all be beggars, but every one provide so much for himself, that he can maintain himself and not impose upon others, and, besides, he should help others, and thus one should contribute to others when it is necessary.

Thus every city should lay up as much as it can for the common need; yes, every parish should have a common treasury for the poor. That would not be unfair, but should be called laying up Christian treasures. For it is not such a treasure as ministers to avarice and lust; as the world does, and as our priests hitherto have gathered money, and with no other purpose than to find their pleasure with it, and to play with the florins like the little girls with their dolls. But when necessity calls for it, when others are to be helped, then there's nobody at home. These are the devil's treasures, against which Christ is here speaking, that we are not to lay up treasures upon earth, that is for one's self and for his own pleasure; in such a way that the heart does not become avaricious, and cling to the temporal mammon, but seek for and lay up another treasure in heaven. But outwardly and secularly you may lay up as much as you can with God and honorably; not for your own satisfaction and avariciousness, but for the need of other people. He who thus accumulates shall have blessing and indulgence besides, as a pious Christian.

But those who are thus avariciously scraping together, so that they cannot cease, and yet do not let any one enjoy it, so that they dare not themselves make a cheerful use of it, with them it shall happen, as is here said, that moth and rust and thieves shall consume, so that as it came so shall it go; although it also often happens, on the other hand, that even where things have been properly gathered, they are nevertheless consumed in this way. For no better treatment can be expected on earth for temporal good at any rate. If this now happens to those who lay up treasures rightly, how much rather to those who seek nothing else than the money, not the use, advantage and fruit of the money. For it is here so denounced that moth and rust must attack it and consume it, and it be stolen, so that no one can succeed who thus avariciously rakes and scrapes together; and although a farmer has gathered a great deal, he still must not use it, that does not become him, but he must bury it, so that it does not benefit him or any one else, otherwise the worms gnaw and bite at it, or it falls to the share of the public servants or scoundrels at court, so that it may not be better spent.

Thus now Christ is trying with these words to reason us out of the idea of thus avariciously grasping after mammon, and he speaks about it so contemptuously that he could not make it more odious to us. For what sort of a god is that, who cannot do so much as to defend himself against moth and rust, but must let himself be daily gnawed at and consumed, and lie there to be plundered by everybody, so that everything that comes along feasts upon him, and every thief steals him, etc. That is vexatious, to have such a helpless god, subject to moth, rust and thieves, who yet rules the whole world. Therefore we ought to be ashamed of ourselves, that we are such people as to be clinging to such a moth-eaten treasure and placing all our confidence upon it. Since you know this, (he means to say), do not set your heart upon it, so that you lay up for yourselves treasures upon earth; but be satisfied with what God here gives you, and hold it liable to be lost or taken from you. For that is all that can be expected; especially if you wish to be a Christian, and confess or preach your Lord, you must be always expecting to be snapped at and cast out, as one that has challenged the world and all the devils. If you are to be really consistent, you must be courageous enough to despise all their treasures and goods, and be assured of another, better treasure.

Therefore he says: Lay up for yourselves treasures in heaven, that is, let the world have its moth-eaten treasures, liable to be robbed and stolen, that are of no more value than that the world may take pleasure and comfort in them. But you that are not of the world, but belong to heaven, and are purchased for heaven by my blood, so that you may have another eternal treasure that is prepared and appointed for you, do not let your heart here be entrapped: but, if your office and worldly calling are such that you must have to do with earthly treasure, do not cling to it or serve it. But let it be your aim to gain those treasures that are laid up for you in heaven. For those are true treasures that neither moth nor rust can reach, and they are altogether safe against everything that can devour or steal. For they are so deposited that they always remain whole and ready, and are so guarded that no one can break through after them.

Let him now who wants to be a Christian apply this stimulus and this logic to himself. For it ought to please an avaricious fellow, and make his heart laugh, when one shows him such a treasure that no rust can corrupt and no thief steal. But the world is said not to regard this, because it neither sees it nor feels after it, but continues clinging to the gold and silver that it sees glittering, although it knows and sees that it is not secure for an

hour against rust and thieves. But we are not preaching to these. He who
will not adhere to Christ, and shape his course with reference to the invisible treasure, let him go his way; we will not drag any hither by main force.
But take notice, if your time comes that you must go hence, then call upon
your treasure that you have laid up, and upon which you have relied for
consolation, and see what you have in it, and what it can help you.

But it happens, as is written in the seventy-sixth Psalm (v. 5): *Dormierunt
somnum suum omnes viri divitiarum, et nihil invenerunt in manibus suis*—
the full-bellied rich that served mammon, when they were to die, found
nothing at all. That is indeed a terrible thing, that those who have served
mammon their whole life long, and have done injustice and wrong unto
many for its sake, and have despised the word of God, yet in the time of
need could not have a hair-breadth of enjoyment. Then for the first time
their eyes are opened so that they look into another world, and go groping
about for what they have gathered as a provision, yet they find nothing,
and are left to pass away empty in disgrace; then they become so anxious
and afraid that they in consequence forget what they have laid up, and they
find nothing also in heaven; and there happens to them just what Christ
says, in Luke 12:19, about the rich man who once had a grand good harvest,
so that he meant to pull down his barns and build greater, and thought to
have a good time, and said: "Soul, thou hast much goods laid up for many
years; take thine ease, eat, drink and be merry." Notice, that is the little
song of the farmers, that all greedy bellies sing; but what follows? "Thou
fool, this night thy soul shall be required of thee: and whose shall those
things be, which thou hast provided?" So he both loses this treasure [his
soul], and must be robbed of his gathered goods, and so disgracefully that
he knows not who shall get them.

For this is the way of the world, since one rarely sees great treasures
divinely gathered, so that they dare not spend them as they would like to
do, or have them benefit some one, but they must be scattered in such a
way that no one knows what has become of them; as I have already often
observed, especially in the case of great, rich, ignorant priests, who have
left large possessions, that, however, soon disappeared after their death, or
fell to the share of those who gave them no thanks for them, but recklessly

squandered and shamefully destroyed them. And especially if a war occurs, then the devil has it all his own way, so that they fall into the hands of the fire-eaters, for whom they never were intended, and who besides pile upon the people for them all sorts of misery.

Therefore, if some one has long been laying up, and any one asks him who is to get it, he has to say that he does not know; and it usually does not turn out as he expected. Therefore he is a great fool, that he risks all his comfort and well-being upon it, and plagues himself with great care and anxiety all his life long, and yet does not know for whom he has gathered it; yet nobody considers this. For man's blindness and wickedness are too great, and the world will still be the world, and have the bother, that it may serve the moth-eaten treasure; and if it has long served, and has angered God, then it must have as its reward that God at last cannot help it, and lets it have the disappointment coupled with insult and injury. That it cannot prevent, as little as fire can be prevented from burning, or water from extinguishing. Therefore let them only go their way, and know that you are taught, as a Christian, to think where you ought to have and find your treasure, where it is safe for you, and always abides, and cannot be displaced or become another's; and meanwhile use this world's goods and make the best of it, as a passing possession. And if you thus gather treasures with God and with honor, then he will also see to it that it remains, if it ought to remain, so that it is nevertheless not lost, but well used, and that much good is done with it.

Christ now ends this with a proverb, and says: Where thy treasure is, there will thy heart be also. That is as much as saying what we Germans say of a greedy belly: Money is his heart; that is, if he only has money, that is his joy and comfort, in short, his God. Again; if he has nothing, that is his death; there there is no heart, no joy, no comfort. Therefore he means to say: Beware, and test your own heart, and know assuredly that your heart will be where your treasure is; as we are else wont to say, what is dear to a man, that is his God. For his heart draws him thitherward, is occupied about it day and night; he sleeps and wakes with it, whether it be money and property, pleasure or honor, etc. Therefore observe your own heart, and you will soon find what is sticking in it, and where your treasure is.

For this may readily be felt, if you have as great a pleasure and diligence in hearing the word of God and living accordingly, and in securing that life, as you have in gathering and storing away money and property.

For, if my heart be so disposed (and also proves itself such, where it can be proved) that I would rather lose not only money and property, but also my neck, rather than to forsake or despise the gospel, and to do wrong or violence to my neighbor for my own benefit, I can conclude that money and property are not my heart's treasure, although I am also gathering and saving; but having freely exposed them to danger and hazard, I am striving for another treasure, in heaven, namely, that hidden in the word of God. Again, however, if it be the case with you that you let others preach and teach and exhort as they will, and you go along, thinking that you have enough, and live in style; never ask whether you are doing right or wrong by your neighbor, if you only have your own, and make your calculation so that with one penny you may gather two, yes ten, and have no concern about God's word and preachers, and about the world with its laws, then you can also understand that your treasure is not above in heaven, but remains with the moth and rust; so completely, that you would rather anger God and the world before you would lose a penny, and give up anything for its sake: as now peasants, citizens, noblemen everywhere shamelessly talk and live, who for the sake of a penny venture to dare defy the government of God in the Church and in the world, so that this saying may remain true and practically convict them, since they will not hear nor be instructed. For it cannot be otherwise, even if we worry long about it and would gladly see it otherwise. Therefore it is best, if we have told it to them, that we let them go their way, and despise and laugh at them as much as they do at us. For God says in the second Psalm that he can laugh too, and laugh so that they will have bitter weeping; that means that he will speak with them in his wrath and will alarm them in his sore displeasure.

36

Verses 22 and 23

"THE LIGHT OF THE BODY IS THE EYE: IF, THEREFORE, THINE EYE BE SINGLE, THY WHOLE BODY SHALL BE FULL OF LIGHT. BUT IF THINE EYE BE EVIL, THY WHOLE BODY SHALL BE FULL OF DARKNESS. IF, THEREFORE, THE LIGHT THAT IS IN THEE BE DARKNESS, HOW GREAT IS THAT DARKNESS!"

That is a warning, that we must not allow ourselves to be deceived by the beautiful color and appearance with which avarice can adorn itself and conceal the villain. For, as I have said, there is no vice among all the natural vices that more readily deceives people and does greater harm both to the gospel and to its fruits. For it hinders wherever it can the preaching of the gospel and its being kept among the people; and although the gospel be preached, the preachers who have fallen under the power of avarice are of no account, so that both are thereby injured, the people who are to hear it, and those who ought to preach it; so that those who indeed have it will not support the preachers, and let them die for hunger, so far as they are concerned; and as the preachers see this, they take special pains not to live at the mercy of the people. These are then more dangerous enemies than the others. For, although a peasant becomes avaricious, and gives nothing to support the gospel, a preacher can still be provided for; although his support is very meagre. But when the preachers themselves become involved in it, the gospel is no longer to their taste, so that they should suffer or venture anything for its sake; but they will lay their plans accordingly, so that their belly does not lack, and they will preach what will please the people and bring the money.

Therefore St. Paul calls this a peculiar vice, a worship of idols or idolatry, that is in direct opposition to the faith, which is the true worship or honoring of God. For it makes mammon and the impotent penny its God and Lord; what it wills, that he does; thus he lives and preaches, and is completely owned and captured by it, so that he no longer asks after the word of God and does not hazard a penny on its account.

Now Christ can do nothing more against all this than to rebuke this vice and warn those against it who are willing to be warned; and this is indeed necessary. For even the pious can hardly prevent their being deceived by it. But others move along serenely, as though completely swallowed up by it, notwithstanding what we preach and declare. The Jews, too, were such a set, immersed in their avarice, so he had to be all the time rebuking them; and all the prophets, when they were holding forth about the faith, were perpetually rebuking and denouncing avarice, against their preachers and false prophets as well as against the mass of the people. But it was of no avail, except in the case of a few who would be thereby influenced, for whose sake Christ and we all must still preach, and let the others go their way, since they will be of the devil's party.

Now Christ used this saying more than once as a common saying, not only in reference to avarice, but also in reference to other matters, especially as to doctrine. For in matters of doctrine it occurs that the factious spirits and lying preachers pretend that they are heartily and truly in earnest, and seek the honor of God and the salvation of souls, so that no one boasts and asseverates as vigorously as they do. To these he utters the warning: Beware, that your eye be single and not evil; that is, that your way of thinking and your boasting is right, and not secretly evil, and that you are not deceiving yourselves with false notions and thoughts.

For it is commonly these people that the devil bewitches, and just as when a man lies in a dream or sleep, and is so completely stupefied that he cannot see that he is dreaming; but he does not think or know anything else than that it is really happening so, and he is so sure of it that he could not feel anything more sure; and yet it is nothing else than a dream, which soon vanishes, and when he awakens it is all gone; and although it seems to him sometimes that it is a dream, or that he is dreaming of a dream, yet he is ensnared, so that he cannot extricate himself, or become master of his senses. So those people are also ensnared, who insist so confidently upon it that their cause is the pure truth, so that they may swear everything upon it, and yet it is all nothing but dreams and the thoughts of crack-brained people. Therefore it is a dangerous thing if one does not cling closely and simply to God's word, and allows himself to be led away from it to the thoughts of men that have an excellent appearance and soon captivate, so that he who falls within their influence cannot afterwards extricate himself from it. For he does not know anything else but that it is the real word of God, and he adheres so firmly to it that he cannot be persuaded to abate a jot or tittle of it; as we see that some have lost their necks for it.

But this is not the place to develop this thought. For here he applies the saying to the common vice of avarice, which, although it is gross and external, yet there is no vice in reference to doctrine that can so adorn itself and wear so beautiful a covering, so that it must not be called avarice, but be seen and praised, as though one were heartily opposed to the vice, and no one were so mild, kind and merciful; and yet he does not himself see that his heart deceives him, and that he is altogether immersed in avarice. We must therefore examine the text a little farther, and exhibit it plainly in illustrations, although it is not possible to comprehend in how many ways the evil eye can contort and help itself; [we do this] in order that one may learn to be on his guard against such influences. For this is also a common temptation among Christians, so that no one believes that so few people are free from it; for the heathen and others are guilty of it in its grossest forms, so that one can easily recognize it.

Christ's now saying: "The eye is the light of the body," is a reference to the natural body. If it had no eye, no sun would be of any use, although it might shine a hundred times so brightly. Therefore the body has no other light that may lead and direct it, than the eye; because one can see with it, we need not be afraid that he will drive alongside of the bridge into the Elbe, or go through hedges and bushes, or rush into the fire or among the

spears; for the light guards him against danger and harm. But he who has
no eye must go forward, and stumbles over wood and stones until he falls
and breaks his neck or is drowned in the water; for there is no light there,
but total darkness.

So (he means to say) it is in the matter of Christianity, especially with
avarice. Here take care that your spiritual body has an eye, that is, an
upright, good intention and understanding, that you may know how you
believe and live, and do not deceive yourself with false notions and darkness. Thus, for example, if you thus reason: "I will work and do something,
that I may gain something and maintain myself with wife and child, with
God and honor; and if God grants that I may also thereby serve and help
my neighbor, that I will gladly do;" see, that is the light or the spiritual eye,
from the word of God, that shows you what belongs to your calling, and
indicates to you how you are to fill it and live in it. For this is right, and has
to be, since the body lives here, so that every one may do something that
he may support himself and keep house.

But now beware that this eye does not become evil and deceive you; that
you do this with a simple intention, and have only this purpose, to work
and do what your calling requires to meet the necessities of yourself and
your neighbor, and not under this pretence to seek something else, namely
how you may thereby gratify you avarice. For flesh and blood is a master
in, misusing this light and employing it as a pretence. So, if it now happens that you have procured some means of living that you are fond of,
and are only concerned how you can keep it and increase it, and, if you
have a gulden, would like to have ten more: see, here the evil eye comes
creeping in, that looks not only at the means of living and the necessary
possession, but also at its avarice, and can still adorn itself [with the pre-
tence] that it is not seeking avarice, but is doing what God has ordered it
to do, and is accepting what God gives.

Well, here no one can look into your heart and judge you; but beware
yourself that your eye is not evil. For it happens very easily, and there is a
strong inclination to it, especially when one sees how profitable it is; love
is thirsty and is never satiated, and nature besides is strongly disposed
that way: so whores and scoundrels come together, and things go as they

ought to, as we say: Occasio facit furem, money makes villains. Therefore Christ warns his own so diligently. For the world is a great whore-house, and quite merged in this vice: and we ourselves must live in it, and these examples and incitements tempt us, so that we are in great danger and have to be well upon our guard that we do not let the devil ride us.

If now your eye is single, (says Christ), your whole body is light; that is, all that you are doing and living in your outward deportment, in accordance with your office and calling, that is all upright, moving in accordance with God's word, with the proper intention, so that it shines like the sun, before God and man, and it stands well before all the world; and all that you do is excellent, and you can use worldly good with a good conscience, as having been honestly and divinely acquired, etc. Again, if your eye is evil, so that you do not act in these things as required by God and your office, but leave the track and are concerned only to gratify your lust and love for money; then your whole body is dark, and everything that you do is condemned by God and lost, although you are called a pious man before the world. For the body lets itself be led with its whole external movement and life as a blind person, and cannot go or live otherwise than as the eye directs.

Thus he means to warn us and charge every one conscientiously to see to it how his mind and heart are disposed, so that he do not flatter himself with the beautiful and yet false idea that he has a good, honest reason, and a real good right to rake and scrape together in this way, and impose upon God, so that he does not observe the scoundrel; as though he said: You may adorn yourself as you will; but if you deceive God, then you have deceived a wise, shrewd, and besides an experienced man. But take care that you are not deceiving yourself, and that your light does not become an evil eye that makes your whole life dark and abominable in the sight of God; for he has a clear, sharp sight, and will not allow himself to be deceived by your extra coat of paint. And he concludes this warning with a threat, to alarm, so that we may not so readily make use of that plausible, invented notion, and says: But if the light that is in thee be darkness, how great is that darkness! That is, although you may invent such plausible ideas, as that you do not mean to accumulate through avarice, as the others, but intend to do it in such a way that you can defend it before God and the world, so that it must not be called avarice, and yet you live just the same, and make thus for yourself a light of your own in your heart; but see to it just here that this light is not also darkness, not alone that it is sheer avarice in your heart, but also that you mean to conceal it as with the light, so that it is not to be called avarice, and thus there is a double darkness, much greater than before.

Just as that was a great darkness under the papacy that completely extinguished the light of Christian doctrine, so that they taught nothing else than to take away sin and be saved by works, etc. But when they besides at once defended this and boasted of it that it was the true divine doctrine, and that he who denied this was a heretic, and was forbidding the worship of God and all good works, etc., then there was the blackness of darkness, so that they adorned this darkness and error with the name of truth, and thus made the darkness greater by the superadded light; just as if one knows the devil, that it is the devil, and makes a god of him. That means to cover darkness with darkness and yet claim that it is bright and luminous, yes, the very sun itself.

Thus Christ now concludes: If the opinion and doctrine that one regards as light is itself darkness, how great must the other darkness be which this brings with it; namely, that one practices this doctrine, and lives accordingly. Thus here, he whom avarice has mastered, so that he rakes and scrapes, he has already a darkness in his heart. But if he goes on, and flatters himself that it is not to be called avarice, and silences his conscience, so as not to be rebuked, that is now a real, thick, double darkness. Just as a fool, who claims to be sensible and not chargeable with folly, is properly called a great, big fool; or an ugly strumpet, who claims to be pretty and adorns herself with her nasty trumpery; that is only making things blacker and worse; and in fact all men are so disposed, that no one wants to have his sin rebuked; but all try to cover their tracks, so as to get approbation and praise, and thus out of one bad sin they make two.

Now when this happens in spiritual affairs, then the great murderous harm is done. For those in this calling cannot easily do things moderately, but, when it comes to dealing with the gospel, they are apt to overdo it with their charities. Again, if they apostatize from the gospel, then there is no end to their avarice; as it used to be hitherto: when they began to give, it fairly snowed with gifts, to churches, public worship and ecclesiastical establishments; as in old times the emperors and princes with good intentions gave whole districts of country for such purposes, and endowed such institutions; but now again hardly anybody gives a penny, and they are avariciously gobbling up everything, as if they were afraid of dying with hunger.

This is the way the monks, priests and prebendaries used to do, whom no one could satisfy with gifts. If one had gathered two, three or four fiefs, he would want to have as many more; and yet they all wore the same mask: Though I would have enough with one prebend, parish or bishoprick, yet something more is needed that I may honorably fill my station as a prince, nobleman, or some other prelate. Then he makes use of all possible means to rake and scrape together all that he can get, and all for the purpose of honorably filling his place; and yet the light is kindled [it is now pretended] that he must not be said to be acting avariciously, but doing it all for the maintenence of his rank. So easily one can find a little gloss with which to kindle a light for the devil; and if one has no other resort, it will have to be this, that one says: "I will gather my money together in such a way that I may afterwards provide for masses and public worship, or give alms for the maintenence of the poor," etc. That is kindling a great, beautiful light; then a man may worry himself to death and always say: "I mean it well; and the simple-minded man, our Lord God, is capitally hoodwinked, so that he cannot see or notice these cunning tricks, and I'll get into his heaven before he is aware of it." But I have also seen many who have thus hoarded, so that guldens by the thousand lay stored up, but afterwards they died off with their property, so that no one knew what had become of it; for it was gained by avarice, it had to be left in avarice, devoured by moth and rust, and never be put to proper use.

This I mention as an example from which one may see how skillfully Squire Avarice can adorn himself and put on pious airs if he has occasion for it; and yet, in fact, he is a two-fold scoundrel and liar. For what does God care for it, that you mean to lead a splendid, knightly life, so that he should be pleased for you to act avariciously, contrary to his command, and live in such a way as if you wanted to get everything for yourself, to display your splendor and pride, and afterward say that you are doing it for God's sake, and for the honor of the Church, and mean to pay for it with benefices and church-services. Just as if some one were to break into your house and open your coffers and take what he could find, and would afterward say he meant to give some of it for alms: ah, that would be a beautiful sacrifice! The right thing is: If you want to give to God, give him of what is your own; for he says: I hate sacrifices that come from robbery. If you have, give what you choose; if you have not, then you are excused. But if you are avariciously scraping together so that you may be able to give, and pretend that you are doing it with that intention, then you are not in earnest, but it is a light that you have yourself taken from the dark lantern wherewith to deceive God and the people.

Thus I might go through all ranks and conditions, and show how men dress themselves up so that avarice takes on the name of a virtue, and mammon is praised and honored as a god. But who is to tell all that the farmers at market, the citizens in towns, the nobleman in office and on his estate, are everywhere doing? The one example that I have given is enough to show clearly and distinctively the darkness that is thick enough to be felt, and also to judge the others accordingly. What are we to think now of the great mass of the nobility that are now undertaking to deal in nearly all kinds of business, even with iron and nails? We must not call this all avarice; but, as God has given it, every one may seek his means of living as best he can, so that he may honorably fill his station, etc. That is also a little light that makes them stock-blind, so that it prevents them from seeing anything at all; whilst yet in ordinary worldly justice it is so ordered that every one may carry on his business and trade so that still his neighbor may also have a chance to get along and maintain himself. But now nobody can do anything for these griffins and lions that monopolize all kinds of business, and besides want to be called pious and honorable people.

But (as was said) who can imagine what a multitude of such tricks are now employed in all ranks and trades? For what is the world, but a great wide sea of all wickedness and scoundrelism, concealed under a covering and color of good that cannot be understood? Especially now in this last age, which is a sign that it cannot long endure, and is going to destruction. For the tendency is, as we say: the older, the stingier; the longer, the worse; and everybody is becoming so avaricious, that almost nobody can get to eat and drink on account of others, although God gives everything in abundance. But that is the reward of the ingratitude and contempt that is shown towards the gospel, as I have said: He who apostatizes from the gospel must be so possessed by the devil that he cannot be avaricious enough: just as, on the other hand, he who has the gospel in his heart becomes mild, so that he not only ceases to rake and scrape together, but gives and risks everything, as much as he ought to and can.

Well, we must still let the world be the world, and although it for a long while avariciously gathers everything for itself, it must nevertheless go back upon itself and leave everything for us; or, if we still must suffer poverty and trouble in the midst of it, we still have no evil portion, as Isaac and Jacob among their brethren. Through us they have gained worldly property and complete freedom from the oppression and burdens of the papacy, so that they may do what they please. That is the portion of Ishmael, a flask with water, that Abraham hung about his neck, and let him go. But we have a different portion, that is called spiritual good and heavenly blessing: and are thus well provided for. Their great possessions that they have we gladly renounce, and would not have them if they would throw them after us; on the other hand, they do not want the spiritual blessings that we have. So we will hold possession of the real territory, and the inheritance that is ours forever, and we will let them boast of their portion that will soon fade away, and rob themselves for its sake of our inheritance, which we would still be glad to share with them. If they, however, rob us of their portion, we have always so much that we can readily recover from the loss.

But let us beware of this, that we do not fall into the false light, along with the world, that is the evil eye, that extinguishes the true light and makes of it a twofold darkness; and see to it that avarice does not perplex you with that sweet notion and beautiful coloring, that you mean to bring yourself or your children into a high, honorable position, and give them a great deal only to better and exalt their position; for thus avarice is the longer the less satisfied, but is always reaching out for something higher and beyond, and nobody is satisfied with his place; but, he who is a citizen would like to be a knight; a nobleman would like to be a prince, and so forth; a prince would like to travel like the emperor. But do you wish to travel like a Christian? then beware of this notion as of the very worst darkness, and conduct your business in such a way, if God, through his blessing, gives you success, that your neighbor also alongside of you may provide for himself and have pleasure in you, so that you may lend him a helping hand. For if you let the evil eye deceive you, then you have already lost the word of God, as driven out by that light, and one thick darkness is added to the other, that makes you totally blind and obdurate, so that nothing more can be done for you.

37

Verse 24

NO MAN CAN SERVE TWO MASTERS; FOR EITHER
HE WILL HATE THE ONE AND LOVE THE OTHER; OR
ELSE HE WILL HOLD TO THE ONE AND DESPISE THE
OTHER. YE CANNOT SERVE GOD AND MAMMON.

Here he pronounces a most fearful sentence against the avaricious: first of all against his Jews, who were the real avaricious bellies, and yet wanted to be holy and very devout, like our priests and ecclesiastics, he means to say: "You think you are all right, and are serving God with great earnestness, and are yet, along with that, avaricious scoundrels, so that you are doing all this for mammon's sake, although you are also serving God." But this is the statement: No man can serve two masters at the same time. If you wish to be the servants of God, then you cannot serve mammon. Here he means two masters who are opposed to one another, not those who reign with one another. For that is not self-contradictory, if I serve my prince or the emperor and God besides; for it passes regularly from one to the other, so that if I obey the lowest one I am obeying the highest also. Just as the head of a family sends his wife or children to the servants, and through them commands these what they are to do: there is no multiplicity, but it is all one lord and from one master. But God and the devil, that means two masters, that are opposed to one another and issue contradictory orders.

God says: Thou shalt not be avaricious, nor have any other God; but the devil, on the contrary, says: You may be avaricious and serve mammon.

Reason itself teaches this, that it is not sufferable to serve two antagonistic masters at the same time; although the world can skillfully do it, and this is called in German, carrying the tree on both shoulders, and blowing hot and cold from the same mouth; as when a nobleman serves a prince, and accepts hire from him, and betrays and sells him to another and accepts money also there, and watches what the weather promises to be, if it will rain here, so that the sun may shine there, and thus betrays and makes merchandise of both. But there is no serving in all this, and even reason must say that such people are traitors and scoundrels. For how would you like it if you should have a servant who would accept wages from you and would be looking with one eye towards some one else, and not be at all concerned about your affairs; but, if something should go wrong to-day or to-morrow, would scamper off to the other and leave you in the lurch?

Therefore it is right to say: He who is a good servant and wants to serve faithfully, must not cling to two masters, but speak thus: "I have my support from this master, him will I serve as long as I am with him, will do the best I can for him and not concern myself about any one else." But if he wants to pilfer here, and steal there, then he's ready for the hangman. For one should kill the hens that eat at home and lay their eggs elsewhere. Thus did the Jews also; they supposed that God should regard them as great saints, and be well satisfied if they sacrificed in the temple and slaughtered their calves and cows, although they meanwhile were acting avariciously wherever they could, until they carried on their merchandizing before and in the temple, and set up their money-changing tables, so that materials could be promptly furnished and no one should leave without sacrificing.

Against these Christ now pronounces this sentence, so that no one may undertake to be the servant of God and mammon. It is not possible to maintain his service, which he has established if you are determined to be avaricious after mammon. For the worship of God means that you cleave to his word alone and make everything bend to that. He who will live according to that, and be consistent, must at once renounce mammon. For this is sure: as soon as a preacher or pastor becomes avaricious he is no longer of any use, and cannot preach any thing good. For he must be on his guard and dare not rebuke any one, allows himself to have his mouth stopped by presents, so that he may let the people do what they please, avoids making any one angry, especially the great and powerful: and thus neglects his duty and office that requires him to rebuke the wicked. Thus also, if a burgomaster or judge or any one who holds an office is to execute his office and see to it that it is rightly administered, he must not be much concerned about how rich he may become and derive benefit from it. Is he, however, a servant of mammon, he allows himself to be bribed with presents, so that he becomes blind and no longer sees how the people live. For he thinks: Am I to punish this one or that one? then I will make enemies and may thereby lose what is mine, etc. And although he has an excellent service, and is occupying the office that God has ordered and given to him, he still cannot administer and exercise it; this is the work of mammon, that has taken possession of his heart.

So it goes now in the world everywhere, so that it supposes it to be a small matter and no great danger with regard to mammon; and it flatters itself with the beautiful, sweet thought, that it can still serve God; but this is a miserable deception by which the devil blinds a person, so that he no longer attends to his official duty, and becomes absorbed in avarice; and this solely for the reason that he fears that he will not receive honor, gifts, or presents.

Therefore Christ (as above said) pronounces a strict sentence that one should not deceive himself with such thoughts and count this a small matter; but should know that he who for the sake of mammon, money or pleasure, or honor or favor, does not administer his office as he should, will not be recognized by God as his servant, but as his enemy, as we will hear; but he who wishes to be found in God's service, and to execute his office properly, so that he may think, with a manly heart, that he can despise the world with its mammon; but this not as an outgrowth of his own evil heart, but as a gift from heaven, with prayer that God, who has bestowed upon you this office, may also give you grace to administer it; and enable you to believe that you have and can do nothing nobler and better on earth than the service that you are to render to him, and not be much concerned as to whether you suffer harm through it or get into trouble; and comfort your-self with this, that you are serving a great Master who can easily make you enjoy your loss, which is better than that you should lose the eternal trea-sure for the sake of the small temporal good that at any rate cannot help you. For if you are to choose a master, would you not much rather serve the living God than the powerless dead knave?

See, thus every Christian does who has God's word, that he may so honor and observe it, and not care whether the world is thereby vexed or fails to get any advantage from it; but he thinks thus: *There* is purse and pocket, house and home, etc.; but *here* is my Christ: if I am now to leave and give up one, then I will let all that go, so that I may keep my Christ. That is what Christ means when he says one cannot serve two masters. For it will happen sooner or later that they will conflict, and one must yield to the other. Therefore there is no use for you to flatter yourself that you mean to keep them both as masters; but you must soon decide to leave one or the other.

Therefore the stress lies here on the little word, *serve*. To have money and property, wife, child, house and home, this is not sinful; but you must not let this be your master, but you must make it serve you, and you be its master; as we say of an honest, excellent, well-disposed man: He is master of his money; not so subservient to it and held captive by it as a stingy greedy-belly, who would rather let God's word go, and everything else, holding back both hand and mouth, than to run any risk with his money. That is a womanly, childish and servile heart, that despises and neglects the eternal treasure for the sake of the scaly mammon which it cannot use or enjoy; yet lives along securely meanwhile, thinks it can attend to God's word at any time, keeps on accumulating as much as it can, so as not to miss a penny for God's sake, until it sinks more and more deeply into avarice, gets farther and farther from God's word, and finally opposes it altogether.

For Christ used hard language and spoke very plainly when he said: "Either he will hate the one and love the other; or he will hold to the one and despise the other." That is as much as to say: The shameful love of mammon makes enemies to God; as some of our priests publicly say: That would indeed be an excellent way of teaching, but it does harm; therefore it is objected to, and not unreasonably (as they think), for it does give occasion to trouble. But mammon is a capital god; he does no harm in the kitchen or in the purse. Therefore here love and friendship come to an issue over the words: "he will hate the one and love the other." For there are two masters, that are opposed to each other, and cannot peaceably dwell together in one heart, as little as two owners in one house; so that when the test comes that one must serve and hold to the one, then one must anger the other or leave him. Thus one becomes the enemy of God, as a matter of course, because he loves money and property.

This is the precious fruit of the service of mammon; as can especially now be seen, since avarice has gained such complete control, that there is a perfect leprosy of avarice among the nobility, peasants, civilians, priests and laymen. Is not that a great piece of sanctity and a beautiful virtue, that one takes the best part of man from God and gives it to mammon? For that is certainly the highest service, to which the heart is sincerely devoted, which the whole body and all the members hanker after; as Christ said above: "Where your treasure is, there will your heart be also." For what one loves, that he will assuredly run after, that he will be glad to talk about, that has all his heart and his thoughts; hence also Augustine says: "*Deus meus, amor meus*," what I love, that is my god. From this you see what kind of people those are to whom Christ applies this title—that they are the enemies of God, who yet feign such great display of serving him, as his best friends; but at heart they are nothing else than real devil's saints, who heartily hate and persecute God and his word and work.

For that is truly to hate God, if one hates his word. This is the way of it: If one rebukes a man for avarice and unbelief, and holds before him the first commandment: "Thou shalt have no other gods before me," that is, thou shalt not incline thy heart, desire and love, to any one else than to me; and he will not hear or endure that rebuke; but begins to rebel and rage against it, until he is quite embittered against it in heart, with rankling hatred against the word and its preachers. Therefore there is in the text of the ten commandments such a word of threatening: "I am a jealous God, visiting the sins of the fathers upon the children of them that hate me," etc., by whom he means these very greedy-bellies and mammon-servers, as the Scriptures call avarice idolatry or the worship of idols. Yet they want (as above said) to be praised as the greatest saints, and as enemies of idolatry and heretics, and by no means to have it said that they hate God. But this is the proof against them that they cannot hear or see the word of God, when it attacks their avarice, and want to be wholly unreproved; and the more one rebukes and threatens them, the more they laugh and mock, and do what they please against God and every one else.

See now, is not this a shameful evil and an abominable sin, that ought to alarm us and make us heartily hostile to mammon, ask God's protection against it, and flee from it as from the devil? For who would not dread falling into it, and hearing this decision concerning himself that he is to be called an enemy of God, who not only depises him, but wishes that God and his word did not exist, that he might only have his free pleasure and will, to God's annoyance and vexation. For reckon yourself what will happen to such a man, and what kind of a person he is loading upon himself, so that at last it will be quite too heavy for him.

And they are indeed very well punished (as the text says), by the fact that they are such miserable people, that their heart, desire, love and pleasure are set upon the out-house, when they ought to be in heaven and set upon that which is God's. How could a man more completely disgrace himself than by turning his consolation away from God, who gives him everything that is good, and well deserves to have our good will, and posting himself behind the devil and taking delight in his stench and hell, and even becoming so hellishly wicked that he not only despises the word of God, but becomes so murderously opposed to it that he wishes there were no God? That is the gratitude that he receives from these greedy-bellies, to whom he daily gives bodily life, sun and moon, and the treasures that they have. But they will find out what they gain thereby, and they have it in part already, so that they must be constantly devouring the devil's stench and filth.

That is one part of the text, spoken of mammon: "Either he will hate the one and love the other;" the other is: "or, he will hold to the one (that is, God) and despise the other." Here he does not merely say: "He will love the one;" but he shows the deed and work of love by the word: "hold to." For he who is to love God and his word, will not find it so very small a matter, but often very hard to do, and the love will become such as the devil will often make sour and bitter. Therefore it is necessary that we be able to hold and hang fast to God's word, and do not let ourselves be torn loose from it, although our own flesh and the example of the whole world, and the devil besides, oppose it and endeavor to take it from us; and he must needs be a man and have knightly courage that can resist so many enemies; yes, there must be a great fiery zeal of love, that is burning so brightly that one can give up everything, house and home, wife and child, honor and property, body and life, yes, despise it too, and trample it under foot, so that he only may preserve the treasure, which he still does not see, and which is despised in the world, but only offered in the mere word and believed on in the heart.

Yet he does not mean thereby that we are not to have money and property, or, if we have it, to throw it away; as some fools among the philosophers, and cranky saints among Christians have taught and done. For he grants that you may be rich, but he does not want you to fix your love upon that; as David taught and proved by his own example: "If riches increase, set not your heart upon them." Ps. 62:10. That is such a state of mind that, in the midst of money and property given by God, can keep the heart free (which the world cannot do), and if it seeks to entice the heart to itself (as the beautiful florins and shining silver goblets and jewels bewitchingly smile), and to bear it away from God, then he can trample it under foot, and so completely despise it as the world clings to it, and on the contrary despises the heavenly treasure. In short, a man must be mammon's master, so that it must lie at his feet; but he must be subject to no one, nor have any one as his master except the word of God. But this is preached to the little flock that believe in Christ, and hold his word to be true; with the others it amounts to nothing.

38

Verse 25

THEREFORE I SAY UNTO YOU, TAKE NO THOUGHT FOR YOUR
LIFE, WHAT YE SHALL EAT OR WHAT YE SHALL DRINK; NOR
YET FOR YOUR BODY, WHAT YE SHALL PUT ON. IS NOT THE
LIFE MORE THAN MEAT, AND THE BODY THAN RAIMENT?

The Lord expatiates here in delivering a strong denunciation of this ruinous vice, because (as said above) it commonly pushes its way in violently along with the gospel, and fiercely assails not only the world but also Christians; especially, however, those who are to preach the word of God and expose themselves to all sorts of danger on its account, who are despised and oppressed by the world, so that they so far as the flesh is concerned have good reason for anxiety. For he who wishes to be a Christian and confess his Lord, he makes the devil (who is a prince of the world) his enemy. Therefore he assails and seizes him, not through the word and faith, but through that which is under his kingdom and power. Now we have our worthless body, flesh and blood, still in his kingdom; that he can indeed torment, and cast into prison, rob of food, and drink, and clothes, so that we, with all we have, must always be in this danger. Flesh and blood, on the other hand, thinks how it can also manage to hold its place securely and escape danger. Thus the temptation arises that is called care for a livelihood; though the world does not consider it a temptation, but rather considers it a virtue, and it praises these people that can scheme for great property and honor, etc.

And here you learn what it means to serve mammon, namely, to care for life and our body, what we are to eat and drink, to have about us and to put on; that is, to think only of this life, how we may become rich here, may gather and heap up money and property, as if we were to remain here forever. For this is not sin, nor serving mammon, that we eat and drink, and clothe ourselves, as the needs of this life and of the body require, so that it may have its food and clothing; also, it is no sin to seek and gain food; but [it is sinful] to be careful about it, that is, to set the heart's comfort and confidence upon it. For care does not inhere in the garment or in the food, but right in the heart; that cannot let it go, it will hanker after it; as we say: Goods give courage, etc., so that caring means hankering after it with the heart. For what the heart does not intend and love, that I am not concerned about; and again, what I care for, that I must have a heart for.

Yet you must not press the text too closely, as though it meant to forbid caring for anything at all. For every office or calling carries with it the duty of caring for that which belongs to it, especially where one is placed over others; as St. Paul says, Rom. 12:8, concerning spiritual offices in Christendom: He that ruleth, let him do it with diligence. Thus the head of a family must care for his children and domestics, that they be well trained and do what they should; and if he neglects this he does wrong. In the same way it is the care of a preacher or a pastor that the preaching and the sacraments are rightly attended to; that he comfort the distressed and sick, rebuke the wicked, pray for all kind of needy ones, etc. For he is commanded to wait upon and direct souls. Thus a prince and other persons in authority must care for the secular government, that it is rightly administered, as their office requires. In like manner also subjects are to care that they faithfully render and accomplish their obedience; servants and maids, that they properly serve their masters and guard their interests, etc.

Christ is not here speaking of this kind of care; for there is an official care that is to be carefully distinguished from avarice. For that is not concerned about itself, but about its neighbor; it does not seek its own, yes, it even neglects its own, and is indifferent about it, and serves another, so

that it is called a care of love, which is godlike and Christian, not that of
selfishness or of mammon, which is both against faith and love, and it is
the very thing that hinders the official care. For he who is in love with his
money and caring for his own advantage will not pay much attention to his
neighbor or his office, which involves his neighbor. As we saw heretofore
in our ecclesiastics, who were not at all concerned about properly caring
for souls, but their whole aim was that the world should contribute enough
to them; and what did not bring them in any money, that they neglected, so
that not one of them would as much as say a *Pater noster* for another without
pay. But a pious pastor cares only for this, that he may rightly administer
his office, that souls may be benefited thereby; is not concerned about it,
that he does not gain much by it, yes, has to suffer much for it, bite himself
with snakes, have the world and the devil as his enemies, lets God see to
it that he gets enough to eat, etc.; but consoles himself with another treasure (for the sake of which he does all this,) in that life, which is so great
that all that he here suffers is quite too small in comparison, etc.

Because now he has forbidden this care of avarice and mammon worship as idolatrous and making men enemies to God, he continues, by adding
many illustrations and comparisons, so that he may make avarice all the
more odious to us, and endeavors to depict it in such hateful colors that
we will feel like spitting upon it, and says, first of all: Is not life more than
food? that is, you can and must entrust God with your life, of body and
soul, and it is not within your power to continue it for a single hour; what
fools then you are that you will not entrust to him your body's nourishment, that he may procure eating and drinking for you? For how can one
imagine greater folly than for one to be painfully solicitous about getting
food and drink, and having no care about getting body and life or retain-
ing them for an hour?—just as if one should be careful to adorn his house
beautifully, and did not know who was to live in it; or, how he might prepare much and excellent food in the kitchen, and should have no one who
was about to eat it. Just so it is that we act with our avariciousness, that
we care for the least and never think of the most important. That is really
unnecessary and superfluous, yes, foolish care. And though we should care
a great deal about our bodily life, there would be nothing gained by that, for

it is not for a moment within our power; just as little as if any one were to worry himself to death, how the grain is to grow in the field, which he has not sowed; or where the silver is to lie in the mine, that he has not put there.

Since then, in the whole matter of our life we must dismiss care, and this, without our thinking or doing anything about it, is hourly maintained by God; why should we worry about little things as if he neither could nor would give us food and covering? We ought to be ashamed that anyone should say of us that we are guilty of such folly. Yet our conduct, especially that of the great, rich bellies, is nothing else than that of the fools, that are ever caring only to have their kitchens full, and have an abundance provided, and yet have no table or guests; or who have many luxurious beds provided and have no one to occupy them; just as if a shoemaker should do nothing else all his life but fill his shop with shoe-lasts, and never think about where he would get leather to make a shoe; ought we not to march him out of the country as a crank and a fool?

See, Christ thus shows us what foolish people we are, so that we might well spit upon ourselves; and nevertheless we live along in this blindness, although it is perfectly plain, that we cannot take care of our bodily life, and if we did care for that we would just thereby have to become Christians and think: See, I do not even have my own life in my hand for a moment. Since then I must entrust my bodily life to God, why shall I then doubt and care how the belly may be nourished for a day or two? Just as if I had a rich father who would gladly present me with a thousand florins, and I would not trust him to give me a penny when I need it.

39

Verses 26 and 27

BEHOLD THE FOWLS OF THE AIR: FOR THEY SOW NOT,
NEITHER DO THEY REAP, NOR GATHER INTO BARNS; YET
YOUR HEAVENLY FATHER FEEDETH THEM. ARE YE NOT
MUCH BETTER THAN THEY? WHICH OF YOU BY TAKING
THOUGHT CAN ADD ONE CUBIT UNTO HIS STATURE?

Here he adds an illustration and a comparison to the exhortation in mockery, ridicule and contempt of the wretched avarice and belly-care, so that he may drive us away from it, and remind us what we ourselves are, so that we may be heartily ashamed of ourselves, since we are far nobler and better than the birds, as we are lords not only of the birds, but of all living creatures, and all things are given to us for service and created for our sake: and yet we have not so much faith as to trust that we may sustain ourselves with all these things that God has given and provided for us: whilst he is daily giving their food and nourishment to the smallest birds, yes, to the very smallest worms, as our servants, without their caring or thinking at all about it, yet they do not gather anything or lay up in store; they neither sow, nor if it be sowed can they gather it in.

Is it not now a shameful disgrace, that we, for whom God has given and provided all creatures, and for whom he causes so much to grow every year, so that we have enough annually to sow, and very much more to reap, cannot trust our belly to him without care and avarice? For if anybody ought to care and gather, it should be done by the little birds; since they cannot do that, and might think when summer is coming: See, now all the world is sowing its grain, so that in summer they may again gather it in; now, or in harvest, everybody is harvesting and accumulating, and as all do not have a little grain to sow or to gather in, where are we throughout the year, especially in the cold winter, to get anything to eat, when everything has been housed and nothing is left in the fields? What would we men do if we for a single summer had nothing to sow? Yes, if we did not know of provision for a fortnight, how would all the world then become desperate, as if we would all have to die of hunger? Now the little birds fly in the air summer and winter, sing and are happy, never worry or care at all, though they do not know where they are to get food to-morrow: and we miserable, greedy bellies, never cease caring, although we have barns and store-houses full, and see grain growing in the fields so abundantly.

See, thus he makes the birds masters and teachers, so that a weak little sparrow must stand in the gospel, to our great, lasting disgrace, as teacher and preacher of the very wisest man, and hold this daily before our eyes and ears; as though he wished to say to us: See, miserable man, you have house and home, money and property, and every year your field full of grain and growth of all kinds, more than you need; yet you have no peace, and are always caring lest you may die of hunger; and if you do not see provision and know that it is before you, you cannot trust God, that he will give you food for one day; whilst there are such multitudes of us, not one of whom is all his life-time ever anxiously concerned, and yet God daily nourishes us. In short, we have as many masters and preachers as there are little birds in the air, that put us to shame with their living example, so that we ought to be ashamed, and not venture to lift up our eyes if we hear a bird singing, that is proclaiming heavenward God's praise and our disgrace; yet we are so obdurate that we pay no attention to it, although we hear this preached and sung daily on every hand.

Yes, see what else they do, the dear little birds; how entirely free from care they live, and look for their food alone from the hand of God. If we cage them, that they shall sing, and give them plenty to eat, so that they ought to think: Now I have enough, so that I need not care where I will get

anything to eat; for I now have a rich master, and my barns are full, etc.;
that they do not do, but they would much rather be free in the air, are fatter
too, and sing better and more sweetly *Laudes* and matins, early in the morning, before they eat; and yet not one of them knows of a little grain in store;
they make a beautiful, long *Benedicite*, and let our Lord God take care, even
when they have little ones that they have to feed. Therefore, when you hear
a nightingale, you hear the cutest preacher, who reminds you of this gospel,
not with poor, mere words, but with the living act and example, because it
sings the whole night long, and screams itself nearly to death, and is mer-
rier in the grove than if it is cooped up in a cage, where we have to attend
to it with all diligence, and where it seldom thrives or remains alive; as if
it were to say: I would much rather be in the kitchen of the Lord, who has
made heaven and earth, and is himself cook and host, and daily feeds and
nourishes innumerable little birds out of his hand, and has not just a sack
full, but heaven and earth full of little grains.

Thus Christ now speaks: Since you daily see how your heavenly Father
feeds the little birds in the field, without their having any care; cannot
you then trust him so much that he will also feed you, because he is your
Father, and calls you his children? Should he not much rather care for
you whom he has made his children, and to whom he gives his word and
all creatures, than for the little birds, that are not his children, but your
servants? And yet he holds them in such high esteem that he daily feeds
them, as if he had only these to care for; and he takes pleasure in it, that
they quite without care fly about and sing, as if they should say: I sing and
am cheerful, and yet I know not of a little grain that I am to eat; my bread
is not yet baked, my grain is not yet sowed; but I have a rich master who
cares for me, while I sing or sleep; he can give me more than all men and
I could get with our caring.

Since now the birds understand the art of trusting him so completely,
and throwing off care from themselves upon God, we, who are his children, should much rather do it. Therefore it is an excellent illustration
that puts us all to shame, so that we, who are people endowed with reason,
and besides have the Scriptures at hand, do not have so much wisdom as
to imitate the birds, and must daily hear ourselves disgraced before God

and the people, as often as we hear little birds sing. But man has become crazy and foolish, since he fell away from God's word and command, so that henceforth there is no creature living that is not wiser than he; and a little finch, that can neither speak nor read, is his teacher and master in the Scriptures, although he has the whole Bible and his reason to help him.

This is the first illustration; to this he appends a saying taken from our own experience, and shows that our caring is useless and accomplishes nothing: Who is there among you, (says he,) who can add one cubit to his stature, although he is concerned about it? If a man should never grow to full size except through his own caring, how large would we grow? or, of what avail would it be for a little dwarf to worry himself to death how he might become larger? What do you accomplish by caring where you are to get food and clothing? just as if it stood in your power to make your body as stout and as tall as you wished. Your body with all its members is of definite size, and has its length and breadth, so that you cannot make it otherwise, and you are defied to make it a hair's-breadth taller. What a fool then you are, that you are concerned about that which is not within your power, and which is already limited both as to time and extent, viz. how long your bodily life shall last, and cannot trust him that he will procure for you also both food and clothing as long as you have to live here, etc.!

40

Verses 28 through 30

AND WHY TAKE YE THOUGHT FOR RAIMENT? CONSIDER
THE LILIES OF THE FIELD, HOW THEY GROW; THEY TOIL
NOT, NEITHER DO THEY SPIN: AND YET I SAY UNTO YOU,
THAT SOLOMON IN ALL HIS GLORY WAS NOT ARRAYED
LIKE ONE OF THESE. WHEREFORE, IF GOD SO CLOTHE
THE GRASS OF THE FIELD, WHICH TO-DAY IS, AND TO-
MORROW IS CAST INTO THE OVEN, SHALL HE NOT
MUCH MORE CLOTHE YOU, O YE OF LITTLE FAITH?

Here you have another illustration and comparison, in which the little flowers of the field, that are trampled upon and eaten by the cattle, must also
become our teachers and masters, so that our disgrace may become still
greater. For see how they grow up, so beautifully ornamented with colors,
and yet not one of them cares and thinks how it is to grow, or what kind of
color it is to have, but it lets God care for this; and, without any care or effort
on its part, God clothes it with such beautiful, lovely colors, that Christ says
that Solomon in all his glory was not as beautiful as one of these; yes, no
empress, with her whole retinue, with all her gold, pearls and jewels. For
he cannot name any king who was richer, more glorious, and more splendidly adorned than Solomon: yet the king, with all his grand display and
splendor, is nothing in comparison with a rose or pink or violet in the field.
Thus our Lord God can adorn whom he will adorn, so that it deserves to
be called adorned, and no man can make or paint such a color, and wish

for or get another still more beautiful adornment; and if we should beautify them with gold and satin, they still would say: I would rather that my Master up there in heaven should adorn me, who adorns the little birds, than all the tailors and embroiderers on earth.

Since now he clothes and adorns so many flowers with such various colors, and each has its own dress, and outranks with it all worldly splendor, why cannot we confide in him that he will also clothe us? For what are the flowers and grass upon the field in comparison with us? Or, for what were they created except to stand there for a day or two, and exhibit themselves, and then to wither and become hay; or, as Christ says, to be cast into the oven, so that one may burn them and heat the oven? Yet our Lord God holds these perishable and insignificant things in such estimation, and bestows so much expense upon them, that he adorns them more splendidly than any king upon earth, though they do not need this ornamentation, and it is even lost upon them, as they soon perish along with the flower. But we, his highest creatures, on whose account he has made all else, and to whom he gives everything, and who are of such account to him that this life is not to be the end of us, but after this life he means to give to us eternal life; should not we have so much confidence in him, that he will clothe us as he clothes the flowers of the field and the birds of the air with manifold beautiful colors and feathers? That is putting the case as so dishonorable for us, and depicting our unbelief as so disgraceful, that he could not make it more contemptible.

But it is the [fault of the] miserable devil and the terrible fall that we made, that we must see the whole world full of these illustrations of the birds against us, who with their example and appearance rebuke our unbelief, and become our highest *Doctores*, sing and preach to us, and smile at us so lovingly, that we should only believe; yet we live on, let ourselves be preached and sung to, and keep on avariciously raking together; but [it is] to our eternal shame and disgrace that every little flower testifies against us and condemns our unbelief before God and all creatures until the judgment day. Therefore he now concludes this sermon before his Christians.

41

Verses 31 and 32

THEREFORE TAKE NO THOUGHT, SAYING, WHAT SHALL
WE EAT? OR, WHAT SHALL WE DRINK? OR, WHEREWITHAL
SHALL WE BE CLOTHED? (FOR AFTER ALL THESE THINGS
DO THE GENTILES SEEK:) FOR YOUR HEAVENLY FATHER
KNOWETH THAT YE HAVE NEED OF ALL THESE THINGS.

Since you daily see these illustrations in everything that lives and grows out
of the earth, how God nourishes and feeds it and most beautifully clothes
and adorns it: be induced to lay aside care and unbelief, and consider that
you are Christians and not heathen. For such caring and avarice belong to
the heathen, who do not know God, or ask about him, and it is real idolatry, as St. Paul says, and as was said also above, where he calls it serving mammon.

Therefore no greedy-belly is a Christian, although he was baptized; but
he has surely lost Christ, and has become a heathen. For the two cannot
endure each other, to be avaricious and full of care and to believe; one must
exclude the other. Now there is nothing more shameful before God and all
creatures, for Christians who hear and know the word of God, than that
they can be said to be like the heathen who do not believe that God nourishes them and gives them everything, and thus fall away from God, deny
the faith, and pay no regard either to his word or to these manifest illustrations. This is a hard sentence that reasonably ought to alarm every one. For

it is a prompt conclusion, that a professed Christian should either reflect, and leave off caring avariciously, or know that he is no Christian, but ten times worse than a heathen.

Besides, (he says,) since you are Christians, you dare not doubt as to your Father's knowing very well that you need all this; namely, that you have a belly that needs eating and drinking, and a body that needs to be clothed. If he did not know it, then you would have cause to care and to think how you might nourish yourselves; but now that he knows it, he will not neglect you. For he is so kind that he gladly attends to it, and especially for you Christians, because (as was said) he cares also for the birds of the air. Therefore drop the care, for at any rate you gain nothing by it. It does not depend upon your caring, but upon his knowing and caring. If nothing grew in the field before we cared for it, we would all have died in our cradles, and nothing could grow after night when we are lying asleep; yes, if we were all to worry ourselves to death, no stalk would grow in the field for our caring; we must ourselves see and comprehend that God gives everything without our caring for it; yet we are such godless people that we will not cease our caring and avarice, nor allow God alone to have the care, to whom alone it belongs, as to a father for his children.

42

Verse 33

SEEK YE FIRST THE KINGDOM OF GOD, AND
HIS RIGHTEOUSNESS; AND ALL THESE
THINGS SHALL BE ADDED UNTO YOU.

The Lord saw very well, as I said, that none among the outward, gross vices so outrageously counteracts the gospel, and hinders [the progress of] God's kingdom, as avarice. For as soon as a preacher lays his plans for becoming rich, he no longer rightly administers his office; for his heart is ensnared by the care for the means of living, as in a net, as St. Paul calls it, so that he can no longer teach and rebuke, as and where he should; concerned lest he might lose favor and friendship among those from whom he can secure it: allows himself to be misled, so that he keeps silent, and misleads other people too; not through heresy, but through his own belly, which is his idol. For he who wants to be the right kind of a preacher, and faithfully perform his duty, must retain and assert his liberty unterrifiedly to tell the truth, without respect of persons, and rebuking if necessary great and small, rich, poor, powerful, friend and foe. This avarice does not do. For it fears, if it should offend many people or good friends, it would find itself in want of bread. Hence it draws in its whistles and keeps silence.

In the same way also the mass of the people, who are not preachers, but who should hear the word of God, and help to further the kingdom of God, every one in his own station and mode of living, are not willing to run any risk or to be prepared for or endure any want, for the sake of the gospel; but they look out for it, first of all, that they have enough, and that their belly is provided for, no matter whether the gospel keeps up or lags behind; thus they go along, raking and scraping, as well as they can, giving the preachers nothing, even besides taking from them what they may have. Thus it goes according to the devil's wishes, so that no one wants to preach or hear any more, and thus both the doctrine and its fruits in the hearts of the people disappear, and the kingdom of God falls entirely away. This is alone the work of the abominably devilish mammon. See, that is the reason why the Lord Christ so faithfully warns his own against it by such a long sermon.

And in order that we may the better guard ourselves against it, he prescribes in these words a very powerful remedy, how we are to treat it, so that we do not need to care; and that we may yet have enough, yes, a much greater and more excellent treasure than mammon can give us, and than we can get through our caring, and this remedy is, to seek the kingdom of God.

But it is very important that it should be deeply impressed upon our heart what the kingdom of God is, and what it imparts. For if we could be made to understand this, so that we would rightly apprehend and could in our heart measure and weigh how great and precious a treasure it is in contrast with mammon or the kingdom of the world, that is, everything upon earth, then we would spit upon mammon. For what more would you have, although you should have the possessions and the power of the king of France, and of the Turkish emperor besides, than a beggar before the door has with his scraps? For the only thing we have to do is daily to fill our belly; we can't do anything more with all our worldly goods and glory; and the poorest beggar has as much of this as the mightiest emperor, yes, his broken victuals taste much better and do him more good than the splendid, royal meal does to the latter. That is the whole of it, and no one gets any more from it, and in a little while we must say good-bye to it all, and we cannot prolong our life with it for a single hour when the time comes. Hence it is a poor, miserable, yes a nasty, stinking kingdom.

What is, however, on the contrary, the kingdom of God, or of the Lord Christ? Count that up for yourself, and say, what is the creature in comparison with the Creator, and the world in comparison with God? For if all heaven and earth were mine alone, what would I have as over against God? Not as much as a little drop of water or a particle of dust in comparison with the entire ocean; besides, it is such a treasure as cannot cease or diminish and become smaller; so that both as to its greatness and durability it cannot be measured or comprehended by any human heart or senses; and shall I so shamefully reject and give up God and his kingdom, that I may take this dirty, deadly belly-kingdom in preference to that divine, imperishable one that gives me eternal life, righteousness, peace, joy and salvation? And everything that I here in time seek and desire I am to have in this one eternally, and everything immeasurably more glorious and superabundant than what I can obtain here upon earth with great difficulty, care and labor; and before I can get it, and can accomplish what I want, I must go away and let everything lie. Is that not a great, shameful folly and blindness, that we do not see this? Yes, a stubborn wickedness of the world, possessed by the devil, that it will not be instructed or give heed when we preach this to it?

Therefore Christ wishes with these words to stir us up, and to say: if you wish to be properly careful and solicitous about having always enough, then seek for that treasure that is called the kingdom of God. Do not be concerned for the temporal, perishable treasure that is destroyed by moth and rust, as he said before. You have a very different treasure in heaven, which I am pointing out to you; care and seek for that, and contemplate what you have in that, and you will easily forget the other. For it is a treasure of such a kind that will sustain you forever, and cannot be lost or taken away, so that because the treasure is enduring and you clinging to it, you must also endure, even though you have not a penny from the world.

It has often been told what the kingdom of God is, namely, most briefly, that it does not consist in external things, eating and drinking, etc., nor other works which we can do; but in this, that we believe in Jesus Christ, who is the head and sole king in this kingdom, in and through whom we have everything, so that no sin, death and misfortune can injure him who abides in it [the kingdom], but he has eternal life, joy and salvation, which here begin in this faith, but in the last day will be revealed and eternally completed.

What now does it mean to seek this kingdom? or how do we attain to it? What way must we take? One points in this direction, another in that. Thus, the pope teaches: Go to Rome and get an indulgence, confess and do penance, read or hear mass, put on a hood, and practice long public worship and a severe, strict life. That is the way we always used to run, just as we were told, as silly and foolish people, and all wanted to find the kingdom of God; but we found just the kingdom of the devil. For there are many ways here, but one and all are aside from the only [true] one, which is to believe in Christ and to diligently apply and use the gospel, upon which faith rests, with preaching, hearing, reading, singing, meditating, and in every possible way, so that one may always at heart be growing and becoming stronger, and give outward evidence by his fruits, so that he may be always promoting it and leading many others to it; as we (thank God) are now doing, and there are still many besides, both preachers and other Christians, who with all diligence are busily urging it on, so that they subordinate all that they have, and would be ready to lose it all, rather than let go of the word.

No monk, nun or priest does or understands this, although they boast that they are God's servants and espoused to Christ. For they all miss the only right way, and ignore the gospel; they know neither God nor Christ and his kingdom. For he who wants to know and find it must not seek for it after his own notion, but hear his word, as the foundation and cornerstone, and see whither he directs you and how he interprets it. Now his word about his kingdom is this: He who believes and is baptized shall be saved. This word was not spun out of our heads, nor did it grow out of the heart of any man; but it descended from heaven, and was proclaimed by the mouth of God, so that we may be perfectly sure and not miss the right way. Where now this is practised, both among preachers and hearers, so that the word and sacraments are diligently employed, where men live accordingly and persevere in so doing, so that it becomes known among the people, and the young people are drawn in and taught: that is what we mean by seeking and promoting and being properly concerned about the kingdom of God.

What is the meaning of his adding: And his righteousness? The kingdom has also a righteousness; it is, however, a different righteousness from that of the world, as it is also a different kingdom. This means now the righteousness that is by faith, that is efficient and active through good works; in this way, that the gospel with me is a very serious matter, and I diligently hear and practice it, and am actually living in accordance with it, and am not a trifling gossip or a hypocrite, who lets it in at one ear and out at the other; but I am one who gives practical proof that the kingdom is here, as St. Paul says, 1 Cor. 4:20: The kingdom of God is not in word, but in power. That we call the gospel with its fruits, that is, doing good works, with diligence and fidelity attending to one's business or office, and suffering variously for it. For he calls righteousness in general the whole life of a Christian with reference to God and man, as the tree with its fruits; but not meaning that it is therefore entirely perfect, but always improving; as he here bids his disciples be always seeking, as those who have not yet actually seized it, nor have already completely learned and lived it. For in the kingdom of Christ it is with us half sin and half holiness. For whatever of faith and of Christ is in us, that is altogether pure and perfect, as not of our own, but of Christ, who through faith is ours, and lives and works in us. But what is still our own, that is altogether sin, yet under and in Christ covered over and obliterated through forgiveness of sin, besides daily through the same grace of the Spirit mortified, until we are entirely dead to this life.

See, this belongs to the righteousness of this kingdom, that it be upright and no hypocrisy. For it is set over against those who talk and boast indeed about the gospel, but have nothing of it in their life. For it is in fact a hard thing to preach the word of God and do good to everybody and suffer all kinds of misfortunes besides; but for that reason it is called the righteousness of God. For the world does not relish it, that it should do right and suffer harm for it; this is not a part of its way of ruling. For there it is not right that he who does right should be punished or suffer violence, but should receive gratitude and some good as his reward. But our reward is not stored away for us upon earth, but in heaven: there we will find it. Now he who knows this, and will do accordingly, will have enough to do, so that he has no need to seek other ways; and he will probably forget also avarice and the cares of mammon. For the world will make it so sour for him that he will not care much for life and temporal good, but he will become so tired of it that he will have to be hourly looking and hoping for death.

This is the exhortation by which he points us from temporal good to eternal treasure, so that we may not esteem this good in comparison with the one that we have in heaven, etc. Along with this he gives also a promise and a consolation, so that we are not to think that he will therefore not give us anything at all upon earth and let us die of hunger, because we have so much to suffer from the world that neither gives nor wishes us anything, and we are hourly expecting that all we have shall be taken from us; but we must know that we are still also here to have what we need for the requirements of this life. Therefore he says: Seek first the kingdom of God, then all these things shall be added unto you; that is, you shall have besides to eat and to drink and to wear, as an addition, without any care of your own, yes, just in order that you may not care for those things and for God's sake risk everything; and it will come to you so that you will not know whence it comes, as our daily experience teaches us. For God still has so much in the world that he can also feed his own, since he feeds all the little birds and worms, and clothes the lilies of the field, as we have heard, yes, since he gives and lets grow so much for us wicked fellows: so that the world nevertheless must let us eat and drink with it, although this vexes it.

What more shall we now desire, if we know this, if we have and handle God's word, and every one does as he should, so that we have enough to eat and to drink and wear, and get just as much ourselves as a king or emperor, namely, that we feed our belly, except that he to suit his rank must have more and grander things, but still does not enjoy anything more; and my bread feeds me just as well, and my clothes cover and warm me just as well as his royal meal and his gold and silver pieces. For how should it be possible that he should die of hunger who serves God faithfully, and advances his kingdom, since he gives in such superfluity to the whole world? There would have to be no more bread upon earth, or the heavens not be able to rain any more, if a Christian should die of hunger; yes, God himself must first have died of hunger.

Since now he has been creating and giving in such superabundance, besides has so certainly promised that he will give enough and so give before we look for or know it: why will you then torment yourself with that hateful caring and avarice? Surely the Scriptures (especially the Psalms) are full of such passages, that he will feed the pious in the time of famine, and never has "seen his seed begging bread." He will not prove a liar in your case, if you can only believe. If now the world, as it is, noblemen, peasants and civilians, does not do it, he will still find people, or other means, through which he can give, and more than they can now take from you.

43

Verse 34

TAKE THEREFORE NO THOUGHT FOR THE MORROW: FOR
THE MORROW SHALL TAKE THOUGHT FOR THE THINGS OF
ITSELF. SUFFICIENT UNTO THE DAY IS THE EVIL THEREOF.

Care for this (he means to say,) how you may keep with you the kingdom of
God, and renounce the other care so completely that you be not concerned
about the morrow. For when the morrow comes it will bring its own care;
as we say: Comes the day, so comes also the counsel. For our caring accomplishes nothing at any rate, though I care for only one day; and experience
teaches that often two or three days slip away from us sooner than to-day;
and he to whom God is propitious and gives success, can often without trouble and care accomplish more in an hour than some one else in four whole
days with great trouble and care; and if he has been long at work and taken
great pains, making it wearisome to himself, another might have accomplished it in an hour; so that no one can do anything except when the time
comes that God gives, granted without our caring; and it is in vain that
you try to anticipate and by your caring (as you suppose) do great things.

For our Lord God understands the art of secretly shortening and lengthening time for us, so that to one an hour may become a fortnight, and again
in such a way that one with long labor and toil gains nothing more than
another with short and easy labor; as one can plainly see daily, that there
are many who by hard, constant labor scarcely gain their daily bread, and

others without special labor have so arranged and ordered their affairs that all moves easily and they succeed. God does everything in such a way that our caring does not necessarily have the blessing. For we will not wait, so that these good things may come to us from God, but we want to find them ourselves before the gift comes from God.

See how it is in the mines, where men are busily digging and seeking; it still often happens, that where one hopes to find the most ore, and where it seems as if it was all to become gold, there nothing is found, or it breaks off suddenly and disappears. Again, in other places, that are regarded as failures and neglected, there are unexpectedly the richest results; and one, who has invested all his property there, gets nothing; another from a beggar becomes a lord; and afterwards, those who have accumulated many thousand guldens before the end of ten years again become beggars, and it does not often happen that these large possessions reach to the third heir. In short, the motto should be: Not sought, but bestowed; not found, but providential, if success and blessing is to come with it. But we would like to make it so that it would come as we plan; but that amounts to nothing; for he thinks, on the other hand: You shall not get it so, or at least not keep it long and enjoy it. For I have myself known many persons who ran their hands into pockets full of guldens, and groschens were beneath their notice; but afterwards they would have been glad if they could have found as many pennies.

Since you now see that there is no use in it, and your caring does not avail, why do you not let it alone and turn your thoughts upon having the kingdom of God? For he will give to you; but not because of your caring, even though you should work. For such care accomplishes nothing; but the care does that belongs to your office; and to the kingdom of God it belongs that you do what is commanded you, preach and propagate the word of God, serve your neighbor according to your calling, and take what God gives you. For those are the best possessions that are not thought about, but are bestowed and providential; and what we have acquired by our caring or are proposing to keep, will be likely first of all to fail us and go to ruin, as often happens to the rich bellies, whose grain and other stores often for their great care are ruined; and it is a great grace that God does not let us care for it how the grain grows in the field, but gives it to us, whilst we are lying and sleeping; else we would ourselves ruin it for us by our caring and would get nothing.

Therefore he now says: Why will you be concerned about more than the present day, and load upon yourself the trouble of two days? Be content with what the present day imposes upon you; to-morrow will bring something else for you. For he calls it an evil or plague that we are compelled to support ourselves by the sweat of our brow, and that we must have other providential daily cares, misfortunes and dangers; as, if something be stolen from you, or some other harm befall you; also, if you become sick, or your domestics, etc., as it happens in this life that we must daily expect and see such trouble. Endure this evil, trouble and misfortune, and do be content with it, for that is enough for you to bear; and drop the anxiety, by which you only make the trouble greater and heavier than it is in itself; and look at these illustrations, that God never made any one rich through his anxious care, whilst many of them are most anxiously caring and yet have nothing. But this indeed he does, if he sees that one is diligently and faithfully attending to his duty, and taking care to do that so as to please God, and lets God care for its success, him he abundantly blesses. For it stands written, Prov. 10:4: "The hand of the diligent maketh rich." For he wants none of those who neither care nor work, like the lazy gormandizing bellies, as if they had only to sit and wait for him to send a roasted goose into their mouth; but his command is, that we honestly lay hold and work, then he will be on hand with his blessing and give enough. Let this suffice about this sermon.

Part III: The Seventh Chapter of St. Matthew

44

Verses 1 and 2

JUDGE NOT, THAT YE BE NOT JUDGED. FOR WITH
WHAT JUDGMENT YE JUDGE, YE SHALL BE
JUDGED: AND WITH WHAT MEASURE YE METE,
IT SHALL BE MEASURED TO YOU AGAIN.

In the previous chapter we heard how the Lord Christ, in accordance with
the doctrine of really good works, delivered a long sermon as a warning
against avarice, as something that greatly hinders the kingdom of God, both
in doctrine and life, and does deadly harm in Christendom. Here he now
begins to warn further against another thing that is also a great, ruinous
vice, and is called self-conceited-wisdom, that judges and blames everybody. For where these two vices rule, there the gospel cannot abide. For
the effect of avarice is either that the preachers keep silence, or that the
hearers pay no regard to the gospel, which thus through contempt is dis-
regarded. But if selfish-wisdom be conjoined with avarice, then every one
claims to be the best preacher and himself master; no one will hear or learn
from others. Then come sects and parties that falsify and corrupt the word
so that it cannot remain pure, and thus again the gospel with its fruits is
undermined. This is what he here now calls judging or passing sentence,
when every one is satisfied only with what he does himself, and whatever
others do must stink. A beautiful, gracious virtue! and the tip-top man

whom we call Mr. Selfconceit, who is not liked either by God or the world, and yet is to be found everywhere.

But, lest we may stumble at this preaching and misunderstand it, if hereby it were altogether forbidden to judge and pass sentence, it is clear from what has often been said above, that Christ is preaching here only to his disciples, and is not at all speaking of the judgment or punishment that must occur in the world; as father and mother at home among the children and servants must judge, rebuke, and also chastise, if they will not do right. Thus, a prince or a judge, if he means to discharge his duty properly, cannot do otherwise than to judge and punish. That belongs to secular government, which has nothing to do with us. Therefore we will not interfere with how things should go in that sphere. But here we are speaking of another kingdom, that does not indeed weaken or annul the other, namely, spiritual life and being among Christians; here it is forbidden for one to judge and condemn another. For there it occurs that the devil always mixes in and carries on his business, so that every one thinks well of himself, and believes that his way alone must avail and be the best, and blames and nullifies everything that is not measured by his standard.

This is now in secular affairs a supreme folly, and may be tolerated, though it is wrong, for it is so gross that every one understands it; as when a harlot imagines herself prettier than all others, and what she sees in others does not please her; or that a young fool will be so handsome and smart, that he does not know his like; and then, among the wise and learned, where this is very much in vogue, so that no one admits the value of anything that another knows or does, and every one claims to be the only one that can do everything better, and finds fault with everybody. Everybody sees and understands this very well; yet everywhere is this Mr. Selfconceit, who knows himself to be so smart, that he can bridle the horse by the tail, when all the rest of the world must bridle it by the mouth.

But when this occurs among us in spiritual affairs, and the devil sows his seed in the kingdom of Christ, so that it takes hold both of doctrine and life, then comes serious trouble. In the matter of doctrine the result is, that, although God has given and entrusted it to some one to preach the gospel, others are found, even among the disciples, who assume to know it ten times better than he, and the gospel must have the worry and misfortune to be judged by everybody, and every one becomes a doctor, and claims to be himself a master in doctrine; just as happened to Moses, Numbers 16, when Korah with his crowd rose up against him and said: "Ye take too much upon you, seeing all the congregation are holy. Should God speak alone through Moses and Aaron?"—just as they say now: Should we not just as well have the Spirit and understand the Scriptures as others? Then there is at once another doctrine dished up and sects started, and judging begins and denouncing, and especially the shameful slandering that one party most bitterly blames and misrepresents the other; as we learn now very well through experience. Hence follows the deadly harm that Christendom is divided and the pure doctrine everywhere suffers wreck.

This Christ dreaded, yes not only dreaded, but also foretold that such would be the case. For nothing else can be made out of the world, even if we were to preach ourselves to death. Therefore, wherever the gospel flourishes, there parties and sects must follow, that again spoil and check it. The reason is: the devil must sow his seed among the good seed, and where God builds a church, he builds a chapel or a tabernacle alongside. For Satan wants to be always among the children of God, as the Scriptures say. Therefore Christ means hereby to warn his apostles and sincere preachers to guard themselves diligently against this vice, and to see to it that they do not let it come in to create separation and disunion, especially in doctrine; as though he meant to say: If you wish to be my disciples, then let your understanding and opinions in doctrine be alike and of one kind, so that no one may wish to be master, and know something new or better, and judge or condemn the rest; and do not pay special regard to persons, but abide by what I command you to preach, and be of one accord, so that one does not despise the other, or start something new.

Yet understand it so, that still it is not forbidden to him who is officially appointed to preach, to judge in regard to doctrine, besides also in regard to life. For it is his official duty publicly to rebuke what is not in accordance with the true doctrine, just for the reason that he may not allow sects to enter and arise; in like manner, when he sees that one is not living aright, that he also rebuke and warn. For he is there for the reason that he may look into this, and he must answer for it. Yes, every Christian, if he sees his neighbor doing wrong, is bound to reprove him and put him on his guard. And this cannot be done without judging. But all this is done by virtue of one's office or authority, about which Christ is not here speaking; as has been sufficiently stated.

But this is forbidden, that every one take his own way for it and make a doctrine and spirit of his own, and imagine himself to be Mr. Extrawise and undertake to master and rebuke everybody, nothing of which has been committed to him. These are the ones whom Christ here rebukes. For he means that nothing should be undertaken or done from one's own notion without being commanded, especially as to the judging of other people. That I now call judging in doctrine, one of the highest, most disgraceful and dangerous vices upon earth, from which all the factious spirits have arisen, and of which hitherto monks, priests, and all that were in the papacy, were guilty of, when every one asserted that his matter was the best and denounced others; of which there is now no need to speak.

The other kind of judging is that regarding the life, when one blames and condemns the life and works of another, and is not pleased with anything that others do; that is indeed a widely diffused, common vice. Now we are under strict orders, so that, just as in regard to doctrine we are to be of one mind and understanding or faith: so also we are to be disposed alike and to have the same sort of heart in external life, although that cannot be all of the same kind as in the case of faith. For, since there are many kinds of callings, the works of them must be unlike and of various kinds. Besides, in this life, that is in itself of various kinds, we find also faults of many kinds, as, some very strange, irascible, impatient people; as it cannot but be among Christian people, since our old Adam is not yet dead, and the flesh is always striving against the spirit.

Here comes in play now a virtue which is called *tolerantia* and *remissio peccatorum*, so that one bears with another, has patience with and forgives him; as St. Paul so beautifully teaches, Rom. 15:1, We that are strong ought to bear the infirmities of the weak, and not to please ourselves; just as Christ says here: Judge not, etc., so that those who have high and better gifts in Christendom, (as some must have, especially the preachers,) still they may not take on any different airs or think themselves any better than those who do not have them: so that in spiritual matters no one should lord it over others. Externally there must be a difference, a prince higher and better than a farmer, a preacher more learned than an ordinary mechanic; thus a master cannot be a servant, a mistress be a maid, etc., but nevertheless in this distinction the hearts are to be similarly disposed and pay no regard to that dissimilarity.

This is done if I bear with my neighbor, although he be of a lower rank and have fewer gifts than I, and I am just as well pleased with his work, in attending as my house-servant to my horse, as with my own, being a preacher or ruler of land and people, although mine is better and of more importance than his. For I must not look at the outward masks, but that he lives in the same faith and in Christ, and has just as much from the grace, baptism and sacrament, although I have a different, higher work and office. For God is all the same, who does and gives all this, and is just as much pleased with the smallest as with the very greatest.

In contrast with this there is ruling in the world the praiseworthy, beautiful virtue of which St. Paul speaks, that every one pleases himself, as, if a man comes along in the devil's name, and cannot look at his own vices, but only at those of others; which adheres to us all by nature, and of which we cannot be rid, even though we are baptized, so that we are fond of beautifying and adorning ourselves and seeing what is good in ourselves, and flattering ourselves with it as if it were our own; and, in order that we may alone be beautiful, we do not look at that which is good in our neighbor; but, leaving that out of view, if we notice a little pimple, we fill our eyes with it, and make it so large, that we see nothing good on account of it, although he may have eyes like a falcon and a face like an angel. Just as if I saw some one in a golden garment, and there were perhaps a seam or a white thread drawn through it, and I would thereupon look amazed, as if it were on that account to be despised, and I on the other hand congratulate myself upon my coarse blouse, with a golden patch upon it. So we do not look at our own vices, of which we are full, yet cannot see anything good in other people. If now this natural evil habit finds its way among Christians, there we begin to judge, so that I readily despise and condemn another if he stumbles a little or is faulty, and he again does the same to me, measures me with the same measure, (as Christ here says,) seeks for and rebukes also only the worst that he can find about me. Thereby love is quite suppressed, and there remains only a biting and devouring of one another until they entirely eat each other up and altogether lose their Christianity.

The same is the case if one looks at the life of another, and will not look at himself, then one soon finds something that displeases him; another finds the same also in us; just as the heathen complain about affairs among them, that no one sees what he carries on his own back, but he who comes after him sees it very well; that is, no one sees where he himself is lacking, but he soon sees it in another. If one looks at other people in this way, the only result is a slandering and judging of one another. The devil instigates this among Christians, and carries it on to such an extent that there is nothing left among them but harsh judging in regard to the way of living, as also in regard to doctrine; so that the kingdom of Christ (which is a harmonious and peaceable kingdom, both in doctrine and life) is divided, and in place of it the spirit of sectism, arrogance and contempt prevails.

Therefore it is highly necessary that we be warned to learn and habituate ourselves to bear with, cover over and adorn our neighbor's faults, if we have attended to our own official duty, whether it be preaching and publicly rebuking, or fraternally exhorting (of which Matthew 18 teaches); and if I see anything in my neighbor that does not altogether please me, that I turn and look at myself, when I will also find much that does not please other people, and which I would be glad to have excused and borne with; thus the itching will soon subside that tickles itself and is amused at the faults of others, and Mr. Self-conceit will scamper off and drop his judging. Yes, you will be glad, so that you may soon settle the matter with your neighbor and first of all say: Lord, forgive me my debt; and then say to your neighbor: If you have sinned against me, or I against you, now let us forgive each other.

But if you see that he is quite too discourteous, and will not cease without your rebuking him, then go and tell him himself about it, as it is now and often has been said, (Matt. 18) that he may reform and desist. That is not judging and condemning, but fraternally exhorting to betterment, and in this way the exhortation would be made in a peaceable way, according to God's command. Otherwise, with your tickling, ridiculing and mocking, you only embitter your neighbor against you, and harden him, and you yourself become much worse than he is, and twice as great a sinner, by withdrawing your love from him and taking pleasure in his sin, and besides you expose yourself to the judgment of God, and condemn him whom God has not condemned, and thus invoke upon yourself so much the heavier judgment, which Christ here gives warning of, and you deserve that God should the more surely condemn you.

See, this shameful evil all comes, as St. Paul says, from our pleasing ourselves, playing and toying with our gifts as if they were our own; but seeing nothing in another except where he is faulty, and thus becoming entirely blind, so that we see neither ourselves nor our neighbor aright. When we should look into our own bosom and see first wherein we fail, that we do not do; but we have a blearness before our eyes, so that we think ourselves good-looking, if we observe a gift in ourselves that our neighbor has not, and by that very thing are spoiled, and we also do not see in our neighbor what is good in him, for we should always find as much of that as we now see of his faults. We should also be pleased with what is good in him and make due allowance, if there be some faultiness in it; as we please ourselves and readily apologize for ourselves.

In short, it is the worst vice and a devilish pride, that we are self-satisfied and merry if we see or feel a good trait in ourselves, and do not thank God for it, but become proud, and despise others, and have our eyes so completely filled with it that we do not care what else we do, thinking we are all right: we plunder and rob God thus of his honor, make an idol out of ourself, and do not see our trouble that we thereby occasion; for we would have enough else upon us, if we would look at it aright, as Apocalypse 3:17, says to a bishop who thought himself more learned than others: Thou sayest, I am rich, and increased with goods, and have need of nothing, and knowest not that thou art wretched, and miserable, and poor, and blind, and naked. For although it is true that thy gift is greater than that of another; as it must be, since thine office is different, higher and greater: but with the disgraceful addendum that thou displayest thyself in it, and thus pleasest thyself, thou dost totally ruin it, and makest the same high ornament viler than the faults of all others.

For the greater the gifts are, the more disgracefully are they perverted if you make an idol out of them, just as if you were to mix poison with excellent malmsey-wine. Thus you have now hit it admirably well, that you judge another on account of a small fault, and fall yourself with your selfesteem into the grievous sin; that you are ungrateful to God, yes, enthrone yourself in his place in your heart, and interfere with his jurisdiction, where one sin is weightier than those of all other men; besides, you become insolent toward your neighbor and so thoroughly blind that you no longer can know or look at God, your neighbor, or yourself.

What else do you accomplish by this judging than that you invoke the judgment of God against yourself? So that he reasonably must say to you: I did not bestow these gifts upon you in order that you might despise your neighbor and serve yourself with them, but that you should serve your neighbor, who is poor and frail, and me. But you go on, and never once thank me for them, as if all had sprung from your own heart, and you employ my own gift against me and your neighbor, and make a tyrant of yourself, a jailor and judge against your neighbor, whom you ought in love to bear with, to improve and to lift up if he should fall. What will you then answer when he thus will address you (as he here gives you timely notice), except that this sentence is justly pronounced against you, that you are making not a mote, as you perhaps see in your neighbor's eye, (as Christ here says,) but a great beam out of a little mote.

I will say nothing about the fact that, with this wretched judging you are not only culpable on account of the act itself; but it usually happens that he who thus judges is himself a greater sinner than others; so that, if he were to go back and read his own record and register, how he has lived from his youth up, he would hear a story that would make him shudder, and which he would be glad to have unnoticed by other people.

But now every one takes it for granted that he is pious, and wants to forget all the past, and blame and condemn a poor man who has once sinned. Thus he is involved in a double calamity, that he disregards his earliest life and forgets what he was; he does not think how it would have grieved him if he had been ridiculed and condemned. That is one sin, that he is ungrateful, and has forgotten the forgiveness of sins, the grace and all the goodness of God. The other, that he loses his piety and sets in array against himself all his former sins, by the very fact that he makes a display of himself in his piety, and becomes seven times worse than before.

For, do you not think that God can lay a list before your nose, and present not only your crimes and the sins of your youth, but also your whole life that you have regarded as excellent? as now the recluse life of the monks; how will you then stand and answer for daily blaspheming and crucifying his Son with your masses and other idolatries? That's the way it goes, if we forget what we have been, we may then well judge others. But the orders are: Jack, take yourself by your own nose, and reach into your own bosom; if you want to seek and judge a scamp you'll find the greatest scamp upon earth, so that you will readily forget other people and be glad at once to let them alone. For you will never find in another as much sin as in yourself. For if you do see many in another, you see only a year or two; in yourself, however, your whole life, especially the dark spots of which others know nothing, so that you must be ashamed of yourself. See, that would be a good cure for the shameful vice, that you do not please yourself but pray God to forgive you and others.

Secondly, that, although you see something bad in your neighbor, you are not on that account to despise and condemn him; but on the other hand to see his good things, and with your own good things and gifts to help, cover over, adorn and advise him; and you should know that, although you were the holiest and most pious, yet you would become the very worst if you judge another. For your gifts were not bestowed upon you that you may tickle yourself with them, but that you may help your neighbor with them, if he needs it, so that with your strength you may bear his weakness, may cover and adorn his sin and shame with your piety and honor, as God through Christ has done to you and still does daily. If you will not do that, and will tickle yourself with them and despise others: then know this, if another in your presence has a mote in his eye, you towards him, before God, have a beam in your own.

So you see why Christ speaks so sharply against this vice and pronounces the strict sentence: He who judges, shall be judged; as is also reasonable. For, since you interfere with God's judgment, and condemn those whom God has not condemned, you give him reason again to damn you to hell with your whole life, although you had been ever so pious, and to raise to honor the neighbor whom you judged and condemned, and besides also to make him a judge over you, and cause him to find ten times as much in you to condemn as you found in him. So you have made a pretty muss of it, that you have angered and turned against you both God and your neighbor; and thus you lose at the same time both the grace of God and Christian life, and become worse than a heathen, who knows nothing about God.

45

Verses 3 through 5

WHY BEHOLDEST THOU THE MOTE THAT IS IN THY
BROTHER'S EYE, BUT CONSIDEREST NOT THE BEAM
THAT IS IN THINE OWN EYE? OR HOW WILT THOU SAY
TO THY BROTHER, LET ME PULL OUT THE MOTE OUT OF
THINE EYE, AND BEHOLD A BEAM IS IN THINE OWN EYE?
THOU HYPOCRITE, FIRST CAST OUT THE BEAM OUT OF
THINE OWN EYE, AND THEN SHALT THOU SEE CLEARLY
TO CAST OUT THE MOTE OUT OF THY BROTHER'S EYE.

In order that he may the more diligently warn us to guard against this vice, he uses a simple comparison and sets it clearly before us, saying that every one who judges his neighbor has a great beam in his eye, whilst he who is judged has only a mote; that he is ten times more deserving of judgment and condemnation, for the very reason that he condemns others. This is indeed a terrible, dreadful sentence. Where are now the factious spirits and Messrs. Wiseacres, who are great at mastering and finding fault with the Bible, and can do nothing else than to judge us and others?—when there is yet nothing to blame, or perhaps they discover a mote in us, for which they bitterly accuse us; as now the papists revile. When they try their best, and adduce great reason for judging and condemning us, this is the greatest, that some of ours hold ecclesiastical properties; or they accuse us of not fasting, and of whatever else that has any semblance of involving some faults. But they cannot notice their beam, that they persecute the gospel, murder the innocent on account of it, whilst they are themselves the great arch-robbers and thieves of monasteries and church properties.

For what robberies are not now committed by pope, bishops and princes? they are doing as they please with all the spiritual establishments; but [they maintain] that no one else is a real bishop, nor has his own with God and honor, and holds his seat as a thief and a robber: and yet all [with them] must be excellent, and not be called stolen or robbed. But, that we do not fast, or so strictly observe their style of righteousness, which they yet do not themselves observe, this must be alone evil, and all their sin and shame be pious and honorable. Thus it is throughout the world, that everywhere a beam judges the mote, and a great rogue condemns a small one.

Now it is true that we are not without faults, yes, no Christian will get so far as to be without a mote. For St. Paul himself could not do it, as he complains in the seventh of Romans; and all Christendom must daily pray: Forgive us our debts, and it confesses the article of the Creed that is called the forgiveness of sins. But these beam-carriers and mote-judges will not endure this article, and will have everything so pure that there may be no want or fault in it; and as soon as they see anything of this kind, they fall to judging and condemning, as if they were so holy as not to need any forgiveness of sins or any praying; they want to reform the Lord's Prayer and obliterate the chief article of the Creed, whilst they are completely full of blindness and devils, and have heart-grief over the motes of other people; and among ourselves, if we too become foolish, those who are full of vices and wickedness cannot cease looking at and condemning the small vices of others, so that the beam is master and judge of the mote.

But he who is a Christian must know (and will surely himself feel) that we cannot get along so faultlessly, without the mote, and the article of the forgiveness of sins must daily rule in us. Therefore one can easily excuse the faults of other people, and include them in the Lord's Prayer, when he says: Forgive us, as we forgive, etc., especially if he sees that one loves and esteems the word, and does not despise or abuse it. For where that is, there is the kingdom of Christ and full forgiveness, by which the mote is consumed. Therefore we should not despise or condemn any one, if we observe this; or we shall also make of our own mote a beam, so that we also do not receive forgiveness, because we are not willing to forgive others.

Thus you say: Shall I then not rebuke if I see that wrong is done, or am I to call it right and sanction it? Or am I to be pleased that they seize the monastic properties, or live so coarsely, do not pray, or fast, etc. No; that is not what I mean. For he confesses here that there is a mote, and that it is to be taken away. But he teaches you how to go about it properly. I must say it is indeed not pleasant, the mote in the eye; but that I must see to it first of all that I do not have a beam in my own eye and first take that out. First make the rogue in your own breast pious, then add to this, that the small one also becomes pious. For it is of no account that the great thieves hang the small ones, (as we say,) and great rogues condemn the little ones. If the pope with his followers would begin here and they would first sweep before their own door, that they would not themselves be archthieves and scoundrels, we would also have to follow suit, or suffer for it. But now they will not let go their beam, and will have it unrebuked, and they condemn us because we still have a mote, and do not keep ourselves as pure as we should; and the result is, that the great heretic, the pope, condemns the other little heretics, and the great thieves, that are openly and continually stealing and robbing, must make the little thieves pious, and hang and pay for them.

This perverted business shall not exist in my kingdom (says Christ), but thus [it shall be], that you first make pious the great rogue that you will find in your own skin, if you properly look at yourself; afterwards, if you have accomplished this, you can easily make pious a little rogue. But you will be astonished at the trouble you will find with the great rogue, so that I may readily become security to you, and give my head as a pledge, that you will never get so far as to remove the mote from another's eye, and must say: Must I first deal with other people and make them pious? Why, I cannot make myself pious, or become rid of the beam; and thus your brother's mote will not be apt to be disturbed by you. See, this is what Christ means to say, that one should gladly forgive another and patiently bear with him, and all should show humility towards one another; as it would necessarily be if we would obey this teaching. Thus everything would move along nicely in Christendom, in true harmony, and God would be with us. But the devil prevents it from coming to this by means of his adherents and rebellious spirit.

And it ought to make us dread this vice, that he holds up before us such a dreadful decision, as I have said, that always he who judges has before God a beam in his eye; and the other, who is judged, only a mote. Now the beam is immeasarably a greater sin than the mote, that is, such a sin as completely condemns us, and for which there is no mercy. For however great otherwise our sins and faults may be, he can forgive them all; as he shows by this, that he calls the sin of the neighbor a mote. But this is the shameful addition and vileness, that ruins everything, that you judge and condemn another on account of his faults, and do not forgive as you wish that God should forgive you; you go along and will not see this beam, thinking that you are without sin. But if you know yourself (as was said), you would also avoid judging your neighbor, and thus also your beam would be small and be called a mote, and attain forgiveness of sin, and you would also gladly forgive and bear with and excuse the mote of another, in view of the fact that God forgives and excuses your beam for you.

But it is rightly called a beam in the eye, that makes a man completely stone and cataract-blind, and which the world cannot see or judge. Yes, it is adorned with such a show that the world supposes it to be a splendid affair and great holiness; and just as Christ before said concerning the evil eye, that the avaricious kindle for themselves a light, and imagine a happy thought, that it must not be called greediness, but divine worship; so it is here also, that those who have the beam will forsooth have no beam or be rebuked, as being blind and miserable people, but praised as those who with true Christian intent judge the doctrine and life of others: as the factious spirits can admirably boast and swear that they do not teach otherwise out of any pride or envy, but they seek only God's glory and their neighbor's welfare, they make it so beautiful and clear, and their humility and regard for God's honor is so great that they see nothing else than that. Thus it is also in life, if people begin to judge and blame one another; then we see the same covering-over and boasting; I do it not from enmity to the person, but from love for righteousness. The person I am favorable to, but the cause I oppose. That tickles then so gently under the beautiful show, that one is never aware of any beam.

But it is all wrong for you to judge and decide yourself, as you choose, without the word and command of God, and then call it God's honor and righteousness; but it is a devilish addition, that ornaments itself with such a covering and beautifies itself. For here you hear that God will not allow us to undertake to be judges, either in doctrine or life; but where judging or rebuking is necessary, that those do it who are officially commanded to do it, preachers, pastors in spiritual affairs, and civil authorities in worldly government; or a brother with a brother, solely from brotherly love, that bears with and corrects the faults of our neighbor.

— CHAPTER

46

Verse 6

GIVE NOT THAT WHICH IS HOLY UNTO THE
DOGS, NEITHER CAST YE YOUR PEARLS BEFORE
SWINE, LEST THEY TRAMPLE THEM UNDER THEIR
FEET, AND TURN AGAIN AND REND YOU.

The Lord Christ has now nearly finished his instructions in regard to
the fruits and works that follow his teaching, and now begins a warning
or exhortation to put us on our guard against other teaching; as he also
exhorts his apostles, when he sends them forth to preach, and says: Behold,
I send you forth as sheep among wolves; therefore be ye wise as serpents
and harmless as doves. For a Christian, who is to minister the word of God
and preach, and confess it in his life, truly lives in a dangerous calling, on
account of the people, and has great reason for impatience, since the world
is so dreadfully wicked, and he lives in it as among serpents and all sorts of
vermin. Therefore says he: Beware that ye cast not your holy things before
swine and dogs. For they might trample them under foot, or turn against
and rend you; meaning thereby to show and teach them that whenever
they come and preach in public before the masses, they will also find dogs
and swine, that do nothing else than trample upon the gospel and then also
persecute the preachers.

Who are they then that trample upon our holy things and turn against
us? This happens now again in two things, doctrine and life. For first of all

the false teachers do it, who take and learn our gospel from us and thus get our jewel and precious treasure, in which we have been baptized, live and boast ourselves, etc., and then go to their own haunts and begin to preach against us, and turn their snouts and teeth against us; as now our swarm of sectaries, that formerly kept very still when the pope was raging and ruling, so that one did not hear them peep; but now, since we opened the way and with great danger to ourselves freed them from the tyranny of the pope, and they have heard our doctrine and can imitate us in preaching, they go and turn against us and are our worst enemies upon earth, and nobody has preached as badly as we, without whom they would have known nothing about it.

Secondly, in the matter of living it is all the same, especially among us, where people despise or have become tired of the gospel, and it has already gone so far that they will hardly sustain a preacher any more; especially squire Greedy-jack in the country, who monopolizes all the property and supports the preachers in such a way that they lose all appetite for preaching, and he makes servants out of them, so that they must preach and do what he chooses. He is followed by Squire Skinflint in town, and Mr. Everybody, who act as if they did not want to have any gospel or word of God, and yet owe to us their freedom from the tyranny of the pope and all other good things that they have. But now they would like to drive us along with the gospel out of the country, or to starve us.

Well, we cannot make it otherwise, we must endure it, that these snakes, dogs and hogs are about us, that are abusing the gospel, both as to teaching and living; and where there are preachers of the right kind, they must always be treated in this way. For this is the fortune of the gospel in the world; and if it ever happens again, (as I have often predicted, and fear it may only too soon happen,) that such people as the popes and bishops reign, then it will be completely put out of the way and trampled under foot, and its preachers will be gone. For the gospel must be everybody's floor-cloth, so that all the world may walk over it and trample upon it, together with its preachers and disciples.

What are we now to do about it? Cast it not (says Christ) before swine and dogs. Yes, dear Lord, they already have it. For, since it is publicly preached, we cannot prevent their falling in with it and seizing it. But they still do not really have it, and we'll prevent them (thank God!) from getting that which is holy; the shells and husks they may indeed have, that is, carnal liberty; but let none of them, whether dog or hog, a greedy-jack, or miser, or peasant, get a letter of the gospel, although he may read all the books, and hear all the sermons, and have the notion that he thoroughly understands it.

Therefore the right thing for us to do, as Christ here teaches, is for us, when we see such a hog or dog before us, to separate ourselves from him as we do from these factious spirits, and to have no fellowship with them, and administer no sacrament to them, impart no gospel consolation to them, but show them that they are not to enjoy anything of Christ, our treasure. If we do this, we have completely withheld from them the pearls and that which is holy. For no skin-flint or boor, fanatic or captious spirit, shall get the gospel and Christ from me unless he beforehand asks me about it and coincides with me, so that I, or any proper preacher, may say yes to it. For he who has the gospel aright, must surely hold it with us and be of one mind, in case we are sure, in advance, that we have the true gospel and the pearls. Therefore he must surely not trample us under foot as Squire Greedy-jack, nor condemn us as the sectaries, nor despise us as the peasants, in towns and villages; but hold the dear word in honor, as well as all that preach and gladly hear it. If not, let us regard them as hogs and dogs, and tell them that they shall get nothing from us; meanwhile let them read and hear and call themselves evangelical, if they will, as I have to do with some miserly fellows and towns. For this is certain, he who despises the ministerial office will not have much regard for the gospel. Since then they trample under foot the preachers and pastors, and treat them more shamefully than the peasants do their swine, we take back again to ourselves our pearls, and we will see what they will have of the gospel without any thanks to us. If you can trample God's word and his preachers under foot, he can trample you too under foot.

This now Christ means to say: If you see that people will despise your preaching and trample it under foot, then have no fellowship with them and get away from them; as he also says in the eighteenth of Matthew: If he neglect to hear thee and the church, let him be unto thee as a heathen man and a publican; in such a way that we say to them that they are not Christians, but damned heathen, and we will not have anything preached to them or let them have any part of our good things, as Peter, in the eighth of Acts, says to Simon Magus. This is the way that I do, and all that preach the gospel in earnest, lest we make ourselves partakers of their sins. For God will not have us to play the hypocrite in this way with our sectaries, as if they were right in their teaching; but we must regard them as enemies, as separated from them with gospel, baptism, sacrament and all their way of teaching and living. Thus we must also say to our own people, if they wish to have part in the gospel, that they must everywhere not despise us, but give practical proof that they are in earnest with it, and at least that they hold the word and sacrament in honor and submit to it with humility.

Yes, (they say,) in this way they want to get into power again, and put themselves again into a position of authority, like that hitherto occupied by the pope; this would be unendurable, and we might rather have remained under the pope. Answer: Yes, indeed, I have myself been much concerned lest that may be the result. But the way that they are taking, by despising and trampling upon them [the preachers of the word] is not the way to accomplish what they are aiming at, viz.: to prevent the tyranny of the pastors, but just the right beginning to effect it. For if these are out of the way, whom they have trampled under foot and driven off, they will still not be able to be without pastors or preachers. For Christ will maintain his rule in the world, so that still his gospel, baptism, sacrament must abide. Although no prince were willing to protect it, he will do it, since the Father has placed him at his right hand, and means that he is to be Lord. Even if they now drive off all the pastors, they will not hurl Christ from his throne. Therefore this will happen to them: because they will not have nor endure the upright, pious preachers, God will make for them others who will force them and tyrannize over them, worse than before.

Therefore they are on the right track, our Greedy-jacks and others, who put their heads together and think they will silence us and compel us to submit to them, not knowing that another One is sitting up there who reigns supreme, and says: If you will not have right preachers, then have the devil with his preachers, who preach lies to you; these you must accept, and besides be ruled and tormented by them; as those parts of our Germany are now already suffering, where they not only refuse the gospel but are persecuting it, so that they have all their corners full of sectaries, fanatics and anabaptists, and cannot prevent it.

But the right way to prevent this is to embrace the gospel earnestly and faithfully, beseech God that he may send true, faithful workmen into his harvest; then there need be no fear. For these preachers would not oppress or force us, or do us any harm in body or soul, but help everybody and do all the good possible; as has been learned in regard to ourselves, who may well boast before God and the world, that we have not sought any authority or advantage for ourselves, but have served all the world with our body and life; we have neither encumbered nor harmed anybody, but have gladly helped everybody, also in temporal things, and besides have suffered for it manifold danger, violence and persecution. But, since they don't want us any more, may God grant that others come after us who will treat them differently, oppress, torment and skin them, so that they may see what they had in us, and they must suffer it from those whom they now do not look at and would not like to have as stable servants. For they deserve nothing better than to have these tyrants whom they must fear, as they had the pope; he was the right sort of a ruler for them. Our cranky princes, too, have already learned it, and think they would like to be rid of compulsion and no longer fear the pope; they begin to protect the priests, but not for their sake, but that they may force them into subjection to themselves, so that they may live by their favor, and they protect them in such fashion that they should rather come over to us, whom they regard as enemies, than to allow themselves to be plucked by them, under the name of protection. But it cannot be otherwise, and they are both rightly served.

But it must not be so among Christians, but upright, pious people should hold their pastors and preachers in high honor, with all humility and love, for the sake of Christ and his word, and have great regard for them as a precious gift and jewel, bestowed by God better than all worldly treasures and possessions. In like manner also true, pious preachers will seek with all fidelity nothing else than the advantage and welfare of all people, without burdening them at all either in their consciences, or even outwardly in temporal affairs or bodily matters. But let him who despises them know that he is no Christian, and has again lost the treasure. We preach to and exhort everybody who will give heed to and join with us; but those who will not, and yet with the semblance and name of the gospel or Christian fellowship despise us, and will tread us under foot, against these we employ the artifice of letting them have the semblance, but in fact taking all back to ourselves, so that they have nothing at all left. For we are commanded to separate ourselves from them, although we are not glad to do it, and would rather that they should remain with us; but as they will not, we must let them go, and not on their account let our treasure perish or be trodden under foot by them.

47

Verses 7 through 11

ASK, AND IT SHALL BE GIVEN YOU; SEEK, AND YE SHALL
FIND; KNOCK, AND IT SHALL BE OPENED UNTO YOU. FOR
EVERY ONE THAT ASKETH RECEIVETH; AND HE THAT
SEEKETH FINDETH; AND TO HIM THAT KNOCKETH IT
SHALL BE OPENED. OR WHAT MAN IS THERE OF YOU,
WHOM IF HIS SON ASK BREAD, WILL HE GIVE HIM A
STONE? OR IF HE ASK A FISH, WILL HE GIVE HIM A
SERPENT? IF YE THEN, BEING EVIL, KNOW HOW TO
GIVE GOOD GIFTS UNTO YOUR CHILDREN, HOW MUCH
MORE SHALL YOUR FATHER WHICH IS IN HEAVEN
GIVE GOOD THINGS TO THEM WHICH ASK HIM?

After the Lord Christ had taught his disciples, and established the office of the ministry, so that they might know what they were to preach and how they were to live, he here adds an exhortation to prayer; he means hereby to teach that prayer next to preaching is the principal work of a Christian, as something always belonging to a sermon; and to show that nothing is more necessary in Christendom, (because we have so many temptations and hindrances,) than that we continue without ceasing in prayer, that God may give his grace and Spirit, that the gospel may become efficient and be in constant use by ourselves and others. Therefore God in the prophet Zechariah (as above quoted) promised that he would pour out upon Christians a spirit of grace and of supplication; he comprehends thus in these two things the whole of Christianity.

Thus he now means to say: I have instructed you, that you may know how you ought to live aright and against what you should be on your guard. Now a necessary part of this is that you also pray, and confidently persevere with seeking and knocking, not becoming sluggish or weary in regard to it. For there will be need of begging, seeking and knocking. For although both doctrine and practice have rightly begun, yet there will be no want of faults and offenses, that daily hinder and obstruct us, so that we cannot advance, and against which we continually contend with all our powers, but without any stronger defense than prayer, so that if we do not use this it is not possible for us to maintain our ground and remain Christians; as we can see very plainly now what kind of hindrances resist the progress of the gospel; but we see, too, that we are not making much account of prayer, and taking it for granted that this warning and exhortation does not apply to us, and that we do not now need to pray, since the useless chattering and muttering of rosaries and other idolatrous little prayers has ceased; which is not a good sign, and it is to be feared that much misfortune will overtake us that we might have been able to prevent.

Therefore every Christian should heed this exhortation, first, as a command, just as well as the previous statement: Judge not, etc., is a command, and he should know that he is in duty bound to practice this Christian work, and not to do as that peasant, who said that he gave his preacher grain, so that he should pray for him; as some think: Of what account is my prayer? If I do not pray, others do; so that we should not think it does not concern us, or that it depends upon our choice, about which I have often more fully treated elsewhere.

Secondly, you have here the consolatory promise and rich assurance which he adds concerning prayer, that one may see that it is of consequence to him, and may learn to regard our prayer as dear and precious before God, since he so earnestly exhorts us to engage in it, so kindly invites and promises that we shall not ask in vain; and if we had no other cause or inducement than this friendly, rich word, this ought to be enough to drive us to do it. I will be silent as to how earnestly he exhorts and commands [us to engage in it] and how heartily we need it.

Besides, as if this were not enough, as we aside from this, for own great need's sake, should ourselves engage in it, he adds a most beautiful comparison (the more to stimulate us) of every father in reference to his son, who although he may be a worthless wretch, yet, if he ask for a fish, he will not give him a serpent, etc. Hence he infers this comforting word: If ye can do this, who are not of a good sort, and have not a vein in you that is good towards God, how then should not God, your Heavenly Father, whose nature is altogether good, not also give to you what is good if you ask him for it? This is the very highest appeal wherewith he ought to or can persuade any one to prayer, if we only would look at these words and lay them to heart.

Now what the need is, for which he gives this exhortation, and which should urge us to pray, has been mentioned, so that, if we have the word of God, and have made a good beginning, both in doctrine and practice, then there cannot fail to occur temptation and opposition, not of one kind only but of thousands of kinds. For, in the first place, there is our own flesh, the old rotten sack, that is soon apathetic, inattentive, and disinclined to the word of God and a good life, so that we are always lacking in wisdom and the word of God, faith, love, patience, etc. This is the first enemy that is daily hanging about our neck so heavily that he is always dragging us in that direction.

Then comes the other enemy, the world, that begrudges us the dear word and faith, and will have no patience with us, however weak we may be; it falls upon us and condemns us for what we do, seeks to take from us what we have, so that we can have no peace with it. These are already two great temptations that inwardly hinder us and outwardly seek to drive us off. Therefore we have no more to do than always to cry to God, that he may strengthen and further his word in us, and restrain the persecutors and sectaries, so that it be not smothered.

The third enemy is now the strongest of all, the very devil, who has the great double advantage that we are not good by nature, and besides are weak in faith and spirit; he gets thus within my own castle and contends against me; he has in addition the world to aid him, so that he stirs up ugly crowds against me, through whom he shoots his poisonous, fiery darts upon me, that he may weary me, so that the word in me may be again smothered and extinguished, and he rule again as he ruled before, and prevent himself from being driven out. See, these are three misfortunes that oppress us heavily enough and lie upon our neck, and will not cease whilst we have life and breath. Therefore we have constant reason to pray and to call. Therefore he adds these words: Ask, seek, knock; to show that we do not yet have everything, but that we are in such a condition that there is failure and want everywhere. For if we had it all we would not need to beg or seek; if we were even in heaven already, we would not need to knock.

Now these are the chief temptations in regard to the serving of God and the keeping of his word. Next we have the common, temporal need of this life upon earth; as that we are to pray that he may grant us gracious peace, good government, and protect us from all kinds of trouble, sickness, pestilence, famine, bloodshed, storms, etc. For you have not yet got beyond the reach of death, nor eaten up all your daily bread, so that you need not pray that he may daily give it to you. Also, thus you have to pray for the secular authority, and against all kinds of vices, that the people may not rob and steal so from one another, since you must daily see that everywhere such shameful conduct abounds. In addition to all this you have at home your wife, child and domestics to be governed; there you will have your hands full. For he who has to observe and carry out in his whole life both Christian and civil righteousness, has undertaken more than one man's work and ability.

What shall we now do? Here we are involved in such manifold great needs and hindrances that we cannot escape, if we should violently shut the door against them. How can I prevent my dying, who am so lazy and indifferent to the word of God and all that is good? or prevent the world from keeping up such a rumpus and racket, and the devil from raging? and how prevent there being so much trouble and misfortune? Now the dear Lord Christ knows this very well. Therefore he means to show us a precious, good remedy, as a kind, faithful physician, and teaches us what we are to do about this, as though he should say: The world is so mad, and undertakes to rid itself of this with wisdom and reason; seeks so many means and ways, help and counsel, how it may escape from these perplexities. But this is the only shortest, surest way, that you go into a little chamber, or into a corner, and there open your heart and pour [out] your desires before God with lamentation and sighing and assured confidence, that he, as your faithful, heavenly Father, will help and counsel in such perplexities; just as we read in Isaiah 37 about king Hezekiah: When the enemy with a great army was lying before the city, and he was so besieged and outnumbered, that no help nor counsel, to human appearance, was to be hoped for, in addition to which the enemy most insolently defied him, and mocked at his misfortune, and wrote him a letter full of blasphemy, so that he well-nigh despaired; then the picus king did nothing else than to go up into the temple, lay the letter before the altar, fall down and heartily pray. Then he was soon heard and helped.

But then we worry and fret, and have the greatest trouble to bring ourselves to do it, and we miserably perplex ourselves, making martyrs of ourselves with our caring and thinking, trying to take our neck from the yoke and be rid of it. For it is a bad, cunning devil that rides me as well as others, and has often played these tricks upon me, when I was tempted or worried, whether in spiritual or secular affairs. He quickly interferes and brings it about that one wears himself out with his trouble; thereby he drags us away from prayer and confuses us to such an extent that one does not think of it, and before one begins to pray, one has already half worried himself to death. For he knows very well what prayer can accomplish, therefore he restrains and disturbs us as much as he can, so that we do not have recourse to it at all.

Therefore we ought to learn to take these words rightly to heart, and accustom ourselves to it, so soon as any trouble and need appears, only at once to fall upon our knees and lay the need before God, according to this exhortation and promise; then we should be helped, so that we need not worry ourselves with our own thoughts about seeking help. For it is a very precious remedy, which assuredly helps, and never fails, if it be only applied.

But how to pray aright has been shown above and elsewhere sufficiently. For here we are speaking only of the power of prayer and of what should urge us to it. The most important thing is that you only at first look at the word of God that may instruct you what you are heartily to believe, so that you are sure of this, that your faith, gospel and Christ are right, and that your calling is pleasing to God; then you will soon see the devil against you, and feel that there is lacking everywhere, internally in faith and externally in your calling, that everything threatens to go wrong, and temptations are swarming on every hand: if you feel this, then be wise and prevail upon your heart to begin at once to pray and say: Dear Lord, I surely have thy word, and am in the calling that pleases thee, that I know. Now thou seest how much I need everywhere, so that I know of no help except in thee; help thou, therefore, since thou hast commanded that we are to pray, seek and knock, and then we shall certainly receive, find and have what we desire.

If you will accept it thus and accustom yourself confidently to pray, and do not receive, then come and call me a liar. If he does not give at the minute, he will still give you so much that meanwhile your heart will experience comfort and strength, till the time that he gives more abundantly than you would have hoped. For this is also a good feature of prayer, if one habitually practices it, and thus meditates upon the word that he has promised, that the heart becomes continually stronger, and more firmly confides, and finally obtains much more than otherwise.

This I could clearly prove by my own example and that of other pious people. For I tried it too, and many people with me, especially at the time when the devil wanted to devour us, at the Diet at Augsburg, and everything stood bad enough, and was in such a turmoil that all the world supposed things would be turned topsy-turvy, as some had insolently threatened, and the swords had already been drawn and the rifles loaded. But God so helped through our prayers, and opened the way, that those screamers, with their scratching and threatening, were completely put to shame, and a good peace and a gracious year was given to us, such as had not been for many a day, and such as we could not have hoped for. If now another danger and need arises, we will pray again and he must again help and deliver, although he may let us meanwhile suffer a little and be oppressed, so that he may the more strengthen us, and we be driven the more earnestly to pray. For what sort of a prayer would it be, if the need were not here and did not oppress us until we felt it? That one rightly feels his need helps to make his prayer the stronger. Therefore let every one learn by no means to despise his prayer, not doubting that it will assuredly be heard, and in due time he shall receive what he desires.

But why Christ uses so many words, that he puts it in three ways: Ask and it shall be given to you; seek, and ye shall find; knock, and it shall be opened unto you, when it was enough to use one; it is easy to see (as has been said,) that he thereby means the more strongly to exhort us to pray. For he knows that we are timid, and we are afraid to present our need to God, as unworthy, unfit, etc.; we feel the need, indeed, but cannot express it; we think God is so great and we so insignificant, that we dare not pray, which is also a great hindrance from the devil that does great harm to prayer. Therefore he entices us away from that bashfulness and hesitation, so that we have no doubt at all, but only draw near confidently and boldly. For although I am unworthy, I am still his creature; and because he has made me worthy to be his creature, I am also worthy to take what he has promised to me and so freely offered. In short, if I am unworthy, he and his promise are not unworthy. Upon this, only venture it promptly and confidently, and lay it with all joy and assurance upon his bosom. But first of all see to it that you truly believe in Christ, and are in your right place, that pleases God, not as the world, that pays no regard to its place, and is only planning day and night to practice its vices and scoundrelism.

One might however interpret the three statements in this way, that he repeats the same thing in other words to indicate perseverance in prayer, concerning which St. Paul exhorts in the twelfth of Romans: Continue instant in prayer; as though he said: It is not enough to begin and give a sigh, and say the prayer and then go your way: but, just as the need is, so should the prayer be. For it does not once take hold of you and then go away, but it hangs on and falls about your neck again, and will not let go. Do the same also, so that you always pray, and besides seek and knock, and do not let go; just as the example of the widow teaches in Luke eighteen, who would not let go of her judge, with persevering entreaty, and so pertinaciously that he was overpowered, and had to help her ungraciously. How much more (Christ there infers) will God give to us if he sees that we do not cease praying, but keep on knocking and knocking, so that he must hear; especially because he has promised it, and shows that he has pleasure in such perseverance. Therefore, as the need is always knocking, so do you continue to knock, and do not cease, because you have his word; so he will have to say: Well, then go, and have what you desire. Of this St. James says in his epistle, that the prayer of the righteous man availeth much, if it is earnestly pressed, and he quotes for this the example of Elijah the prophet from the Scriptures, etc. Thus God also does it for the reason that he drives you not only simply to pray but to knock, so that he means to try whether you can keep a firm hold, and to teach you that your prayer is not for that reason unpleasant or unanswered, although he delays and lets you often seek and knock, etc.

— CHAPTER

48

Verse 12

THEREFORE ALL THINGS WHATSOEVER YE WOULD
THAT MEN SHOULD DO TO YOU, DO YE EVEN SO TO
THEM: FOR THIS IS THE LAW AND THE PROPHETS.

With these words he now concludes his teaching, given in these three chapters, and gathers them all up in a little bundle in which one can find it all,
and every one can put it in his bosom and keep it well; as if he said: Would
you like to know what I have preached, and what Moses and all the prophets teach you? then I will tell you in a very few words, and state it so that
you dare not complain of its being too long or hard to keep. For it is such
a sermon that one can stretch out far and wide, and also make short; and
all teaching and preaching flow out from it and spread themselves, and
here they come together again. How could it be expressed more briefly
and clearly than in these words? except that the world and our old Adam
prevent us from catching his meaning and contrasting our life with this
teaching; we let it go into one ear and out at the other. Were we always to
hold it in contrast with our living and doing, we would not live so rudely
and be so neglectful, but always have enough to do, and become our own
masters and teach what we ought to do, so that we would not need to run
after holy living and works, and would also not need many jurists and law-
books for this purpose. For it is briefly stated and easily learned, if only we
were diligent and earnest to do and live accordingly.

Thus, that we may see it in plain illustrations, there is surely no one who would like to be robbed, and if he asks his own heart about it, he must say that he really would not like that. Why does he not then conclude that he should not rob another? As, if you see at market that everybody makes his goods as dear as he chooses, that he wants to give for thirty pennies what is not worth ten, and you ask him: My friend, would you like to be treated that way? then he cannot be so coarse and unreasonable, but must say: I would buy it at its market value, and what would be reasonable and right, so that I be not overreached. See, there is your heart that tells you truly how you would like to be treated, and your conscience that concludes that you should also do thus to others, and it can properly teach you how you are to deal with your neighbor in buying and selling and all sorts of dealing; all of which belongs to the seventh commandment: Thou shalt not steal.

The same in regard to the other commandments: If you have a wife, daughter or maid, you would not like to have her disgraced or badly spoken about, but you want to have her honored and well treated and highly spoken of by everybody. Why then are you so perverse as to hanker after another man's wife and yourself put her to shame; or to refrain from honoring her when you should do it, and to find pleasure in traducing and slandering? Also, you would not like to be injured by any one, or badly spoken of, or any thing of that kind; why do you not here yourself keep to the rule and measure that you demand and will have from others, and why do you soon judge, blame and condemn another if he does not do it to you, and yet will not yourself act according to your own rule? Thus go through all the commands of the second table, and you will find that this is the real sum of all the preaching that we can do; as he himself says here.

Therefore it is well called a short sermon; but again, if we were to spread it out through all its applications, it is so far-reaching that there would be no end to it; for we cannot count up all that will be done upon earth till the last day; and he is a splendid master who can compress and embrace in a summary such a long, diffuse sermon, so that every one can take it home with him, and daily remind himself of it, as written in his own heart, yes, in all his living and doing (as we shall hear further on) and see where he has been wanting in his whole life.

And I believe too that its force would be felt and its fruits realized if we would only accustom ourselves to remember it, and not be so very indolent and careless. For I do not think that any one is so coarse, or so wicked, if he would bear this in mind, that he would still shun it or take offense at it; and it is surely a wise device that Christ puts it in such a way that he takes no other illustration than ourselves, and he applies it in the closest possible way, laying it upon our heart, body and life, and all our members, so that no one need go far after it or spend much trouble or cost upon it; but he has laid the book in your own bosom, and besides so clear that you need no glasses to understand Moses and the law, so that you are your own Bible, master, doctor and preacher. He gives you such directions that you need only to look at them to find how the book reaches through all your doings, words, thoughts, heart, body and soul. Regulate yourself only according to that, and you will be wise and learned enough, above all jurists, art and books.

So, to take a rough illustration, are you a mechanic, you find the Bible lying in your workshop, in your hand, in your heart, that teaches you and preaches to you how you are to deal with your neighbor. Look only at your tool, your needle, your thimble, your beer-cask, your wares, your scales, your yard-stick, and you read this motto written upon them; so that you cannot look in any direction that it does not stare at you, and no one thing is so small, with which you daily have to do, that does not constantly say this to you, if you will hear it, and there is no lack of preaching. For you have just as many preachers as you have dealings, wares, tools and other apparatus in your house and home. That is always calling to you: Dear friend, deal with me towards your neighbor just as you would like you neighbor to deal with you in his line of business.

See, thus would this teaching be written upon everything that we look at, and enstamped upon our whole life, if we only had ears that were willing to hear and eyes that were willing to see; and it is so richly preached to us that no one can excuse himself as not knowing it or not having it sufficiently told and preached to him. But we are like the adders that stop their ears and become deaf if we attempt to charm them; we will not see or hear what is written in our own heart and thoughts, and we rush ahead recklessly: Ha, what do others concern me! I can do with my own what I choose, and sell my goods as dear as I can; who will hinder me, etc.? as Squires Skin-flint and Gag do at market; and if one rebukes and threatens them by the word of God, they merely laugh and ridicule and only harden themselves in their wickedness. But we do not preach to these, nor does Christ, and he will have nothing to do with them, and just as completely despises them as they do [him], and he will let them go to the devil.

But those that want to be pious, and still fear God and think how they will live and act, must know that they are not to deal with and handle their property as they may wish, as though they were themselves masters of everything: but they are bound to do what is right and orderly, for which reason we have laws of the land and of the city. For so every one wishes to be dealt with by his neighbor; therefore he should do likewise, both taking and giving good wares. This is his seriously meant command, and he will not allow any liberty or arbitrariness to be made out of it, as if one could do it or not without sin; and he will insist upon it, however much the world may view it as an insult and despise it. If you do it not, he will deal with you according to your own measure, and it will come home to you, so that you will have no blessing in what you have gained contrary to this teaching, but all trouble and sorrow, and your children after you. For he will have his command kept, or there shall be no good or success enjoyed.

Secondly, it is not only brought so close home (as now stated) that we must see it in everything that occurs; but it is also presented in such a way that one has to blush at his own conduct. For there is no one who would like to do a base act so that other people should see it, and no one is as ready to sin publicly before the people as if it occurred secretly, so that no one sees it. Thus Christ means to set us here as witnesses against ourselves, and to make us afraid of ourselves, so that if we do wrong our conscience will oppose us with this command, as a perpetual witness, and say: See, what are you doing? This you ought to sell at such a price, according to common fair usage; now you are asking too much. Also, these wares you would not like to take from some one else, as you are depreciating or misrepresent-ing them, etc. How you should be vexed if some one would give you for a gulden what would be worth hardly ten groschen? so that, if you have a drop of honest blood in your body, you ought to be ashamed of yourself.

For if some one else would do it you would call him a thief and a scoundrel. Why, then, are you not ashamed of yourself, as not some one else but you yourself must thus blame yourself, condemned by your own conscience? But that is all very well for a hard, shameless forehead, that feels no disgrace before the people, before itself, still less before God. But if another does it to you then you can readily cry out: Is not this a sin and a shame, and cunningly stolen from the purse? You can easily see a thief and scoundrel in another; but the one who hides in your own breast, and whom you can easily catch and feel, him you will not see.

O, how many such fellows there are in all trades and occupations, that live along securely, deceiving and cheating the people, wherever they can, and yet not willing to be counted thieves and scoundrels, if they only do it secretly and smartly. But if everybody was to give back what he has stolen and robbed in his business or trade, few people would retain anything; yet they live along as pious people, because they cannot be publicly criminated and punished, and they imagine too that they have not sinned; and if they look about themselves, every corner of the house and home is full of thievery, and God is witness that they do not have a gulden or two in the house that has not been stolen; and yet all this must not be called stealing. Yes, if it were only stealing, and not also murder besides, for with bad, injurious wares, food or drink, people are made weak and sick, etc., and not only robbed of their money, but also of their health, so that many a one eats and drinks, so that he afterwards must pine away and often die in consequence of it. My good friend, is not that just the same as if you were to break into his house or chest, or to strike him a deadly wound?—only it goes by a different name.

If you were not so wicked and shameless, you should be ashamed of yourself when your conscience says this to you, and holds this saying before you so that you must reflect; yes, it would make you so fearful that you would not be able to stay anywhere on account of it. For it is a burden that is always oppressing and disturbing, yes is always condemning, as a perpetual witness against ourselves, so that it cannot possibly be borne. That would then soon teach you that you must quit plundering and stealing, and such things that you would not like to have done to you by some one else, etc. Thus accustom yourself then to look a little at this saying, and practice it upon yourself, then you will have a daily preacher in your heart, in whatever way you may be dealing with your neighbor; thereby you can readily learn to understand every commandment and the whole law, and to govern and conduct yourself in your intercourse with others, so that you may well decide accordingly what is right and wrong in the world.

But do you say: How does he say that this is the law and the prophets? The Scriptures of the law and the prophets contain much more than this. For the Scriptures have the doctrine of faith and the promises, of which nothing is said here. Answer: Christ names here the law and the prophets in direct contrast with the gospel or the promise. For he is not preaching here about the important article, namely, concerning faith in Christ, but only of good works. For those are two different kinds of preaching; we must preach them both, but each in its proper time and place. That you see also clearly in the text, in the words where he says: Whatsoever ye would that men should do to you, that do ye unto them likewise. Thereby he shows that his preaching now extends no further than to the dealings which people have with us and we with them, and says nothing about the grace of Christ which we receive from God. Therefore he now means to say: If one is to preach about good life and works, which we are to practice in dealing with our neighbor, then you will find in all the law and the prophets nothing else than what this saying teaches you. Therefore he uses the words: the people, and: that do ye to them, etc., to indicate that he is speaking only about the commandments of the second table.

And this is the best in the saying, viz., that he does not say: Other people shall do it to you; but: Ye shall do it to other people. For every one would like others to do good to him, and there are many scoundrels and bad fellows who would have no objection to other people being good and doing good to them; but they will not do it to anybody: as now our peasants imagine it is wrong and great oppression that they are to give fair measure; and yet they can loudly cry and complain that they are robbed or are taxed. But these are nothing but vile reptiles. Some, however, are a little better, who say: I would take my turn and gladly do what I ought, if other people would first do it to me. But this saying puts it in this way: Do thou what thou wouldst have from another. Thou shalt begin, and be the first, if thou wilt that others should do it to thee; or, if they will not, do thou it nevertheless. For if thou wilt not be good, and do good, before thou seest it in another, nothing will come of it. If others will not, thou art none the less obliged to do it, according to the law, and what is acknowledged to be right, as thou wouldst be glad to have done to thee. He who wants to be good must not regard the example of other people; and it will not do for you to say: He deceived me, and I must befoul him again; but because you do not like it, do not do it to him, and begin with that which you wish to be done to you. Thus you may then influence other people through your example, so that they will do good again to you, even those who before did you harm. But if you do not do it yourself, you have as your reward that no one does good to you; and you are served right, before God and the people.

49

Verses 13 and 14

ENTER YE IN AT THE STRAIT GATE: FOR WIDE IS THE GATE, AND BROAD IS THE WAY, THAT LEADETH TO DESTRUCTION, AND MANY THERE BE WHICH GO IN THEREAT: BECAUSE STRAIT IS THE GATE, AND NARROW IS THE WAY, WHICH LEADETH UNTO LIFE, AND FEW THERE BE THAT FIND IT.

He has now ended his sermon, our dear Lord, and finally concludes the same sermon with several warnings to equip us against all kinds of hindrances and vexations, both in doctrine and life, that we meet with in the world. For of a truth the teaching has been beautiful and precious, at the same time widely spread out and also briefly enough condensed, in a single word, so that it can readily be told and understood; but then comes the trouble and the labor to put it in practice; and it is indeed a difficult and hard life to be a Christian or pious, for that will not be sweet for us; as that good girl said: Much belongs to honor; yes, indeed, and still much more to a Christian life. This is what our dear Lord is here thinking of, that it may seem desirable and occur to them: I would indeed like to live in that way; but a great deal is required for that. Yes, I say that too (says he), therefore I warn you, be careful, and do not mind if it is a little sour and difficult; for it cannot be otherwise in the world.

This a Christian must know, and he must be prepared for it, so that he does not allow himself to be hindered or vexed, if the whole world lives otherwise, and he must by no means adapt himself to the course of the great mass, as Moses also prohibited already in the twenty-third of Exodus: Thou shalt not follow a multitude to do evil, etc., as though he should say: Offenses you will always find existing in the world; as also Christ here says: The way to destruction is broad and very many are walking upon it; and the gate is very wide, so that crowds pass through it.

That is the great offense that startles a great many people, and causes them to apostatize, yes, it has greatly perplexed the prophets and the holy people; as David in the Psalms often laments, especially in Psalm 73 at length: I was envious at the foolish, when I saw the prosperity of the wicked. For there are no bands in their death, but their strength is firm. They are not in trouble as other men; neither are they plagued like other men. In short, they are fortunate upon earth (says he) and become rich, have house and home full, live in luxury and do just what they please. But what do I do, on the other hand? I must be pious and suffer, and am plagued daily and chastened every morning, that is, if I slightly transgress, he is quickly behind me with the rod. That is what I get for it. There everything is in honor and joy; therefore all the world falls in with them, everybody praises and congratulates. As we saw under the papacy; if any one only put on a priest's robe, him all the world had to praise and honor; everybody contributed to this, and she was a happy mother who bore him. And it is just the same now: He who only is an enemy to us is held in high honor and esteem among them, let him live as he may. That was a great cross to the dear fathers, that they had to see this success and wickedness in the world, so that every one highly regarded it and ran after it, and they were to be pious and have nothing with it but misfortune, and suffer contempt and persecution from everybody.

Christ wishes to show this also, and to warn his own that every one should so live in the world as if he were alone, and regard his word and preaching as the very greatest thing upon earth, so that he would think thus: Although I see that my neighbor and the whole city, yes the whole world lives differently, and all that are great, noble, rich, princes and lords, side with it; yet I have an associate who is greater than they all, namely Christ and his word. Therefore, though I am alone, I am yet not alone. For, because I have the word of God, I have Christ with me, together with all the dear angels and all the saints from the beginning of the world; so that really there is a greater crowd and more glorious procession about me than there could now be in the whole world; only, that it is not visible to mortal eye, and I must see and bear the vexation that so many people fall away from me, or live and act in hostility to me.

You must firmly hold on to this, if you expect to endure; otherwise this vexation will carry you away, if you are influenced by how other people live and believe. For the Turks hence conclude, as their strongest argument [against us]: Do you suppose that God is so cruel as to condemn a great world? In like manner also the papists: Yes, do you think that what you bring forth from your corner is the only right thing, and that the whole world is damned? Should so many popes, bishops, holy fathers, kings and princes altogether have erred, etc.? They insist so doggedly upon this that no man can tear them away from it, and they conclude most assuredly that our doctrine is not right; and their only argument is: There are many of us, there are few of them; we are pious, learned, wise, God's people, occupy the apostles' seat, etc., therefore we cannot be in error. Christ has surely not forsaken his church nor God his people. It is not possible, that God will damn so many people for the sake of a few; for he has not created heaven in vain.

But against all this Christ teaches thus: Only out with your eyes, or turn them the other way, so that you don't by any means look at the great crowd, but only at God's word; and be assured that it cannot be otherwise than that the way to destruction is broad, and the gate wide, and many going upon it; and again, the gate to life is narrow and the way strait, and very few going upon it. Therefore it is of no avail that the Turk and pope boast about those of their faith: We are many and have long believed as we do; therefore, it must be right. For Christ bluntly asserts the contrary, and he calls that the way to destruction that is broad and well travelled, and warns that we should not be worried because there are so few of us and the other crowd is so large. But it is very hard to digest this little mouthful, if one rightly feels it, so that I have myself often choked at it, and thought: We are such a little, poor company, despised and damned by all that is high and great upon earth; ought we then to be boastful and defiant against all the world, to assert that our side alone is right, and to decide in regard to all of them that pope, bishop, and all that adhere to them, belong to the devil? Yet we must get over this, and conclude: I know that my cause is right, though the whole world should talk otherwise.

How must the dear virgin Mary have felt when the angel came and brought her the message that she was to be mother of the Highest? Who then was about her that believed this, or stood by her? Ought she to have taken it into the account that there were the daughters of so many rich, noble, great lords and princes there, and should God not have known how to find any other one for this high duty, to which no virgin had ever been called but herself, a poor, unknown, despised maiden? Also, how did the patriarch Abraham act, when he had to go forth from Chaldaea, and travel alone, as if he alone were a Christian and all the world condemned? But he had to give himself no concern about that, nor look around upon others, but had to speak thus: "How God manages with the whole world, I will let him see to that; but I will stick to his word and follow that, although I see all the world going differently;" as also Mary must have thought: "What God will do with others, that I will let him care for; but I will abide by the word that I hear, and that tells me what he will do to me." So we must also conclude: I see that the pope, bishops, princes, sectaries, civilians, and peasants, do as they please, despise and ridicule us with the greatest assurance, so that I might say: Do you then think that you alone are right against all of them? But go along pope, princes, learned men, and all the world; I know that the doctrine is right, and that it is the word of God: I will abide by that, whatever may happen.

Thus Christ now means to say: I have given you this instruction, so that you may see how extremely few people agree with you, and how many will teach and live to the contrary, so that it will greatly perplex you; but be firm, and do not let it worry you, and know that it cannot be otherwise, and remember that I told you beforehand that the gate to life is strait and the way narrow; but the other broad and wide, etc. Therefore pay no attention to that, but hear what I say to you, and follow me. For I, with all the saints, have taken the narrow way; you must take it too, if you would come to me; let the others go their wide way. For you will see how narrow the pit will be into which they will have to go; on the other hand ye, who now must go by the narrow way through the strait gate, will come into a beautiful space, as large and wide as heaven and earth.

Now, what makes then the way so narrow and small? No one does but the very devil, the world and just our own flesh, which is lazy, resists and refuses, and will not move forward, to trust God and rely upon his word, cannot bear the world's contempt, poverty, perils, etc. In short, it likes also to travel the broad road, therefore it makes this path for us sour and difficult.

Then comes the world, that persecutes us, hangs, murders, burns and drowns, because we will not go with it in the broad way; and if it can do no worse it slanders and abuses us most poisonously, drives us out with sword, fire, and water: so that it is a hard battle, to stand there and fight against our own flesh, so that one may trust God, love his neighbor, live chastely, and abide in his lot; and if we do all this in a hard struggle, then the world must come too with its persecuting and reviling us as the worst criminals upon earth, just to make our life hard.

Along with this comes the devil himself and torments the heart with evil thoughts, unbelief, fear, dread, despair, makes out of our good deeds sin and shame, and yet we have to remain among these enemies and exposed to their assaults. Under these circumstances one may be vexed and tempted to apostatize and say: I see indeed that those have rest and a good time, pass their days in quiet peace, and have the same glory and honor of being the true servants of God: why shall I then alone suffer myself to be so wretchedly persecuted, vexed and abused? Where they all stay, there will I stay too.

The ancients have admirably depicted this in the legend of the Knight Tondalo (except that they did not rightly apply it, and interpreted it of purgatory or the punishment of souls after this life,) how he had to pass over a small bridge that was scarcely as broad as a hand, with a burden on his back, and under him a sulphurous pool full of dragons, and besides there was one coming towards him to whom he had to give place. That coincides well with this statement. For a Christian leads a life as hard as if he were walking upon a narrow path, yes, upon nothing but razors; thus the devil is beneath us in the world, he is incessantly snapping at us with his jaws, that he may drive us into impatience, despair and murmuring against God; besides the world opposes us and it neither will yield to us nor let us pass by, and our flesh hangs about our neck; so that we are crowded on every side, and the way in itself is so narrow, that of itself there would be trouble enough even if there were no danger or hindrance in the way: yet we must go through or fall into the hands of the world and the devil.

Therefore reflect and act accordingly: if you will be a Christian, let it be so. For things will remain as they are: you will not make the way any broader, and must observe that a few go here, and the great crowd there. But let this be your comfort, first, that God is with you; then, that after you have gotten through you will come into a beautiful, wide place. For if you only adhere to the word and act according to it, not according to sight, then he is assuredly with you, and so effectively that your spirit will overcome the flesh, the world and the devil, so that he can accomplish nothing through your flesh, nor through the world, nor of himself. For the word upon which you rely through faith is too strong for him, although it appears little and we do not see it. But he knows very well what it can do, as he has often tested it and felt what a force and power it is, if one believes in it. Therefore the prophet so confidently boasts in Psalm 118: "The Lord is on my side: I will not fear: what can man do unto me? They compassed me about like bees; they are quenched as the fire of thorns; for in the name of the Lord I will destroy them. Thou hast thrust sore at me that I might fall: but the Lord helped me," etc. See, he too has nothing else than the word and faith, that the Lord is with him, whom he still does not see; but he feels indeed the world and the flesh that make his way narrow and embitter his life. Yet he remains firm, finds his satisfaction in the fact that the Lord is with him and approves his course, and he is sure that he will be on the Lord's side and conquer, though all the world should oppose him.

We must also avail ourselves of this consolation, that we learn to make for ourselves out of the strait gate and narrow way a wide space, and out of the little company a great crowd, so that we do not stare at what we see, but through faith and the word look at the invisible, namely, that Christ himself and all the heavenly host are with me, and have gone the very same way, and in a beautiful long procession have preceded me to heaven, and that all Christendom till the last day are still traveling the same road. For where he goes and stays, there they must all go and stay. Thus our way becomes light and easy, so that we confidently pass through; as Christ also invites thither and says: Come unto me all ye that labor and are heavy-laden, I will give you rest; for my yoke is easy and my burden is light; as if he meant to say: Do not be grieved by what I lay upon you in the world. For it is a yoke and a burden to the flesh, and is called a narrow way and a strait gate; but only adhere to me and I will make it very easy and pleasant for you, and give you so much strength that you can easily go that way; and not only so, but you shall also experience that it will become lovely and sweet for you.

For this is certainly true, if we rightly look at both sides, that believers have the advantage, so that they ought not willingly to exchange with the ungodly. Although these live in luxury and those must suffer much; yet these trouble and worry themselves ten times as much as we do, with their poisonous, restless hatred, and with so many fruitless schemes, how they may harm us, and all sorts of evil practices and tricks, with which they criminate themselves, so that they still have no good conscience nor a real cheerful hour, and they are their own devil here upon earth; and yet they do not accomplish anything more thereby against us, than to befoul and oppress us somewhat, as much as God allows them.

But those who believe in Christ do not need these cares and troubles, and can still have a cheerful heart and conscience. Although we are somewhat distressed, and the devil annoys us: yet he must again refrain, and we are refreshed by the word, so that our burden and distress become sweet and we have only half a torment, outwardly in the external man; but they are doubly tormented by the devil, they have their hell both here and there, with perpetual torment and unrest of conscience, of murder and blood, so that they cannot have any cheerful, good thoughts toward God, although outwardly they may have a little joy and pleasure. So they are rightly served, as the Scripture says: *Duplici contritione conteres eos Domine,* Lord, destroy them with double destruction.

See, thus the Lord means with all fidelity both to have us warned and comforted, so that we do not care if our life is embittered, and we must see and feel so much vexation in the world, because if we look at it aright, it is only half-embittered, and through Christ, on whom we believe, everything in our heart becomes sweet and conduces to life and eternal joy. What harms it then, if the old Adam is somewhat worried about it?

50

Verse 15

BEWARE OF FALSE PROPHETS, WHICH COME TO YOU IN SHEEP'S CLOTHING, BUT INWARDLY THEY ARE RAVENING WOLVES.

Hitherto the Lord has been correctly presenting both doctrine and life, and warning against that which is contrary to it, and injures or hinders. In addition to that he now also adds a warning, so that we beware lest, whilst all is right both in doctrine and practice, teachers may secretly arise among us who under the name and semblance of genuine preachers and of the gospel, may introduce something else, and pervert and ruin both the doctrine and life.

For it cannot be otherwise than that the true, pure teaching of the gospel must on every hand be attacked by the devil in all sorts of ways, both externally and internally, as Christ taught from the beginning of this sermon: that he who means to be a Christian must consider this; that he will have as enemies, first, those who are outside of Christendom, who will oppose, hate and injure him, striking and throttling him, or at least reviling, cursing and condemning; and it is settled that he who has no haters, revilers, and persecutors is not a Christian, or at least has not yet proved his Christianity by outward act and confession. For, as soon as he makes a profession, the world becomes his enemy, and if it can it will surely kill him for it. These are now open enemies and outside of Christendom, that every one can see and readily feel.

But in addition to these (Christ means to say here), you will have another kind of enemies that are not without and deny the doctrine, but who grow up among you, bear and boast of your name—these, first of all, do the great harm. For the others, though they make a great ado, cannot do more than take body and goods; but my heart and my faith they cannot take from me by violence. But these are not after body and goods, but let me keep what I have; but they cunningly reach after the doctrine, that they may take the treasure itself out of my heart, namely, the dear word, on account of which we suffer persecution from those enemies. This is indeed a lamentable business, that those who are called our brethren, and profess also the Christian doctrine, set themselves up against us and under the same name set aside the true doctrine and introduce another; as St. Paul also warns his Ephesians, and predicts (Acts 20): Of your own selves shall men arise, speaking perverse things, etc. That is (I say) especially a lamentable thing that those should do it who are among us and of us, whom we regard as upright, and against whom we cannot protect ourselves until they have begun to do harm.

This is the persecution in Christendom that was predicted throughout the Scriptures, and has lasted in fact from the beginning of the world. For so it was with Moses among his people, yes, Jacob, Isaac and Abraham in their families, and Adam, who had only two sons, yet one of them had to instigate mischief.

And I think we have now had sufficient experience of it ourselves. How many there were who at first held with us and began [to follow] the gospel against the pope, so that it seemed as though we would have the whole world with us? But just when we were about to carry everything before us, our own people fall to work and do us more harm than all the princes, kings and emperors could have done. Well, what shall we do about it? They do us great injury, and besides strengthen our enemies against us, who cry out, There one can see what our teaching is, since we are not a unit among ourselves, and the Holy Ghost cannot be with us, since we ourselves persecute, abuse and revile one another, etc. We must endure this, that the enemies be strengthened by this scandal, and we be weakened and reviled, and thus have both our enemies and our brethren against us, so that in fact there is no greater tribulation in Christendom, in external matters, so far as our teaching is concerned.

Since now we must always expect this, and cannot avoid it, Christ gives us along with this sermon both a consolation and a warning. The consolation is, that we are not to be alarmed, or to trouble ourselves to death in regard to this wretched tribulation, as we see and feel it, that we who confess the word of God are not a unit among ourselves; but, taught by his word, say thus in response to it: That I knew very well before, when I wanted to be a Christian, that it would be just as my Lord Christ beforehand predicted, that I must have two kinds of enemies, both from without and also from within, from my own dearest friends and brethren. Therefore this shall not frighten me off and make me apostatize from the doctrine, as if it were to be wrong for the reason that those set themselves against me who have been my brethren. Why, Christ himself had Judas, his betrayer, with him, and what he taught and did was not false or wrong because his dearest disciple deserted him and did the mischief. Therefore, we must not mind our Judases.

But the warning is, that we should certainly expect this and diligently take care and be on our guard that these parties do not deceive us, but we must arm ourselves against them and learn to know them. For by his saying: Beware, he means to teach that we are not to be yielding or impatient, but to open our eyes, be wakeful, cautious and wise. For against those external enemies we need nothing more than patience, that we may suffer what they lay upon us, and be firm; but here it avails not to suffer, or yield, but to beware and see to it that I do not entrust a word even to my brother in confidence, but look with sharp, wakeful eyes only at the word, and trust no man who is now with me, who to-day can preach with me, but to-morrow perhaps against me. And no one should think himself safe, as not needing this exhortation. For it is such a dangerous, subtle temptation, that even the most spiritually minded have trouble enough to avoid being deceived by it. But the rest, that are secure and careless, cannot at all prevent their being misled. Therefore he does not without reason add the word: Beware.

For the semblance and name is too attractive, so that no one can recognize it (as we shall hear) who does not have the correct understanding of the word of God, and besides with all diligence gives heed to it, and lets it be his supreme care to hold it pure and undiluted.

For see how he depicts them, the false teachers, according to their appearance and aspect. In the first place he gives the name, that they are called and are prophets, that is teachers and preachers; and are proud of it that they are not otherwise called or regarded, have just the same ministerial office, the same Scriptures, and the same God whom they boast of as the others; and yet they are false prophets. For he is speaking here of those who preach by virtue of their office. For the others, who act without official authority, are not fit to be called false prophets; but tramps and scamps, that ought to be turned over to the rabble, and are not to be endured, (even if they do teach aright,) when they want to interfere with the office and sphere of others, in violation of established order; or secretly and thievishly to creep into corners, where no one unauthorized ought to offer a sermon of his own, or to insinuate himself, although he may hear and know that the public preaching is false, as he is not responsible for that. For God established this office, as others, so that we are not to act contrary to it; but he who does not rightly discharge it will have to answer for himself, and will surely find his judge.

Secondly, says he, that they come in sheep's clothing, so that one cannot blame them, nor outwardly distinguish them from other true preachers. These two things it is that do harm, that they hold the true office, and besides come with such beautiful attire and semblance, that one cannot say anything else than that they are true, pious preachers, who seek every one's welfare; as they charmingly profess, and can swear to it, handling only the name and word of God. This spreads very rapidly and hurries the people violently along, like a flood, so that one cannot resist it. For who is there among the rabble that can or dare set himself against these and rebuke them? Yes, who knows how to guard himself against them, since they come with God's name and word (as they boast)?

But Christ herewith warns us against both, so that we are not to be influenced by the fact that they hold the office, although this is necessary,

and belongs to a preacher; but no one is thereby assured that he is therefore to believe him, as if he could not in the office be a scoundrel: as it is
not unusual in the world that there be in all offices and grades in society
many scamps and low fellows that abuse their position. They may be called
prophets indeed (says Christ); but beware, and see to it that they are not
false prophets. In like manner, be not misled, if they come in sheep's clothing with the precious name and semblance. For here you are told that under
that there may be hidden a ravening wolf. Therefore beware again that the
sheep's clothing do not deceive you. For they must all wear that beautiful
covering and semblance if they are to deceive the people.

And this is just the difference between these secret and the other open
enemies. For the latter rush in among us openly, so that every one readily knows them; but these come among us in the same office that we have,
employ also the same Scriptures and words for appearance sake; but they
come (says Christ,) of their own accord; that is, although they have the
office, yet they bring the word and doctrine that God has not entrusted to
them, nor did he send them for that, but their own dreams and devil's doctrine, adorned with God's name. Therefore be especially warned against the
sheep's clothing, so that you trust no one, however great a show he makes,
but look only at the word, whether he rightly handles that, or under cover
of it is selling his own wares.

See, if we would now accept this warning, and regulate ourselves
according to the words of Christ, we could easily guard ourselves against
all false prophets and preachers. But that they are so rapidly multiplying is
owing to the fact that we who hear the true gospel do not earnestly accept
it, do not take care that we truly have and hold it; move along in such a
sleepy, lazy way, as if we could not go astray. That is the reason why we
are deceived by this excellent show and semblance, before we are aware
of it. For as soon as another new teacher comes and begins, then the word:
attendite, beware, is forgotten, with which we ought to be equipped, and
we ought so to hear every one as though we did not hear him, but were
looking at and attending to the word alone. Those are trifling, unsettled
spirits, that look only into the preachers' mouths, and suddenly run after
them, through curiosity that makes them eager for novelties, so that they

think: O, I heard that one before, now I must hear this one too, he is a fine, learned, holy man, etc. There the devil has already gained a foothold, and ensnared them before they are aware of it, drives and leads them as he pleases, from one conspiracy into another; as St. Paul says of these (Eph. 4:14) that they are like a reed, tossed to and fro, and carried about with every wind of doctrine. If to-day or to-morrow some one else appears, they rush after and listen to him.

The reason is, they have no certain understanding in their heart of God's word, have little regard besides for the gospel; think, if they have heard it once or twice, that they know it and now have it all: they are soon tired of it, open their eyes and ears if some one comes that brings something new; and it happens with them, as with Adam and Eve, misled by the serpent; who gazed at the forbidden tree and imagined these beautiful thoughts against the word of God: Why should we not eat just from this tree? because thus eager and curious, so that they became tired of all the other trees in the whole of Paradise and gazed only at this one, etc.

But if it were a serious matter with us in regard to the gospel, and we were carefully living so as to keep the treasure pure and clean, we would not be so easily deceived. For I hope indeed that no factious spirit shall so easily upset me, because I know that the gospel is true, and I would not like to lose it. But if some one comes in beautiful sheep's clothing, I will not look at his mask, as if I wanted to hear something else or new: but [I ask] whether he agrees with my gospel. If not, then thank God, I am thoroughly assured that he is a false prophet and a ravening wolf under his sheep's clothing.

Thus the devilish spirits have the twofold advantage, that we are such heedless, secure and frivolous people, and they can trick themselves out in the beautiful wool of the sheep. For by sheep's clothing he means not bad conduct and gross sin, as of the heathen and unchristian people; but the excellent name and reputation of real Christians, that have holy baptism, sacrament, Christ, and everything that belongs to Christ. They must bring all this along. For no one must come along and say: This I say; but thus: Dear friends, this Christ says, here you have God's word and the Scriptures, this you must believe, if you wish to be saved; he who teaches otherwise deceives you, etc.; they make use of the precious name of Christ, and God, and the awful, grand words: God's honor, truth, eternal salvation, and whatever other words like these thereto belonging. If now any one hears these excellent words, and is so earnestly exhorted in view of his soul's salvation and destruction, he becomes alarmed; and surrenders himself at once, if he is not well furnished and decided against it. For it cuts like a sharp razor, and strikes through body and soul. That is a part of the sheep's clothing.

Besides, they embellish themselves with wonderful works and ways, go about in gray coats, look morose, and lead a hard, strict life with fasting, bodily mortifications, hard couches, etc., and do not live at all like other ordinary people. That makes again a great impression, and captivates the people admirably, so that they fall in by crowds; and such a villain with a single sermon can mislead a whole city that has had the word of God for a long while, and make them forget in an hour what they have heard for ten years; so that even I, if I wished, would easily undertake in two or three sermons to preach my people back again into the papacy, and get up new pilgrimages and masses, by means of this show and special sanctity. For the rabble is, as was said, easily thereby persuaded, and at any rate curious and eager to hear what is new.

See, thus must they embellish themselves, both in doctrine and practice, so that they employ the same words that we hear, and along with this lead a beautiful attractive life; as now our anabaptist sectaries, in fact, mislead many people by crying out that we do not have the real gospel, because one may see that it yields no fruit, and the people continue to be bad, proud, avaricious, etc.; that there must be something more than the mere word and letter: the Spirit must do it, and they must honestly strive to live better; if it were the word of God it would surely also produce fruit. Then they go on and say they have the true understanding, and the right fruits and life. If a simple, inexperienced man hears this, he says: O, that is really so! lets himself thus be carried away by the taking words: Spirit, and fruits of the Spirit. Then they go further, and say: He who wants to be a Christian must not share in civil authority, or bear a sword, or have anything of his own, as it is with us; but he is a true Christian who proves

it by his works, forsakes everything, does not accept any secular authority and rule; dresses in a gray coat; suffers hunger and sorrow, etc. These
they call fruits of the Spirit. See, these are nothing but sheep's clothing;
with these they carry away crowds of the poor people.

Who can now recognize the wolf under this and guard against him?
Answer: I know no other counsel than, as I have said, that every one first
see to it that he is sure of his case and of the doctrine, and have so settled it
in his heart that he can adhere to the doctrine, although he see everybody
upon earth teaching and living otherwise. For he who wishes to get along
safely must absolutely not look at any outward marks in Christendom and
shape his course after them, but must look alone to the word that shows
the true way of living that avails before God. As, for example, the principal topic and sum of the Christian doctrine is this, that God has sent and
given his Son, Christ, and alone through him forgives us all our sins, jus-
tifies and saves us. That you are to cling to, and nothing else. Then, if you
look about you, you will see a great variety of dissimilar personalities and
modes of living, that one is a man, woman, master, servant, prince, subject, rich, poor, representing the various callings or offices that are in the
world, and all so mixed up together that I can see nothing that has a peculiar appearance [about any of them]. But as I am so settled in mind, and
know that main topic in which I have the whole summed up, my heart concludes thus: Suppose I see a husband or a girl, master or servant, learned
man or layman, clothed in gray or red, fasting or eating, looking grave
or laughing; what have I to do with that? In short, what that difference is
that I see [in them], that is all the same to me. For I understand this, that a
maid in a red dress, or a prince in his golden garment, can be just as good a
Christian as a beggar in a gray coat or a monk in a woolen or hair shirt, and
I am with such an understanding safe against all sorts of external masks.

But he who does not hold this main truth, or know how to regulate
everything by it, cannot avoid being deceived by these masks, when he sees
one happy with his wife and children, or splendidly and richly dressed,
etc., and another looking demure, fasting much, barefoot, and in a gray
cowl, and he concludes at once: O, that is a holy man! the others are of no
account; and keeps gaping thus after the masks, out of humor; is not smart

enough to say: Can there be a rogue lying hidden under the gray coat? as a Christian can conclude and say: Dear monk, if you wear your gray coat not of necessity, but with the peculiar notion that you will be regarded by others as something peculiar, then you are a desperate, double scoundrel, making the people gape by your pretended sanctity; otherwise you would have to say: If a farmer, who is ploughing or manuring upon his field is just as good a Christian as I, and will get to heaven, what do I want with my peculiar way of living?

But, as I have said, the great common mass hankers after these masks that fill their eyes and make a special show, so that it amounts to nothing if one preaches long against them. And we are besides naturally inclined to this doctrine and works. For it is well pleasing to reason, which always likes to deal with God with its own works. Thus it happens that the devil through these teachers prompts and agitates until he has quite persuaded us.

But we who want to go safely must before anything else see to it, as I have always taught, that we are firmly rooted in our main point, concerning Christ; then we can correctly judge concerning all outward masks and styles, and the Spirit will duly teach and lead us. Thus every one will find enough real good works to do in his calling, if he wants to be pious, so that he need not seek for anything special.

For, are you a prince, judge, husband, servant, maid, etc., and are you to practice and prove your faith, to fill your place and calling properly, and do what is right: then you will surely get so much to do and to work, that no Carthusian will have a harder order to work for than you. For what sort of great trouble and hard work is that, for him to wear a gray coat or hood, or walk in wooden shoes, or mortify his body a little, if he be somewhat strict, and yet along with that live without care and worry, and have enough to gormandize and guzzle? But this one must eat his daily bread in the sweat of his face and with hard work, and must let not alone his body but rather his heart be plagued by the wicked world and his neighbors, and expect and endure all misfortune, discord and affliction; so that a true citizen's calling, conducted in a Christian way, is more than a ten-fold Carthusian order; except that it does not make a show, like the monk, who wears a hood, is separated from the people, etc., and yet, if we open our eyes and rightly compare the two, even reason must come to the same conclusion. Thus also a prince, although he wears golden chains and a cloak of marten fur, but is pious, yet he is under the marten cloak such a plagued and miserable man, that you cannot find his like in any monastery. Thus go through all offices and callings. If you find a pious man or woman, you need not look there for a monk or a nun; for he or she is already monk or nun enough, and is living in a harder order than all the hood and tonsure wearers; yes, it is all tomfoolery before God with all the monks and hermits, in contrast with a pious child, servant or maid, who is obedient to duty. Only do what a pious man or woman ought to do, there you have a rule that is harder to follow than the rules, hoods and tonsures of St. Francis and of all the monks, which cover rather a scoundrel than a pious Christian.

But proud reason will not look at this, but disregards it and thinks: O that is a common affair, that every one may have at home! gapes after something else that is strange and odd, looks in wonder, follows the continual bawling; which is all a mere false show, with which they come along and so dress up their trifling way of living as to put contempt upon all else that are God's ordinances and callings, as if they were of no account. But it is all owing to this, that we do not take hold of the word of God with real earnestness, or we would soon say: Let the Carthusians come on, and the Anabaptists, the devil himself or his mother, they could not make better callings or ways of living than God has made.

Therefore we must count every calling as excellent, high, divine, whether it be that of a pious husband, servant, maid or faithful laborer, and could thus rightly judge according to the word about all works and callings, and every one could rightly teach and live, and everything would move along splendidly. Those would be the right callings which God has ordered and established, and which he approves; and if God granted that we could bring it to pass that a city would have many of these pious citizens, women, children, masters, servants and maids, we should have heaven upon earth, and would need no monasteries, and should have no need of fasting, or praying and singing all day long in the churches, but simply of doing what their various offices and callings require.

Thus you see what the kinds of sheep's clothing are with which they set the people gaping. But what are they inside and in fact? Nothing else (says Christ) than ravening wolves. That is what they seek, the desperate scamps, that they with a beautiful show of doctrine and life may ruin and destroy souls. Not outwardly, as the tyrants and persecutors, who destroy life and property; also, not as the preachers, who publicly preach against us and condemn our doctrine, etc.: but inwardly, that they secretly tear away the treasure of our heart, which has now become the throne or kingdom and dwelling-place of God. That is, all their scoundrelism that they so adorn with doctrine and life, aims at destroying the faith and the foundation article concerning Christ; as now the Anabaptists outwardly bear our name, and indeed acknowledge that we have the gospel, with the word and preaching; but there follows (they say) no fruit. Just with this word: No fruit, they turn the attention of the people from faith to works, and they push aside the main thing, which is faith in Christ, and they lead us away so that we are to look alone at the fruits; if these appear, then it is the true gospel, and *vice versa*; and their whole teaching is nothing else than that one must do his utmost and make a display with the fruits, have no private property, forsake everything, etc.; fall back again upon their works, and place their confidence in them, as thereby to be saved. And what is the worst, they do not teach the true fruits, which the gospel teaches and demands after faith, but what they dream about and imagine; say nothing about how every one is to follow his calling properly and faithfully, and abide in it, but just the contrary; lead the people away from these callings, teach them to forsake them as worldly, and run away from them, and look at something that is peculiar; look morose, live severely, stop eating, drinking, dressing like other people, let themselves be tortured and killed willingly and when not required. Else (say they) the gospel yields no fruit in you, and you are still no Christian, although you have long been believing, etc.

And these their dreams they adorn with the Scriptures and quotations from the gospel, though Christ never taught or required this, neither by word nor example, that we are to run away from the community, forsake everything, have nothing of our own, except when it becomes necessary that we must either do this or give up his word. Therefore you must not forsake these things before he orders you, or you are forced to do it. If it comes to that, then say: Before I will forsake Christ and the gospel, rather may go wife, child, body and goods, sun, moon, and all creatures. But apart from necessity you have God's command, that you are to love your neighbor, serve and help him with body and goods, in like manner to love and rule your wife, child, domestics, not run off from them and desert them, as these [fanatics] do, against the word and ordinance of God, altogether without necessity, and yet they want to boast of the great fruits of the gospel, as special saints.

Learn thus to recognize these spirits, as they under the sheep's clothing inwardly raven, and take away the faith, lead you from Christ back upon yourself, and call this fruits of the gospel, which they themselves imagine, by which they destroy the real fruits. That is what these ravening wolves are in sheep's clothing that have always been injuring Christianity. Hitherto they have been called monks; now they are Anabaptists, as a new sort of monks; in old times they were Pelagians, Ishmælites, Esauites, Canaanites. For this faith has continued since the beginning of the world; and although these Anabaptists may get out of the way, others will certainly come.

In short, monkery will endure as long as the world stands, although with other new names and methods. For all that go about getting up something peculiar, beyond faith and ordinary callings, these are and remain monks, although they do not use the same kind of style, clothing or methods. It is true we can easily be on our guard against these that go about with hood and tonsure; for they are now sufficiently marked, so that every one knows them. But beware of the new monks, that do not wear hoods, but yet start some other odd notions, pretend great devotion and sanctity, with demure looks, gray coats, and a strict mode of living; they say, one must not wear satin or silk, red or variegated clothes, just as those monks also taught, so that still it is monkery all the same, only with a different mask. Therefore, the artists have hit it exactly, when they paint the devil in a monk's hood with his devil's claws sticking out below. For he has been doing nothing else from the beginning of the world than to mislead the world by monkery.

51

Verses 16 through 20

YE SHALL KNOW THEM BY THEIR FRUITS. DO MEN
GATHER GRAPES OF THORNS, OR FIGS OF THISTLES?
EVEN SO EVERY GOOD TREE BRINGETH FORTH GOOD
FRUIT; BUT A CORRUPT TREE BRINGETH FORTH EVIL
FRUIT. A GOOD TREE CANNOT BRING FORTH EVIL
FRUIT, NEITHER CAN A CORRUPT TREE BRING FORTH
GOOD FRUIT. EVERY TREE THAT BRINGETH NOT FORTH
GOOD FRUIT IS HEWN DOWN AND CAST INTO THE FIRE.
WHEREFORE BY THEIR FRUITS YE SHALL KNOW THEM.

Since the Lord Christ has warned his followers to hold firmly to his doctrine, and to beware of their being misled by others who under sheep's
clothing are ravening wolves: he now instructs them also, as an additional
warning, how they are to recognize them by their fruits, and he uses an
illustration in plain, simple words that even a child can understand. For no
one is so simple as not to know that a thorn-bush bears no figs or grapes,
etc. But however simple the words are, yet no one sees how much they mean
unless he diligently considers the word of God. But it all depends upon this,
that we understand what he means by a good or bad tree or fruit. For it is
easily said: This is a fig-tree or a thistle, a good apple or a sour wild plum,
and with the eyes and reason it can be easily seen and understood; but as
Christ here uses it, there is no other way to explain it except by spiritual
comprehension, according to God's word. For we heard above how these

same false teachers employ such semblances and smooth words, that reason cannot judge them, or guard itself against them. Yes, it is just that kind of doctrine and life that grows out of reason and suits it, and is naturally pleasing to us, because it teaches about our own doing and working, which we understand and can do.

By a good tree that brings forth good fruit is meant, in short, one who lives and conducts his walk and conversation according to the word of God, pure and simple. For he means to tell hereafter also of many who have heard the word of God, and also say: Lord, Lord, and besides have done many wonderful works, and yet are false and hypocritical. Therefore we must here completely silence reason and follow the word of God alone, and then infer, if we wish to judge about life and works, that we may know what God's word calls a good tree or good fruits. For this is too much for reason, (as I said,) if it sees a man who wears nothing but a gray coat, fasts every week, as the Pharisee in the gospel, yes who also does wonderful works and miracles, that he should not be a good tree with good fruits. For it cannot look any higher, or think and understand any better, is badly caught by it, so that it concludes he who leads a different life from other people, he must be a peculiar, holy man; she sees not, the blind fool, that these works are all still far, far from the word of God.

And if you now ask: Whence do you know that these works are so precious as you make them out to be? it can give no other answer than: I think so. There, go to the dogs with your thinking, if I am to trust my soul's salvation upon it. The rule is: you must know, and not imagine or think, and you must have a sure basis and evidence from the word of God, so that he is satisfied, and you can say: The work is well done, the calling is well pleasing to God, that I know; not according to my own light or star, so that it appears good or evil to me; but that is decided by the word and command of God. It does not seem to me that a husband, or wife, or prince, or judge is as holy as one who creeps into corners or goes into the wilderness: but it does not avail to decide according to my thinking; and although some one should exorcise devils and do all the miracles that the apostles did, I would rather be servant to a shoemaker or a dishwasher according to God's word, and I will consider this calling superior to your thinking, even if you could raise the dead. Therefore adhere to it that bringing forth good fruits means that kind of life and good works that are in the line of God's word and command.

Thus these words—by their fruits ye shall know them—are given as a token and set as a sign whereby they can be judged and recognized. If we are deceived, it is no one's fault but our own. For he has not left us in doubt, but has drawn the picture clear and distinct. If you cannot judge them (says he,) because of their sheep's clothing, then observe their fruits and works, whether these are upright and good.

Yes, (you say,) how am I to recognize these? they too may themselves be deceptive. Answer: You surely know what God's commands are; then see whether they agree with them. For I will assuredly warrant you that no captious spirit will come without making it perfectly sure and leaving a stench behind him that one may see that the devil has been there; and there has never yet a false doctrine or heresy made its appearance without bringing the characteristic mark along with it which he here indicates, that it has proposed other works than those which God has commanded and ordained. That now the world is misled is owing entirely to its following wild reason and neglecting the word of God, paying no attention to what he commands and gaping after the pretenders, if it only sees something odd.

He who wishes to judge rightly here, let him do as Christ teaches, and set before himself their works and fruits, and contrast them with the word or command of God, and he will soon see how these coincide. Look at the very holiest Carthusian monk with his strict order, and St. Paul on the other hand with the ten commandments, and you will see that St. Paul preaches in this style: If you have Christ through faith, then let every one be obedient and subject to the authorities, and exercise love toward one another in all callings. See, there you have a true mirror of a Christian life, according to God's command and ordinance. In contrast with this comes that factious spirit and says: O that is of no account! There are many bad people in the [different] callings, and it is all a worldly matter, etc.; ah, we must seek something better. So he goes along and makes something peculiar and odd, comes parading along in a hood or a gray coat; that must now be a grand life and a perfect calling.

But if you are firmly rooted in God's word, you can soon judge and say: Where has God commanded you to get special callings and works in opposition to the common callings that he has ordained? I know very well that there are many bad fellows and pious people in all callings; but what concern is that of mine how they abuse them? I will still abide by the word that teaches me that such callings are good, although there are bad people in them. That is what I look at and regulate myself by; and because the calling is good, the works and fruits, performed according to the word of God, just as the calling demands, must also be right and good. But because your calling has no word of God for it, the works, done in the calling, cannot be good, and both tree and fruit are rotten and of no use.

Thus you have a sure judgment, that cannot deceive you, as Christ teaches you, to know them by their fruits. For I have also read about all the heretics and fanatics, and have found that they one and all every time put forth something different from what God had ordered and commanded, one on this subject and another on that. One forbade to eat all kinds of food; another marriage; the third denounced the civil authority; and each one took up something peculiar to himself, so that they all must walk in this track.

Therefore it lies (as I have said), entirely in this, that one properly knows and holds the definition, what Christ calls good works or fruits, namely, that a good work is that which is ordered or commanded by the word of God and is covered by that command. As a married woman who is pious and deports herself rightly can say this and boast that her calling is commanded by God and has the right, pure, unadulterated word of God, and heartily pleases God. Therefore her works are all good fruits; so that one is to judge and decide a thing to be good not because we think so, but because God says so and pronounces it good. Adhere to this, and you cannot go astray as they must do. For the judgment stands, that they cannot teach any proper fruits. God also thinks the same way about this, so that they must preach nothing else than about purely invented juggleries; and, because they despise real fruits and works, as not having any special show about them, he too despises their foul works that they put forth with great show, and presume to do things better than he has done.

It is a proverb, invented by the priests, and I think the devil himself mocked them with it: When our Lord God made a priest the devil was looking on, and wanted to imitate him, and he made the tonsure too broad and it turned out a monk; therefore they are the devil's creatures. That is said by way of a joke, but it is nevertheless the pure truth. For where the devil sees that God orders obedience and love to one another, and constitutes an excellent, spiritual little assemblage, he cannot refrain from building his chapel or beer-shop alongside of the church, and also afterwards teaching his monkery, poverty, gray coats, etc., so that always the monks are the devil's priests; for they preach the doctrine of devils (as Paul also calls it) wrought out of their own imaginings, and they claim to be wiser than God and to do his work better than he does.

Therefore Christ now means to say: If you wish to know and judge them, keep to the pure word of God, that you may be sure what the right fruits are and see how they accord with them: thus you will surely find that they teach and practice otherwise than as God has commanded; from that you can certainly also test the tree, that it is not good; and they consider this a coarse, childish comparison. Can one gather grapes from thorns or figs from thistles? Yes, very well, (they think) should not we be able to do that? Why one may gather pure sugar from them. For these works are by far more valuable, according to their notion, than those God has ordered. But look at the two kinds of trees, the vine or fig-tree, and in contrast the thorn-bush or thistle. Thistles and thorns may also bloom, but what kind of fruit do they produce? But the fig-tree, however, is such a simple tree, makes no boast of its fruits or leaves, puts forth no leaves before the fruit is at hand, but before you are aware it produces fruit. So also the vine, it is more completely destitute of show and glory than any other tree, a mere thin, weak wood; yet it bears the very sweetest grapes, better than any other growth, whilst other trees plume themselves upon their leaves and flowers, so that one should think that they would yield pure sugar; and yet they produce nothing but these sour fruits that are of no use. Thus also here these have the show and make a racket with their boasting of special works as if they alone were doing it: and when the bloom is over, there are nothing but medlars that are quite full of stones, neither nourishing nor feeding anybody,

or thistle heads that only prick or scratch if one takes hold of them. For
if one contrasts with them the command of God, whether God has commanded and ordered these works, and whether they have been done for
the service and benefit of a neighbor, it is seen that they are of no account
and only hinder the real good works. Again, as to the other callings, they
make no show, do not shine and glitter, and yet they yield the very finest,
best fruits, and cause the greatest benefit upon earth, but [they do this]
before God, and before those who are enlightened through spiritual eyes,
so that they can rightly look at and judge the matter.

Therefore he now speaks thus: Can one also gather figs from thorns? As
if he would say: It may bloom beautifully, but wait a little, and see when
the time comes to gather the fruit what you will find then. For nothing
more will come of it than that people are thereby deceived that have been
waiting for large, valuable fruit, and yet find nothing which they or others
can comfort themselves with or enjoy; besides the harm is done, that even
the very highest reason is deceived and misled by this phantom, gotten up
by the devil, which has not God's word and sound understanding, but follows its own notion and devotion and supposes if this pleases it, this must
also please God; but it should be turned the other way, so that I am glad
to hear what pleases him, although there are vexatious things in all God's
callings, and besides there are many bad people in them that injure these
fruits, just like miserable worms.

And this comparison he concludes with a common saying which he
was fond of using elsewhere: Every good tree bringeth forth good fruit,
and an evil tree bringeth forth evil fruit. But what is the need of teaching
this in so many words? Who does not know this already? Why a blind man
could tell it by the bush; and he thinks us such fools that we don't know
this? Well, he who knows it, let him know it; but we are willing to learn it
and remain Christ's scholars. For, as was said, it is not such an easy art to
decide in regard to this doing, of which Christ is speaking. But this saying
serves to comfort and strengthen such as are in those callings that reason
does not consider desirable or respectable so that there is much vexation
in them and much evil is done in them, by which many people are startled,
so that they are considered dangerous, as if one could not easily serve God

in them, etc.; with this St. Augustine worried and plagued himself greatly, even when he was already a great doctor, so that he would have been glad to see everything right, and to separate from the callings what was bad, and the Pelagian heretics made him a great deal of trouble with this matter: as nearly all the heretics have aimed at making things perfectly pure, and, (pardon the expression) have totally befouled them.

But why need we go far to find it? It is here admirably put, and in a few words: The calling that God has created and ordained, and the man who moves and lives in this calling according to the word of God, he can produce nothing but good fruits. With that you can now console your heart against these thoughts: Alas, this or that one has put me into this calling! There is nothing but disgust and trouble in it! This has often assailed me in regard to my office, and it still does, so that, if it were not for the word of God, I would long since have foresworn the preaching of a sermon, and would have given good-bye to the world; as the monks used to do. But that is the work of the devil himself, who makes every one's calling so burdensome to him, and so blinds proud reason that it cannot recognize the office and work that God assigns to us and which is heartily pleasing to him, and thus it ruins its own calling and fruits. For it would surely be a good tree and a good calling; but reason does not see it and stands in its own light, so that it cannot bring forth good fruits.

Therefore learn to look at your calling thus according to this saying, so that you may thence conclude: Now I know, thank God, that I am in a good, happy calling, that pleases God; although it is vexatious to the flesh, has much trouble and dissatisfaction, all that I will cheerfully endure. For here I have the consolation that Christ says: A good tree yields good fruit, in all callings comprehended in God's word, although they are despised and depreciated by the world and the special saints. On the other hand, I hear the decision, that every evil tree brings forth evil fruit: so that when I see the holiest Carthusian, I see a worthless, evil tree, although he makes a fine display and has not so much worry and opposition. For the devil does not embitter and burden him as he does the true, divine callings. Therefore those callings and works they are well pleased with.

But just as little as I can see in my calling that my fruit is good, just so little also can he see that his calling and fruit is evil and of no value; and this saying must be inverted among them, and read thus: An evil tree brings forth good fruit, and a good tree brings forth evil fruit; so that, in short, here reason cannot judge, nor see the goodness of its calling and its works, or derive joy or pleasure from them; but it praises the opposite. For, if we could see it, we should move along in constant joy, and should suffer and endure everything with a cheerful heart that God lays upon us, assured that because the tree is good its fruits must also be good; so that if a pious farming servant hauls a wagonload of manure to the field he is hauling a load of valuable figs and grapes; but [this he does] in the sight of God, not in our eyes, who do not believe, hence every one becomes tired of his calling and gapes after another.

That is now what Christ means when he concludes so bluntly and directly: A good tree brings forth good fruit, and the opposite; and, to make it still stronger, he adds with seeming superfluity, and says: A good tree cannot bring forth evil fruit, and an evil tree cannot bring forth good fruit. How, cannot a servant or a maid be a scoundrel? Cannot a man or a woman commit adultery? Cannot a prince be a tyrant, or a preacher be an impostor? You have said the same yourself. Where are we to look for scamps and scoundrels except in the various trades and callings? Answer; Yes, that is only too true; but in that case he is no longer a good tree, for he goes beyond his calling and lives in opposition to God's command. But if he abides in his calling or office, and does what this demands, he canot be an evil tree. Therefore says he: Only be careful to remain a good tree and I will warrant you that what you do cannot be evil. For the works that God has ordered must have the praise that they cannot be called evil.

What better thing could we now desire than to have this praise and testimony from Christ himself, against all factious spirits and such as make special claims to sanctity, that we know that we are in such a calling in which we cannot do evil, if we live in accordance with God's word and do what is our duty. Yes, even if something evil should intervene, if we overdo things not purposely or wilfully, but through ignorance or weakness, this must also be good and pardoned. In short you cannot spoil it, because you are in the divine office and word, only abide in that and it cannot be evil; or, although it would otherwise be sin, yet it must not be called evil, but be covered over and forgiven; so richly shall you be blessed through the word of God. Just as a fig-tree, or other tree, although it sometimes bears a worm-eaten fruit, yet this is still a good fruit, after its kind, without prickle or thorn; yes, rather than have no fruit at all, it must have fruit that is worm-eaten, yet innocently so; thus all the works of a Christian are of a good kind, because the tree is good, and he so lives that he would gladly bring forth only good fruit, although sometimes through the weakness of the flesh, or some other hindrance, something evil slips in.

On the other hand, those thorn-bushes and thistles, if they should do their best, cannot bring forth any good fruit that may be called a good apple or fig. And no Carthusian or barefooted monk, if he should pray and torture himself to death, could say a Lord's Prayer that God would call good or do any good work; but the more he would do, and worry himself to do good works, the worse he would make it. For it is decided: A thistle bears no figs, and a thorn-bush no grapes; and in short: an evil tree cannot bring forth good fruit. That sounds like severe and strict denunciation of all self-constituted orders and callings, that they cannot do a single good work; and on the other hand like admirably comforting us, so that we who live according to God's word cannot do evil.

Thereupon he now concludes: Every tree that bringeth not forth good fruit is cut off and cast into the fire. There you have the decision stated that shall be proclaimed in regard to all who teach and maintain their own works, aside from the word of God, who mean to accomplish and effect it that their cause must ever abide and think that God must spare them, as valuable trees and plants, and fence them in and take the best care of them: but do not perceive what a sentence has been pronounced against them, so that he has already detected the kind and marked it on the tree, as Christ elsewhere says, and that they are fit for nothing but the fire of hell. For it stands written: Every plant that my heavenly Father hath not planted shall be rooted up, etc.

This he has now spoken through comparisons, and as *in parabolis* or dark words. Now he goes further and means to explain what he meant thereby, and he adds the right comment, with clear, plain words, and says:

52

Verse 21

NOT EVERY ONE THAT SAITH UNTO ME, LORD, LORD, SHALL
ENTER INTO THE KINGDOM OF HEAVEN; BUT HE THAT
DOETH THE WILL OF MY FATHER WHICH IS IN HEAVEN.

That is, just those who serve me, and regard their way of worship as the
very best, and are earnestly concerned about entering into the kingdom
of heaven, and think they have it before all others, against these I will shut
heaven. That is a terrible decision, that no one is farther down in hell than
the greatest devotees, that is the most holy monks; as the devil also has
made a proverb, and himself made a mock of his saints, as a scoundrel who
himself cannot conceal his villainy, so that it is said: Hell is paved with the
tonsures of priests and monks. That is just what he says here, that those
who claim to be the greatest saints shall not enter the kingdom of heaven.
Why? For they say: Lord, Lord, (says he,) but they do not the will of my
Father which is in heaven. How is this? Are they not doing the will of God,
when they are serving God night and day, and besides are working miracles,
as is presently said? What shall become of the other great crowd if these
are not to be saved? Answer: You hear very plainly that he says No to this,
and makes a distinction between saying: Lord, Lord, and doing the will of
his Father; and he says; I do not want those who solemnly cry: Lord, Lord,
and come with their great devotion, as if I must lift them to heaven; but
those I want who do my Father's will. They hope and presume that they will

not only get to heaven, but will also by their merit bring others in, and will have high seats and receive special crowns, etc; as they confidently boast: Shall not a Carthusian merit more, and have a higher grade in heaven than a mere layman or a married woman? Else what does he gain in the monastery with his strict disciplines, etc.? But it is not: Carthusians or servants of God enter heaven, but those who do the will of God.

For to do the will of God does not mean to put on hoods or wear gray coats, and to run off from the community into monasteries, etc., for the scriptures have not a word about that; but it means this, that Christ has preached and taught, namely, that we believe in Christ, and be found in that calling that has [the sanction of] God's word, and do in it what he has commanded. Turn to the ten commandments and see how St. Paul out of these teaches those in all callings, how inferiors are to render fidelity and obedience to superiors, the others to love and serve each other, etc., and every one to be faithful in his office. There you find nothing about priestliness or monkery, gray coats, or other specialties. He now who lives in this way, he does the will of God, which he has himself indicated. These are fit for heaven, not those who neglect the word of God, and yet have meant to serve God with great earnestness and devotion, so that they say over and over again: Lord, Lord, whilst the rest of us hardly say it once. For these same persons are always busier and livelier in their worship than the real Christians; but since they have done their own will, they may also seek another Lord who may hear them and open heaven for them.

Therefore he means hereby to warn us again to be careful not to be misled by these who offer such great splendid worship (although they may even work miracles); but be content with what he calls good, so that everything is done in accordance with his command, although it makes no display, nor is pleasing to reason, because we have the test, that no factious spirit can be content with that, nor teach or bring forth good fruit, but they are busied merely with their own thoughts, spun out of their own head. These are now the first whom Christ rejects, that come and make the world full of forms of worship; as he predicted about them in Matt. 24:23: For there shall arise false Christ's and false prophets and shall say: Lo here is Christ, or there, and shall deceive many. Then others shall come who

not only say: Lord, Lord, but also do great wonders and signs. Concerning
this he now adds:

53

Verses 22 and 23

MANY WILL SAY TO ME IN THAT DAY, LORD, LORD, HAVE WE
NOT PROPHESIED IN THY NAME? AND IN THY NAME CAST
OUT DEVILS? AND IN THY NAME DONE MANY WONDERFUL
WORKS? AND THEN WILL I PROFESS UNTO THEM, I NEVER
KNEW YOU: DEPART FROM ME, YE THAT WORK INIQUITY.

These are now high, excellent people, and yet they are shamefully deceived
and altogether unexpectedly go to hell. The others of whom he has just been
speaking, go to the same place as a genial crowd, unless they are at the very
last converted; as I hope that, nevertheless, many of them have been saved
on their death-bed, converted from that error. But these claim to be sure
of heaven, begin to call God to account, and say: Are we not to be saved?
Surely we have preached in thy name and done so many wonderful works.

How can this now be, that they do wonderful works, and besides in the
name of Christ, and yet can be counted among false Christians and damned,
wicked people? I always thought, as it is also true, that God gives no sign
or testimony to confirm lies, as Moses says, Deut. 18:20, etc.: "If a prophet
shall presume to speak in my name, which I have not commanded him to
speak—and if thou say in thy heart, How shall we know the word which
the Lord hath spoken? When a prophet speaketh in the name of the Lord,
if the thing follow not, nor come to pass, that is the thing which the Lord

hath not spoken." And yet here the contrary is stated, that they do miracles in his name, and yet are false, wicked people.

First, this may be an answer, that they were once real Christians and truly preached and did wonderful works, but afterwards became apostates. For this is the very devil's [work], (against which also St. Paul warns his Corinthians,) if a Christian begins to feel that he is in advance of others, and has superior understanding, wisdom, and other gifts, so that he is self-satisfied and becomes proud, and he turns out to be such a man as shells himself out of the grain and nothing is left but the empty husk; he thinks nevertheless that he is pious and well off; as there have been many such people, and there are still many such. For it is an extremely dangerous thing, if God endows a man with high, excellent gifts, that he do not become proud, but continue humble. Thus we read about an ancient father in the wilderness, who had a peculiar gift to exorcise devils, and helped many people, so that all the world ran after him and regarded him almost as a God. Then he began to be tempted by the vain honor, and when he felt that, he besought God to guard him and not let him fall into [the sin of] pride. Then God let him be possessed and plagued by the devil for four weeks, so that he lost all his reputation, and everybody said: See, he helped others, now he lies there and cannot help himself! Thus he was rid of the temptation and remained humble. I give this as an example, to show how dangerous a thing it is with great, high gifts, and how pride is always apt to attach itself to them; as we see also in gross outward things, yes, in the beggar's staff of temporal possessions and authority. In short, God's gifts are so grandly noble, but we are so befouled, that we cannot avoid becoming proud and taking on airs if we are conscious of them; on the other hand, of becoming desperate if we do not have them.

That (I say) would be indeed an answer, but we will not press it here, although it is fair. For the principal thought is that he is here speaking of false prophesying and wonder-working as he says also in Matt. 24:24: For there shall arise false Christs, and false prophets, and shall show great signs and wonders; insomuch that, if it were possible, they shall deceive the very elect; and St. Paul says of Antichrist, 2 Thess 2:9. Who will come with all power and signs and lying wonders, and with all deceivableness of unrighteousness, etc., because they received not the love of the truth, that they might be saved; so that assuredly false miracles must be performed in Christendom, and the false Christians must regard them as real, true miracles.

Now that has been abundantly verified in the papacy; although in Turkey there are many of these priests and peculiar saints. One need only read their books and legends, especially those written by the monks, what a hotch-potch it is, brim-full of wonders; that are all however nothing but lies and knavery. How have people nowadays been fooled with so many pilgrimages to the valley of the Grim, to Eichen, to Treves, etc., and I have myself seen some monks, shameless, bad fellows and reckless men, who nevertheless exorcised the devil and played with him as with a child.

But who could relate all the knavery and raising of the devil that has been practiced under the holy name of Christ, of Mary, of the holy cross, St. Cyprian, etc., all of which the monks have carried on with vigor, and all the world has fallen in with them and no one dared peep against it. There was no pope or bishop that would preach against it, but all helped it along; and if any body resisted it, he was overwhelmed and silenced with violence; as not long ago bishop Ernst, of Saxony once pulled down such a devil's chapel; but he had to suffer for it, so that he fell sick in consequence and was glad to rebuild it. Along with this devil-raising business there have now been started and confirmed purgatory, masses for the dead, and worship of all saints, pilgrimages, monasteries, churches and chapels. Yes, many have also prophesied about future times, as Liechtenberg and others; but all this has been done by the devil, that he might endorse his abominable lies, and bewitch the people and hold them captive in error, so that no one could escape him.

For that is a small matter for the devil, to let himself be driven out, if he chooses, by a bad fellow, and yet remain unexorcised; for by that very performance he more completely possesses and ensnares the people with the shameful deception. Thus he can also guess at what is future, as a shrewd, experienced spirit; although he commonly mocks the people with his prophesying, and juggles in such a way that one may interpret him in various ways, and however it turns out he still has hit it; as he used to do in ancient times by his heathenish priests. Thus the people then are infatuated and bounce in: O here God lives! Here one sees and touches the miracles and signs! They cannot reckon that the devil does it only for the purpose of deceiving and misleading the people; and they do not think, the fools, that Christ clearly foretold all this and faithfully warned us against it through himself and his apostles. But it had to be so, and we have been rightly served, because we despised the word of God and did not take into the account that we must lose Christ and accept the miracles of the devil; and it was just real sport for the devil, whereby he ruled with full power in Christendom, as he sought to do.

Since we have now seen this, and alas quite too often experienced how great harm the devil has done through these lying spirits and false miracles, we should be made wise and not (as those before us have done) let the word of Christ lie and be spoken in vain, so that it may not go with us as it went with them. For it is a sermon, yes a prediction, written as a warning; but alas too late for those who lived before us; but early enough for us, if we will only heed it, so that we do not care how they boast of the signs and wonders that Mary and other saints have done, and dress them up beautifully wherewith to lead us away from the word; but to be so wise, since we hear this warning that these false miracles must occur, as not to believe in any mere miracles.

For he faithfully and earnestly warned, as he was speaking of these wonderful works, Matt. 24:25: "Behold, I have told you before;" as though he would say: Beware, and heed my warning; otherwise you will surely be misled. For you have my word, so that you know what is the will of my Father. Contrast these two together. Here you have my doctrine, which shows you how you ought to live and act: there you see the miracles that stand opposed to this doctrine, so that you can decide thus: Since I see there such excellent signs, and on the contrary have here the doctrine and the warning besides, I will first see to it what the miracles tend to, and will carefully examine whether they really serve to strengthen my faith in the word, namely, that Christ died for me, that I through him may before God become pious and be saved; then, that I may pursue my calling and faithfully attend to the same. Thus I learn the opposite fact, that they want thereby to strengthen and confirm their silly notion, and teach thus: Run to this or that saint, creep into a hood, etc., there so many miracles and wonders daily occur, there is such a holy order, etc. That means led away from Christ, from my church, pulpit, baptism and sacrament, that I should adhere to, also from my calling and the works demanded of me.

Therefore I will not hear or know it, even though an angel should come from heaven and awaken the dead before my eyes. For Christ has taught and warned me thus: Cling to my word, pulpit and sacrament; where this is, there you will find me. Abide there, you need not go or seek any farther; I will not come any nearer to you than where my gospel, baptism, office of the ministry is, through which I enter your heart and speak with you. Also, that he says: Be thou father or mother, prince, master, subject, and obedient, etc., and abide in thy calling, there thou hearest him speak, and present in person. Why do you then still run, as a senseless man, to stock and stone, where no word of God is preached, and yet through the devil's miracles open wide your eyes as though Christ would be there where his word is not!

See, thus they should have done against the papists, who come crowding with their custom, fathers, councils, and so many wonders and miracles, by which they want to have their matter confirmed, and should have answered only in a few words: Well, let us hold the two in contrast; there I have the word of Christ, of that I am sure, and it is most powerfully confirmed, through all the world: and you show me on the other hand your doctrine and miracles, that lead one to rosaries, pilgrimages, worship of saints, masses, monkery and other peculiar self-chosen works. There is nothing about Christ, nor faith, baptism, sacrament, obedience, and good works which I am to do in my calling towards my neighbor, as Christ teaches me; but just the contrary. Therefore they cannot be true miracles, but both the doctrine and the miracles are a delusion of the devil.

Thus we could readily know and judge all false miracles, and say: Miracles hither, miracles thither, I do not care for them, though you were to raise the dead before my eyes. For all that can be deceptive: but God's word does not deceive me. For the devil can readily befool and bewitch the people, so that he holds a man awhile as dead and then lets him come to himself again, as if he were awaked from the dead; or he can ruin one's eye or other member and then restore it again, so that one should think it was done by a miracle. Thus God decrees also that truly real miracles may occur as the punishment of those who pay no regard to the truth, as St. Paul says, and as a warning to others. For there is such excessive disregard for his word and such ingratitude, that no wrath is sufficient to punish it; as will be the case with us again, if the world stands long, who have sinned to such a degree that it must become much worse with all kinds of error and wonders.

For since the world absolutely will despise the word, and not hear it, and gape after something else: he will send it enough so that it may be led astray into the depth of all error; as was hitherto the case, when in all churches, monasteries, schools, nothing else was preached and taught, all books were stuffed full of these lying miracles, and with no other reason than that these miracles had occurred; as if it had not been sufficiently predicted that this should happen, and the people be deceived thereby, so that even the elect should hardly be saved from the error; and those are rightly served who so easily let themselves be misled and will not heed this warning. For he gave the word, how we are to believe and live, and besides confirmed it with miracles enough. He means to let that be enough, and stop there, and do nothing else; but they want to get up a different new doctrine and better callings against God's word and the true miracles.

Therefore Christ now says: I will pay no regard to it, although they boast: Lord, have we not in thy name done many wonderful works; but will pronounce this sentence upon them: I never knew you; depart from me, ye workers of iniquity, etc. How so, dear Lord? Are not the signs and wonders here, so that we cannot deny it? Yes, (he will say,) why then have you neglected my word, confirmed by my miracles, and have gotten up something else of which I know nothing, and have controlled the world according to your notion and have followed that? Because then you have despised my word, and have not done my Father's will, I will also not know you or have any mercy. They are mistaken about this now upon earth, supposing that they shall be the nearest to God; but they will find it out all too suddenly. This is now the right meaning of this text, so that he is speaking of false miracles, which the false teachers perform to establish their doctrine, whom he will not know, neither with their miracles nor prophesying, etc.

But in regard to this it is now earnestly asserted (and I do not know if this is the proper place for the discussion of it) that God sometimes allows real miracles to be performed by bad people, which God does through them; as Caiaphas, the high priest, prophesied, John 11:50, and Balaam, Num. 24:17, who uttered the most beautiful announcement concerning Christ, as Moses himself says, that the Holy Ghost entered into him, and he had to prophesy against his will, as also Caiaphas; and it cannot be denied that also Judas, as an apostle of Christ, did many miracles, as well as the other apostles and disciples. What shall we say to this? St. John himself answers, when he says concerning Caiaphas: Because he was high-priest that year he prophesied. For this can easily happen, that such a person, being in public office, or a ruling person, prophesies or works miracles and does a great deal of good, bringing many people to God; and yet the person himself may not be pious, and be going to the devil. Thus, a preacher is in a public calling and an official person, and if we look at it aright, such a person performs the very greatest work, miracle and wonder that happens on earth. For through his office, word and sacrament that he applies to you he brings you to faith, saves you from the devil's power and from eternal death, and leads you to heaven and eternal life; which is far above all external signs and wonders, and yet he may still be himself an unbelieving, bad man.

Therefore in this matter we must always look to the word of God, and judge according to that, not according to the person. Now you have heard above concerning those miracles that are performed in order to confirm something else than God's word, of which there is nothing in the Scriptures. But here are those miracles that relate to something that God has spoken and confirmed. Thus, the prophecy of the high-priest Caiaphas announced that Christ with his death should redeem the world, etc. This was a true, precious prophecy, although his motive was poisonous and evil. Thus also the prophet Balaam, although he was a villain, yet he predicts truly, as a prophet, concerning God's people and Christ, and God speaks through him. If now a preacher properly administers his office, and in virtue of it performs miracles, we should hear him. But if he wanted to get off the track and go another way, to start something else, aside from his office, he would no longer be a true but a false prophet. Thus, also, if the apostle Judas preached and performed miracles, who belonged to the devil, as Christ says, it was done by virtue of the apostolic office, to establish Christ, so that thereby the people might believe on him.

In accordance with this, judge concerning all who hold an office in Christendom. For they are not all Christians, or pious people, who are in office and preach. God does not ask about that; but let the person be as it may, the office is still right and good, and does not belong to man, but to God himself. Thus, Caiaphas prophesies not as Caiaphas, a murderer and bad fellow, but as a high-priest. So, the pastor or preacher baptizes and brings to eternal life, not as Mr. John Pommer, but as a pastor. For to honor and confirm the office God causes this to be done. Since now Judas is in the right public office, which Christ has appointed, therefore the office is honored in him, not the person.

For this is also the case in worldly affairs, as Solomon says in Prov. 16:10: *Divinatio in labiis regis*, a divine sentence is in the lips of the king; that is, everything that the authorities order, is right, and God confirms it. Therefore if they condemn criminals and punish them officially, that is God's judgment, which he utters in heaven above and will have executed, although it otherwise, aside from the office, is forbidden. Thus the Scriptures make all who are in the sacred office prophets or predictors, although personally they are often villains and tyrants; as Solomon again says, 8:15: "By me kings reign;" that is, their law and sentence is my law and sentence, and all that they do officially, if they rightly rule; and yet nevertheless for the most part in the world there are great scoundrels among them, that boldly make a bad use of their position and power; yet, if they remain in their office, and do what right demands, it is all God's business. It is just the same, to use an humble comparison, as when a prince or lord gives orders to a servant, or sends forth his ambassadors, that one hears and honors them, although they are bad fellows: not for their own sake, but for the sake of their lord, whose office and command they bring with them, etc.

Since now God does this in secular affairs, much more will he insist upon it in spiritual affairs, so that his office and service shall be efficient and effective. Therefore, as was said, it is a purely miraculous event, if a pastor preaches or baptizes, in so far as he properly administers the gospel and baptism, whether he be pious or wicked; and if he himself, as not being a Christian, does not have the treasure, yet he receives it who accepts the word and believes. If now these miracles and wonders are effected through the ministerial office, so that thereby souls are redeemed from sin, death and the devil; how much more can it be done with small, external miracles, in corporeal matters, that do not affect the soul?

Therefore we must here also carefully distinguish the two things, office and person, so that we do not reject the office for the sake of the person; as commonly happens, if one be pious, there are twenty of them wicked: but we must inquire carefully whether the office and the miracle tend and serve to praise and confirm the doctrine, so that one may believe on Christ, and whether they harmonize with what he has spoken, commanded and established. If you see that, then say: This sermon is right, though the person may be of no account. The miracle I will accept, but as to the person I will not ask, etc. If that be not the case, thou must not accept or believe it, the miracle may be ever so great, and the person ever so holy and excellent. But here are also many bishops, preachers, and those in other offices, who suppose that God must regard their persons, and they are thereby misled, as I said above. Therefore it will be of no avail for them to boast at the last day and say: Lord, we have surely in thy name done wonderful works. For God did not bestow this upon them for the sake of their person, but of their office, and he did the works not for their sake personally, but in view of their office, to confirm it. This is now said concerning public officials, by whom signs and wonders are performed, some of whom are pious, and some wicked, which neither detracts from the office nor adds to it.

But what do you say about those who perform miracles and prophesy and are yet not in office? as we read in Luke 9 of some who performed miracles and yet were not Christ's disciples, so that the apostles told Christ of it and said: Master, we saw one who drove out devils in thy name, and we rebuked him; for he did not follow thee. But he answered: Do not hinder him; for he who is not against us is for us, etc. Now that was a single person to whom the office had not been entrusted by Christ, and yet he says they should not hinder him, and he adds the reason, Mark 9:39: There is no man which shall do a miracle in my name that can lightly speak evil of me. Answer: That is true, as I have said, that God does not allow miracles to be done by bad men, unless they are in public office; because God does not give miracles on account of their person, but of their office. But if real miracles are done by a single person, that person must certainly be pious, as some are, who have special revelations, through dreams, visions, etc.; but these miracles must have the tendency to praise and further Christ and the gospel.

Thus you have two kinds of miracles that are good and honest, first, those which are done by pious persons who are Christians; then also those done by wicked persons, who yet are in office and teach correctly; but that we are always to judge according to this sure test, which is to be applied to all kinds of persons, whether pious or impious, in office or out of office, whether the miracles have the tendency to praise Christ and to strengthen your faith. But if you discover that they are pointing you in a different direction, as to go upon pilgrimages, pray to saints, deliver souls from purgatory, and in short, to rely upon your works and establish a righteousness of your own; then say: If you would perform all miracles for me, so that I could see and make sure of them, I would still not believe you; for Christ has sufficiently warned me against that.

This rule God himself stated through Moses in Deut. 13:1-3: "If there arise among you a prophet, or a dreamer of dreams, and giveth thee a sign or a wonder, and the sign or the wonder come to pass whereof he spake unto thee, saying: Let us go after other gods which thou hast not known, and let us serve them; thou shalt not hearken unto the words of that prophet, or that dreamer of dreams, etc." There he stated also the *causam finalem*, by which one can recognize them and proceed aright. If they try to persuade you to establish a different divine worship, that is, not to adhere to the one, pure doctrine, but to begin something else alongside of it, then we are not to believe, although it snows miracles. And he explains it further, and says: For the Lord your God proveth you to know whether you love the Lord your God with all your heart and with all your soul. As though he were to say: He wants to test you, how firmly you hold to the doctrine that has already been established and is in vogue.

In short, our orders are to accept no wonders or miracles, however great and numerous they may be, that are opposed to the well-established doctrine. For we have the command of God, who has given it from heaven: Hear ye him, Christ alone ye are to hear. Besides we have also this warning, that false prophets shall come, and perform great miracles, but all of them lead the wrong way, from Christ to something else. Therefore there is no other way to avoid this than to be well-grounded in the doctrine and keep it constantly in view; thus we can properly judge everything according to that, whether it is taught by the gospel or your faith, which you repeat every day, which declares: I believe on Christ alone, who died for me, etc., or whatever else it is.

Now, we have been warned enough, whoever is willing to heed it. But it avails nevertheless little with the great mass, as it availed but little heretofore; and I verily believe that if some one would arise here to-day and perform only one miracle, great crowds would fall in with it. For that is the way of the senseless crowd, when one puts forth something new before it and makes it stare, that it drops everything, word and doctrine, and gapes after that, although one should yell himself to death against it: as it has allowed itself heretofore to be fooled and led by the nose with coarse, palpable lies and unblushing fraud, whenever a villain has turned up and lied about a new relic, new pilgrimages, etc., and it has run after these things like crazy. This comes of the shameful overcuriousness and surfeit of our flesh and blood, along with the very devil himself, so that always the signs and wonders, especially those that are false, prove more attractive than even the genuine. For, that Christ and his apostles and others have performed miracles, that one does not see and regard; but that any one drives out a devil, that beats all. Well, he who will not take warning, and wants to be deceived, dare not lay the blame upon us.

54

Verses 24 through 27

THEREFORE WHOSOEVER HEARETH THESE SAYINGS
OF MINE, AND DOETH THEM, I WILL LIKEN HIM UNTO
A WISE MAN, WHICH BUILT HIS HOUSE UPON A ROCK;
AND THE RAIN DESCENDED, AND THE FLOODS CAME;
AND THE WINDS BLEW, AND BEAT UPON THAT HOUSE;
AND IT FELL NOT, FOR IT WAS FOUNDED UPON A ROCK.
AND EVERY ONE THAT HEARETH THESE SAYINGS OF
MINE, AND DOETH THEM NOT, SHALL BE LIKENED UNTO
A FOOLISH MAN, WHICH BUILT HIS HOUSE UPON THE
SAND: AND THE RAIN DESCENDED, AND THE FLOODS
CAME, AND THE WINDS BLEW, AND BEAT UPON THAT
HOUSE; AND IT FELL: AND GREAT WAS THE FALL OF IT.

That is the conclusion and the end of it, upon which it all depends: He who
not only hears this sermon with his ears, but who does it, he is a wise man.
For the doctrine is indeed good and excellent, but it is not preached in order
to be heard, but that it be applied to practical life; and especially because
we are always exposed to danger from false prophets and wonder-workers,
so that we may reflect, and accept this doctrine and warning, since we hear
and have it, both teachers and scholars. For if one wants to postpone it till
the hour comes when death and the devil come storming in upon us, with
his rain-storms and tempests, then it has been put off too long. Therefore
we are not bidden only to hear and become able, but to do and struggle.

Those also hear it who say: Lord, Lord, as heretofore the pope, bishops, and kings and all the world have heard, and the mass-priests and monks have daily read, sung, and intoned: but none has done it or preached it; but they have clung to their false worship and false miracles, and have encouraged others to do the same. Therefore, although they have heard much, and have also performed miracles, yet they have not done the will of God. For they do not continue in the doctrine of Christ and real good works, but they fall back upon their own works, done without faith and love, so that among all the monks and priests not a single genuine work is to be found. For they do none of them to serve or help their neighbor, but seek only their own thereby, and thus are entirely without faith, love and patience. Therefore among them nothing at all is done, as Christ says, although they hear the true doctrine; for it takes no hold upon them, for their hearts are nothing but mere sand.

But they nevertheless (as was said) have much to do and to teach, even more than the true preachers and Christians; by this too they lead the people astray. For a hermit or a Carthusian seems to be doing much more, with his strict spiritual living and doing, than St. Paul or any true preacher or Christian. For the external masks of special works and divine worship make people stare so that an ordinary Christian life makes no show in comparison. Therefore they are not lacking in doing, teaching and believing. But here is the difference (says Christ,) that they hear my teaching indeed, but they will do nothing except what they have themselves invented; on that track I cannot keep them, so that they would do what I teach them. If we Christians were as diligent in our works as they are in theirs, we should be altogether saints. But neither side amounts to anything. We are lazy and idle; they do quite too much, but of real works they do none at all. Thus we still have the advantage (thank God!) that we have begun a little to believe and love, and are upon the right track, however slowly we move.

He closes this now with a beautiful comparison, how it will finally be with both of these: He who hears and practices my teaching is an excellent, prudent builder, who does not build upon the sand, but seeks first a strong rock as a foundation. If he has this, he builds upon it, so that it may stand firm and endure. When then storms and showers come, around and above, and waters underneath (the wind meanwhile howling) seek to soften the earth and overturn the building, it stands against these immovable, as if to defy them all. But he who places his building upon sand will find that it stands only till the waters wash it away and the wind overturns it, so that it lies upon a heap or falls to pieces of itself.

With this comparison he means to warn us faithfully, so that we take good care to hold firmly to his doctrine and not let Christ be taken out of our heart as our only sure foundation and cornerstone of our salvation, as St. Paul and St. Peter (from Isaiah 28) call him. If we stand founded and built upon that, we will surely abide unmoved, and can let the world and the devil, with all false teachers and captious spirits pour down upon us hail and slags, and beset and assail us with all sorts of danger and trouble.

This confidence and security those miserable, foolish people cannot have. For they are not standing upon the rock, that is, upon the doctrine concerning Christ, but upon the drifting sand of their own imaginings and dreams. Therefore, when trouble comes, so that they have to struggle with the devil and death, they feel how they have rested their confidence upon loose sand, and their callings and works cannot endure; as I have myself seen and known many of these poor people, especially in monasteries, who have deeply felt this, so that at last they became crazy through fright and timidity of conscience, and some continued in perpetual despair! The reason was, that they had built upon their own doing, devotion and good intentions, and knew nothing about Christ. That was just the kind of a structure for the devil, that he could joyfully overturn and throw all into a heap.

St. Bernard himself had also to feel and acknowledge this, who had nevertheless led a very strict life, with praying, fasting, bodily mortification, etc., so that he was deficient in no respect, and served as an example for all others, so that I know of no one among the monks who wrote or lived better than he. Yet, when he came to die, he had himself to pronounce this judgment upon his entire holy life: O, I lived a damnable life, and spent my life shamefully! Ah, how so, dear St. Bernard? You were surely a pious monk all your life. Is then chastity, obedience, your preaching, fasting, praying, not an admirable thing? No (says he,) it is all lost and belongs to the devil.

There comes the wind and rain, and throws foundation, basis and building all into a heap, so that he would have had to be eternally damned, by
his own judgment, if he had not turned about, and, made wiser by his loss,
deserted monkery, seized upon another foundation and clung to Christ,
and been kept in the faith that the children use in their prayers, when he
said: "Although I am not worthy of eternal life, nor can attain it by my own
merit, yet my Lord Christ has a double right to it, once as Lord and heir to
it, inherited from eternity; secondly, attained through his suffering and
death. The first he retains for himself; the other he bestows upon me," etc.

Thus all the monks and priests, and all that claimed to be holy, that
were ever saved, had to creep out of their hoods and all their works, and
cling to Christ; although it went very hard with them. For it is very difficult
for a man who has spent his whole life in this self-made holiness, and has
depended upon it, to tear himself loose from it in an hour and cast himself
upon Christ. Therefore he warns and exhorts us to lay hold of and practice his teaching whilst we have the time, before the last agonies overtake
us. Thus our dear Lord has now completed this beautiful sermon. Now the
evangelist states in conclusion how the whole world had to testify that this
was a very different style of preaching from any they had heard before,
and to which they had been accustomed.

55

Verses 28 and 29

AND IT CAME TO PASS, WHEN JESUS HAD ENDED
THESE SAYINGS, THE PEOPLE WERE ASTONISHED
AT HIS DOCTRINE: FOR HE TAUGHT THEM AS ONE
HAVING AUTHORITY, AND NOT AS THE SCRIBES.

Thereby the evangelist shows what kind of preachers and teachers the
scribes had been, namely, that [their teaching] had been a mere cold,
vain, idle babbling; that they had not urged or insisted upon God's commands with earnestness or energy; just as our rag-washers have hitherto
upon the pulpit been drivelling about nothing else than purgatory, indulgences, hoods, rosaries, lighting of candles. But he took hold quite differently, showed what they had never heard before, the true doctrine and
life, and rebuked vices in such a way that they all felt that the man taught
with authority, and everything had life and a voice, as if it had hands and
feet, and they had to say that this was preaching with authority, whilst
that of the others was vain, empty, yes a mere dead wish-wash. Therefore
our papists now act shrewdly in that they are ashamed of their filthy rags,
and keep silence [in regard to those other topics] and begin also to preach
a little, after us and our books, about faith and good works; although they
still twist and butcher it, as not being really in earnest about preaching
right, or having grace to be able to understand it.

There remains yet at the end one question to be treated of, because we heard in this sermon that Christ insisted so strenuously upon works, when he says: The poor shall inherit the kingdom of heaven; the merciful shall obtain mercy; also, those shall be rewarded in heaven who suffer persecution for his sake; and what is said about this at the end of the fifth chapter: If you love those who love you, what kind of reward shall you have? and in the sixth chapter concerning alms, fasting and praying: Thy Father which seeth in secret, shall reward you openly, etc.; from which sayings the senseless, false preachers conclude that we get to heaven and are saved by our own working and doing, and thereupon they build upon this their endowments, monasteries, pilgrimages, masses, etc.

Although, however, this question is somewhat sharp, and belongs rather to the university, among the learned, than to the pulpit, before ordinary, simple-minded people; yet, as it occurs so often in our text, we must not overlook it altogether, but must have something to say about it. For it is very necessary that every one should have some idea of the difference between grace and merit. For the two do not accord with one another. If one is preaching grace, he surely cannot be preaching merit; and what is grace cannot be merit, else grace would not be grace, says St. Paul in Rom. 11:6. There is no doubt about that. Therefore, he who confounds these two confuses the people and misleads both himself and those who hear him.

Well, we will ignore for the present the sharp answer, and discuss this question in the plainest way that we can; and in the first place we must distinctly remember this, that there is a great difference between faith, or essential Christianity, and its fruits, as I have often said. For, according to the Christian name and nature one is not different from another; all have at once the same treasure and the same kind of possessions. For St. Peter has no different or better baptism than St. Paul, and a child born yesterday no inferior baptism to that of John the Baptist or St. Peter and all the apostles; thus they have also no other, better Christ than the least Christian.

If we now look at this, there avails no merit, or difference. For the least Christian receives just as well the same body and blood of Christ in the sacrament, and when he hears the gospel he hears the very same word of God that Peter and Paul heard and preached. Also, no saint can pray another or better *pater noster*, or pronounce and confess a creed and ten commandments different from those prayed daily by me and every child. That is now so plain that every one can easily understand it; so that in what entitles us to be called Christians there is no inequality or preference of persons, but one is just like the other, man, woman, young, old, learned, unlearned, noble, ignoble, prince, peasant, master and servant, great and small saint, as there is only one kind of Christ and creed: just as the sun in the heavens is of one kind towards everybody, shines upon a peasant as well as upon a king; upon a blind man as well as upon one who sees well; upon the sow upon the street as upon the most beautiful woman upon earth, and shines as readily upon a thorn as upon a rose, upon filth as upon purple, and it is the very same sun that shines upon the poorest beggar as upon the greatest king or emperor.

But thereafter, if we begin to consider external matters and what we are doing, as that I, who am a Christian and baptized, am in addition to this also a preacher, whilst I could be a Christian without that; then the inequality begins and it extends to the various distinctions among Christians; not as Christians, or as to the nature of Christianity, but as to its fruits. Thus I am a preacher, that is, such a Christian who is to present the word to the people, to comfort the distressed, to instruct the erring and ignorant, etc. And this one is the head of a family or a mechanic, who is to rule his house, attend to his business, provide for his wife and children. There is a man, different from you and me; yet I must say: He is just as much a Christian, and gets as much from baptism, the grace of God and eternal life, as I and all the others, and is no less in Christ than I; and there is here no difference between women or men, etc. Yet the woman's work is different from that of the man, that of a servant from that of his master, that of a preacher from that of a civilian; likewise, a child compared with its father, a scholar or disciple with the teacher, each of them having his own work or fruits; and thus everywhere there is a difference in external circumstances, whilst yet all are at the same time Christians and one according to the inner life. For there is no more than one Christianity and only one natural condition of all men. That we see too in the heavens (says St. Paul, 1 Cor. 15:41,) that there are so many kinds of stars, and differing from one another, one great, the other small, one shining clearly, the other dimly, and yet there is but one sun in our heavens. In this respect they are all alike, that all stand in one heavens and have one kind of sun; and yet they are unlike as to size and brightness. Thus it is also upon earth (says St. Paul, further,) not all flesh is the same flesh, but there is one flesh of man, another of beasts, another of birds. In the fact that they are flesh they are all alike, and one has his members, head, heart, stomach, etc., just as well as the others; yet there is a great difference between men, beasts, birds and fishes.

If now you wish to speak about a Christian, or to depict him, you must paint him so that he is in no wise different from others, and one must be in all respects as the others. For you must not describe him as a man or woman, a preacher or layman, prince or beggar, mechanic or Carthusian monk. For these distinctions have nothing to do with him; but so far as his essential character is concerned, he is just as good and holy as Peter and Paul, and no one is any more and better than he. For if St. Peter were better than I, as to the true essentials of Christianity, he would have to have a better Christ, gospel and baptism than I. But because the great treasure that we have is altogether one and the same, we must in this respect be all alike and no one must be raised above the other. It may well be that one does more and greater things than another, as, that St. Peter raised person's from the dead. But thereby, that he does miracles which I do not, he is indeed a greater, brighter star than I in the heavens, but not a different kind of star, and he has no other heavens. St. Paul did and labored more than all the other apostles; but he did not for this reason have a better apostolic office, nor did he preach a different and better Christ.

This is what we now say about merit. If we are speaking about that which concerns the essence of Christianity [or the Christian life] according to which we are all equal, how we become pious before God, and attain forgiveness of sins and eternal life, here all our merit is totally excluded, and we must neither hear nor know anything about it. For you have not at all deserved the gospel, or Christ, or baptism, but it is a pure grant, freely given; so that our sins are gratuitously forgiven, we become God's children and are assigned to heaven without our doing anything towards it.

And here we contend against the abomination of the sophists who so greatly exalt our works, that we thereby secure a gracious God, and merit heaven. Yes, they venture shamelessly to say that a man even in mortal sins can do so much of his own accord, and perform such acts of devotion or accomplish such good works that he may thereby allay and propitiate the wrath of God. That means hurling the roof to the ground, quite upsetting the foundation, building salvation upon nothing but water, driving Christ entirely from his throne and setting up our works instead. For it must follow from that, that we have no need at all of baptism, of Christ, or gospel, or faith, because even when in mortal sin I find so much virtue and power in me that I can extricate myself by my own works and merit forgiveness of the same and eternal life. From this you see that God is slandered and blasphemed by all that they drivel about merit, on the subject about which we are now disputing, how and whereby we are to attain to the grace of God and eternal life. Yet they are not satisfied with teaching this shameful blasphemy of God; but they are actually fighting for it and denouncing us as heretics on account of it.

This every one can now readily understand, that one of these two must be false: either that we cannot by our doing merit grace, or Christ with his baptism must be of no account and nothing; and Christ must have acted like a fool, to let himself be martyred and shed his blood so dearly, and to have undergone so much, in order to acquire and bestow upon us what was not at all necessary and what we already have by ourselves. Therefore, although they revile us as heretics on this account, that we do not agree with them about this merit of works, we will gladly submit to their calling us heretics and leave the matter in the hands of God our judge; but only the more firmly resist them and reply to them that they are not heretics, but the very worst blasphemers of God that the sun ever shone upon, who most shamefully deny and curse Christ, as Peter prophesied about them, and as the epistle to the Hebrews says, they smite Christ on the mouth and trample him under foot, with his baptism, sacrament and entire gospel, and what God has given us through him.

And I would really like to hear what they could say to it, the miserable people: If they assert that we by our works can begin by securing grace,

and when this is done, and so much is merited, that we, over and above
the first grace (as they call it), merit in addition the kingdom of heaven
and eternal salvation; what does one then merit by the other subsequent
works? For I will suppose that a papist has done his mass or other work in
grace, and has thereby merited the kingdom of heaven, as such an excellent work that is worthy of eternal life, which they call *meritum de con-
digno*; what will he then merit by the works and masses that he does next
day and afterwards in the same grace? Then they begin, (as they do not
know what else to say,) and make *essentiale* and *accidentale premium*, and
say: These following works enable one to merit something additional, as
a little gift into the bargain, which God gives to us over and above eternal
life. Is this true? then I am to understand that the first works are the best,
but the others are not so good. Otherwise they must merit just the same;
yet commonly the following works are accustomed to be better, because
they are now more diligently practiced.

Since now the last works do not merit the kingdom of heaven, the first
must also not merit it; or, if they are equally good, and every work can
merit this, then God must build as many heavens as the good works that
are done; and where would our Lord God at last get so many heavens as to
pay for every good work? Those are really smart people, that can measure
it off so smoothly and accurately. But what shall we say? All that they say is
nothing but lies and deception, for there is not a word of it true; first, that
any one can merit grace by any work of his own, much less if one is lying
in mortal sin; and then, although a man were in grace by works (as they
say), that these works, done in grace, should be so precious as to merit the
kingdom of heaven. For there stands Christ and asserts the contrary with
clear, plain words. Luke 17:10: "When ye shall have done all those things
which are commanded you, say, We are unprofitable servants."

Therefore we ought to hold fast to our doctrine, so that we never allow
any work to put in a claim for securing the favor and grace of God, delivering from sin and entitling to heaven. For this, in short, my merit is to
be nothing; and if one should want to use it in that way, I must trample it under foot, and damn it to the devil himself in hell, as something
that would hinder my faith and lead me to deny Christ. For here the truth

stands, that God has bestowed all this gratuitously, out of pure grace, in that he sends his Son and lets him die for me, and announce and give this to me, commanding me only to believe this and be baptzied in it. My works have nothing to do with this, but it is a pure gift, granted from heaven and brought to me by Christ. Therefore let all merit in this matter be entirely thrown away, and let us conclude that one cannot secure grace and the forgiveness of sin in any other way, manner or measure than by the word of God concerning Christ, and receiving it by faith. And that God may hear us, why should we boast of our merit, since they themselves and all the saints must daily pray, in the Lord's prayer, as long as we live: Forgive us our debts, etc.? And the desperate saints dare unblushingly to say that a man, though lying in mortal sin, can prepare himself for grace and afterwards also merit everlasting life.

But how do you account for it that there are so many passages concerning merit and reward? To this we reply now, for the benefit of the simple-minded, that these are merely for a consolation to Christians. For if you now have become a Christian, and have a gracious God and forgiveness of sins, both of those past and of those that you are daily committing [I say to you], that you must do and suffer much on account of your faith and your baptism. For the devil himself, together with the world and the flesh, will besiege you and on every hand torment you, as has been abundantly shown in these three chapters, so that you may feel as if the world was too narrow for you. Now if [our Saviour] would allow us to be thus perplexed, without word or consolation, we should be led to despair and to say: Who is willing to be a Christian, preach, or do good works? He sees surely how it goes with them, and the world tramples upon them, reviles and abuses them, treats them cunningly and wickedly, and finally robs them of honor, property and life itself; and he [my Saviour] calls me nothing else than poor, distressed, hungry, soft-hearted, peaceable, afflicted and persecuted: is it always to be so, and never different?

Then he must talk out, encourage and comfort, and say: You are now in grace and the children of God; although you must now suffer for that in the world, do not be alarmed at that, but hold on, and do not let yourselves be made weary or weak whatever you may see, but let every one do just what he should. If he suffers on that account, it will not harm him, and he may know that the kingdom of heaven is his, and he shall be richly repaid. Ah, how paid? Why we have it already, through Christ, without and in advance of all our doing. Thus, as St. Paul says, that God will make a great, bright star out of you, and grant you a special gift, even in this life. For a Christian can even here upon earth accomplish so much with God through his prayers and works, that he may spare an entire land, prevent wars, famines, pestilence, etc.; not that the work on account of its worthiness is so valuable, but for this reason, that he has promised it, for our invigoration and consolation, so that we are not to think that our works, plagues and misery are lost and forgotten.

Now there is here no merit, by which we are to earn grace, or our baptism, Christ and heaven (of which they speak when they are talking of merit); but it all refers to the fruits of Christianity. For Christ says also (as we have seen) in this sermon nothing about how we become Christians, but only about the works and fruits which no one can do unless he is already a Christian, and in grace; as the words prove, that they must endure poverty, misery, persecution, just for the reason that they are Christians and have the kingdom of heaven, etc. If we now speak of those fruits that follow being in grace and having forgiveness of sin, we may consent to speak of a merit and reward; but we object to calling those works of ours the chief good, which must be there beforehand, and without which they could not be performed, or be pleasing to God. If now we only insist upon this point, that there is no merit but only pure grace [by which we are saved], then we will not object to giving the name to the fruits that follow; but, so that one does not falsely pervert those passages, and refer them contrary to the Scriptures to our meriting grace, but interprets them properly, as intended, to comfort Christians, especially amid suffering and hostility, when one feels and it seems as if our life, suffering and doing, were in vain and accomplishing nothing; as the Scriptures everywhere console, where they exhort to perseverance in good works, as in Jer. 31:16: *Est merces operi tuo*, thy work is not in vain; also, St. Paul, in 1 Cor. 15:58: *Labor vester non est inanis in domino*, your labor is not in vain in the Lord. For, if we had not this consolation, we could not endure this wretchedness, persecution and misery, that we should do so much good, and let our teaching and preaching be rewarded with sheer ingratitude and disgrace; and would have at last to cease from doing and suffering what was plainly our duty. But God means to arouse and confirm us by this beautiful promise, so that we pay no regard to the ingratitude, hatred, envy and contempt of the world, but regard him who says: "I am thy God. If the world will not thank you, and robs you of honor, property, and even of life on that account, then cling to me and take comfort from this, that I have a heaven, and so much in it that I can easily recompense you, and ten times more than can now be taken from you;" so that we can have this answer for the world: Well, if it will not treat us with favor, let it go along with its favor, and all that it has; I did not begin anything on its account, and I will henceforth neither do nor omit anything on its account. But I will do and suffer everything for his sake who gives me such rich promises, and says: Although you have already, aside from this, all treasure in heaven through Christ, and more than enough; yet I will give you still more, as additional, so that you shall have the kingdom of heaven fully revealed, and you shall visibly behold Christ in everlasting glory and joy, (whom you now have in faith), so much the more as you now suffer and labor.

Here are applicable the charming passages and exhortations, such as Heb. 10:35: *Magnum habetis remunerationem*, etc. Cast not away, therefore, your confidence, which hath great recompense of reward; and Christ, in Matt. 19:29: "And every one that hath forsaken houses, or brethren, or sisters, or father or mother, or wife, or children, or lands, for my name's sake, shall receive a hundredfold, and shall inherit everlasting life." Thus he speaks also here: *Merces vestra magna est in coelo*, you shall be well rewarded in heaven; by which he shows that they already have the kingdom of heaven, and yet shall have it so much the more glorious when it now is revealed.

See, if we turn these passages in this direction, they are rightly used, so that they have no reference to our confiding in our works contrary to faith, but to the consolation of Christians and believers; and if the sophists had aimed their talk about merit in this direction, it would have been all right. But they based their own work-holiness and monkery upon it, so that God should thereby regard them as peculiar saints, and sell heaven for these, and should give them the highest seats, as those with whom common Christians were not to be compared; and they acted indeed not unwisely in the matter, for that did not bring poverty, misery, mourning, persecution, but money, property, honor, and no order was established for the purpose of using in it the word of Christ, sacrament, faith, love and patience; but only with their hoods, and rigid, peculiar mode of living, they want to be highly esteemed and exalted before God, as those who need no Christ or faith.

In this way now we admit that Christians have merit and reward with God; not for the purpose of becoming children of God and heirs of eternal life; but for the consolation of believers who already have this, that they may know that he will not let that be unrewarded that they suffer here for Christ's sake; but, if they suffer and labor much, then he will specially adorn them at the last day, more and more gloriously than others, as stars especially great in comparison with others. Thus St. Paul will shine forth bright and clear above others most splendidly. That does not mean forgiveness of sins, or meriting heaven, but compensation for suffering with so much the greater glory.

But we will not suffer the matter to stand where they put it; for that is to slander and blaspheme Christ, God and the Holy Ghost, and everything that God has given us by them, and we would rather be denounced as heretics and scoundrels, and be burned with fire, than give up or deny this treasure: but we will also insist upon this consolation even if we must suffer for it all trouble, shame and persecution. For this will be the result at any rate. The devil will not agree to this, or accord with us; but means to maintain the pope's doctrine and bring us to believe as he believes; and as he sees that we won't do it, he lays himself out against us with all his might. For he knows very well, if this point is settled, that Christ and the forgiveness of sins are a perfectly free gift, that any one can count it off on his fingers and conclude that the papacy with its masses, monkery, purgatory, worship of saints, etc., must be nothing, and all will fall to pieces of its own accord.

Now learn to answer in this way about those passages that refer to merit and reward. I hear indeed that Christ says: Blessed are the poor, for they shall have the kingdom of heaven; and, Blessed are ye when ye suffer persecution for my sake; for great is your reward in heaven, etc. But he does not thereby teach me to rest my salvation upon that, but gives me a promise that is to be a comfort to me in my sufferings and in my Christian life. You must not confound these things for me and mix the two together, nor make my merit out of that which God gives me in Christ through baptism and the gospel. For we are not here told that we can merit that, and that we need no Christ and baptism for it; but that those who are Christ's disciples, to whom he has here preached, and who must undergo all manner of suffering for his sake, may know how they are to comfort themselves, because they have a hard time of it on earth, namely, that they because of this shall have everything so much the more abundantly in heaven; and he who does and suffers the most shall be so much the more gloriously recompensed.

For although (as I said) in Christ all are alike, and grace is bestowed equally upon all, and brings full salvation to every one, as the highest, most common possession, so that he who has Christ has all: yet there will be a difference in the brightness and the glory with which we shall be adorned and shine; just as in this life there is a difference in the gifts, so that one labors and suffers more than another; but in that life it will all be manifest, so that all the world shall see what each one has done, and shall have so much the greater glory, at which the whole heavenly host will rejoice. Let this be enough about that.

God preserve us in his grace, revealed in Christ. Amen.